FUTURE GREATS

GREATS

AND

HEARTBREAKS

FUTURE GREATS

AND HEARTBREAKS

A YEAR UNDERCOVER IN THE SECRET WORLD OF NHL SCOUTS

GARE JOYCE

DOUBLEDAY CANADA

To Susan

Doubleday Canada and colophon are trademarks.

LIBRARY AND ARCHIVES CANADA CATALOGUING IN PUBLICATION

Joyce, Gare
Future greats and heartbreaks : a year undercover in the secret world of NHL scouts / Gare Joyce.

ISBN 978-0-385-66440-0

1. Joyce, Gare. 2. Hockey. 3. Hockey players. 4. Hockey scouts.
I. Title.

GV847.J69 2007   796.962'62   C2007-903899-9

Jacket image: Tom Feiler / Photonica / Getty Images
Book design: Leah Springate
Printed and bound in the USA

Published in Canada by
Doubleday Canada, a division of
Random House of Canada Limited

Visit Random House of Canada Limited's website: www.randomhouse.ca

BVG   10   9   8   7   6   5   4   3   2   1

CONTENTS

PROLOGUE

August 12, 2006, Zimny Stadion, Breclav, Czech Republic

I T'S THE FIRST SATURDAY NIGHT OF THE HOCKEY SEASON, but it's a long way from *Hockey Night in Canada*. It's six time zones away from the foot of Bay Street or rue de la Gauchetière Ouest. It's not a game between NHLers, not even pros, not even men, really. Most of the best seventeen-year-old hockey players from Canada and the United States are squaring off for gold medals and bragging rights at the Ivan Hlinka World Cup. The final of the eight-team tournament, the game isn't broadcast back to North America, and the outcome won't be headline news there. It will barely be noted in Canadian newspapers, even in the hometowns of the players here, and it won't be mentioned in U.S. sports pages at all. But make no mistake, this tournament and this game have been circled on calendars in National Hockey League front offices for months now. Flights and hotels were booked back in the spring. It's a more meaningful game than many hockey nights in Canada that will be watched by millions this winter.

The NHL isn't on the ice. The NHL is in the stands. A hundred and fifty scouts and executives with NHL teams, several more scouts with the NHL's Central Scouting Service, a dozen or so agents certified by the NHL Players' Association. You won't find this many heavy hitters at NHL games—lucky if you have ten pro scouts up in the press box and a few execs from the teams that are playing.

A couple of Czech photographers are working the game. So are a couple of young reporters who work for local papers. I'm the only

North American sportswriter in attendance—I might be the only
North American sportswriter who's really paying attention to the
tournament. I have a couple of freelance assignments to knock off—
the main one a profile of Angelo Esposito, the captain of the
Canadian team, the top-rated prospect eligible for the 2007 NHL
entry draft, a kid who has been playing in the spotlight since he
turned fourteen. I also want to get a look at Nick Petrecki, a
defenceman with the U.S. team who's billed by some as the best
blueline prospect going into the season. The assignments will just
cover the expenses, really. It's a busman's holiday—eight games in
five days. I was looking for a way to get here. It was circled on my
calendar, just like the scouts'.

As I say, the NHL is in the stands, not on the ice. The players in
the starting lineups stand on their blue lines and listen to the playing of "O Canada" and "The Star-Spangled Banner." When the
final notes echo around the arena they slap their sticks on the ice
and yell and whoop. And when the puck is dropped, they yell and
whoop some more, overexcited teenagers acting like overexcited
teenagers. Some of them on the ice and on bench will end up
becoming millionaires and some will never make a buck playing the
game. Some of them will get beyond youthful overexcitement and
respect the game; others won't. The NHL is here in the stands, trying to sort one bunch from the other, and so am I.

I was an unlikely pick, I'll admit that. They'd probably call it "a
reach." Fact is, even I thought so. *The Globe and Mail*'s hockey
columnist had bolted back in the summer of '94. I'd only written a
few magazine articles about hockey, more about the business of
the NHL than about the game itself—I'd written a book about
baseball, and my idea of winter sport was basketball. I had been to
a dozen Maple Leaf games in my life. I wouldn't have described
myself as a fan. I was a lapsed fan. I went to junior games Friday
nights and Sunday afternoons as a teenager. As a kid I went with
my father to Bobby Orr's last junior game, Oshawa vs. Edmonton
for the Memorial Cup at Maple Leaf Gardens. I saw Wayne

Gretzky play as a junior when I was in university in Ottawa. But even junior hockey I gave up, along with other childhood things. For all those who applied, writing a hockey column for the national newspaper was a job they dreamed of; for me, it was one I hadn't even thought of.

One day the phone rang. On the other end was an editor from *The Globe and Mail* asking if I had seen the ad. I told him I had seen it. He asked me if I'd come in to talk. Sure, I said, it doesn't cost anything to talk.

After an uncomfortable and thoroughly puzzling interview, I passed on a note thanking the editor for his interest, something to the effect of "Sorry this didn't work out . . . please stay in touch . . ."

And a couple of days later, the editor called me and told me I was hired.

Serendipity. A series of fortunate events. That's how I ended up working in the game.

Some would have taken it as a bad sign that my first week on the job coincided with the NHL lockout of 1994. In effect, I was hired to cover a league that immediately shut down on my arrival. It's a game of constant motion, but come October arenas were dark and Zambonis parked. There's only so much reporting on collective bargaining that a hockey scribe can write and still sustain the interest of readers. So I cast around looking for other stories. I started to look at the games far from the spotlight, games not tracked by the national media. In some circles it would be called "colour," in others "filler." To me it was neither. Fact is, there was a lot of despair about the state of hockey: that the game was in crisis, that fans would be alienated, that young people were tuning out the game. Above all there was the idea that the supposed caretakers of the game—the commissioner heading the league and the boss of the players' association—cared only about business. That's how I ended up in junior hockey rinks, looking for signs of hockey life.

I thought that was going to distance me from the NHL. As it turned out, it brought me inside it.

I remember going to a game in Peterborough that fall. An early-season game between the Petes and the Oshawa Generals. In the first intermission I saw Bob Gainey in the halls of the arena. Gainey was then the general manager of the Dallas Stars. He is also a native of Peterborough, a former Pete. At first I thought he was back in Peterborough on family business. But after a brief chat—a brief one, because he wouldn't broach questions about the lockout, especially with a hockey media greenhorn—he said he had made the trip to scout Jamie Langenbrunner, a Minnesota native playing for the Petes and a second-round pick of the Stars at the 1993 draft. Which struck me as sort of odd, the idea that he made a long trip to keep tabs on a player already drafted. Before I could ask a follow-up he spun around and was in deep confab with a couple of other guys carrying clipboards that featured Stars logos. Scouts who reported to him. And by the time the puck was dropped for the second period, I spotted Gainey amid a dozen guys carrying clipboards, not all from the same organization and not all there to see Jamie Langenbrunner, but all there for the same sort of thing. They were easy to pick out in the crowd. When the fans cheered, the scouts had their heads down and scribbled notes. When the fans booed and cursed the ref, the scouts looked on stone-faced.

The doors of NHL arenas were deadbolted. CBC was showing movies in the time slot reserved for *Hockey Night in Canada*. But these guys were working.

I saw them wherever I went that fall and early winter. I expected to see them at the usual places, the easy-to-get-to spots, the arenas closest to Toronto: Oshawa, Belleville, Guelph. I saw them in droves at the CHL all-star game in Kitchener. But I saw them when I didn't expect it. Owen Sound was the one place they tried to avoid. It was a bad drive, and the Owen Sound Platers weren't much of a team because the best prospects let the management know that they had no intention of reporting if Owen Sound drafted them, that they'd hold out and force a trade or go to college in the U.S. if the team called their bluffs. I drove up through an ice storm to Owen Sound on a Saturday night when the opponents were the worst team in all of junior hockey—the

London Knights, winless after two months, so hopelessly outmatched they looked like a threat to go winless all season. After a three-hour white-knuckle crawl along the winding two-lane highway, I made it to the rink thirty minutes before the drop of the puck . . . and a half dozen scouts were already seated in the corners of the rink, watching the teams take their warmups, checking the scratches and lines.

Their commitment to the game was as plain as the lines on the ice. They would leaf through league schedules, trying to pack in as many games as possible, trying to see eighteen-year-old prospects who were going to be eligible for the draft next June. They automatically made the leap of faith, presuming that there'd be a league and a draft in several months' time. Trying to keep tabs on players like Jamie Langenbrunner, players already drafted. Fact is, they were complete counterpoints to the two names that played out most prominently in the sports pages at that moment: Gary Bettman and Bob Goodenow. The commissioner and the players' association director. Just as wars are ultimately settled by politicians and diplomats in suits, so was the game brought to a standstill by these two men and the ring of lawyers and bean counters around them.

Eventually the keepers of the game got their act together and the NHL opened shop once more. But that didn't mark the end of my education. I didn't give up the "colour" and the "filler." I kept going to junior games when my work schedule allowed it. I made it out to Memorial Cup tournaments. I made the world junior tournament a fixture on my schedule. I started to see the scouts' work and lives in sharper focus.

I realized that they didn't just care about the game more than anyone else, but that they *had* to care more than anyone else. More than a player, because the player stands to make millions. More than a coach, because the coach wields power, finds the spotlight and cashes a cheque smaller only than the player's. More than a general manager, because the general manager works in the comfort of an oak-panelled office and lives in executive comfort.

The scouts' jobs were tough. The travel was awful—long drives, often alone. At the end of a long day they booked into budget hotels.

But before crashing on rock-hard mattresses, they filed reports for an hour or two while the names, games and impressions were still fresh in their heads. From September through May, the scouts rarely had a weekend at home. For trips to more distant leagues, a week or ten days away from home was just a matter of course. So was scouting three games in the course of a day. Not that there was overtime pay. No, the pay was, in many cases, nothing special. One Eastern Conference scout told me that a waitress in a cocktail joint was set to fast-track a relationship with him after hearing that he worked for a NHL team — at least until he told her that he was making about thirty grand. "She got up to make a phone call and never came back," he said. Relationships, though, were more secure than their jobs. NHL scouting has always been a business of one-year contracts, and the first topic of gossip around the rink is usually who among them might be in trouble with his outfit. Scouts of long and distinguished service were thrown overboard when a new general manager was hired and brought with him a new crew.

And yet they carried on. As hard as their jobs were, the scouts seemed happy at the rink — happier than me. It couldn't simply be that they liked the game. No, if anyone was at risk of getting too much of the stuff they loved it would be a hockey scout. But one told me early on that it came down to being needed: "It's not just that our teams need us to find the best players. It's more than that. The NHL needs talent. It needs talent desperately. The league is only as good as we are. If there are bad coaches or bad general managers, there are bad teams. But if scouts are bad, you'll end up with a bad league and a bad game."

Soon enough, I was able to put names to scouts' faces.

Some were recognizable to any kid who collected hockey cards. Harry Howell's card must have been like Dorian Gray's portrait. Howell, the last defenceman to win the Norris Trophy before Bobby Orr took ownership, was always at games filing reports for the Edmonton Oilers, but deep into his sixties and seventies he looked like he could still play. Who with a washboard stomach collects a pension? Don Luce was the same sort of story. The Buffalo Sabres were the only outfit he had worked for in his life, first as an industrious forward in the '70s and early '80s, then as a savvy scout. And Guy Lapointe—the first time I sat beside him at a game he introduced himself simply as a scout for Calgary. A Hall of Fame defenceman, Lapointe was oblivious to the fact that anyone who watched the Montreal Canadiens' nonpareil teams back in the '70s would recognize him in an instant. The mop of black hair, the sideburns, the beak. Maybe it was a mind-set of the scouts, a presumption that as soon as they became scouts, fame waned and obscurity waxed. Maybe scouting was a trade meant for the humble, or those who need to be humbled.

Others had names that hockey fans would recognize, yet no public profile at all. When the Edmonton Oilers reigned in the '80s a lot of the credit for finding players like Jari Kurri and Paul Coffey went to a scout named Barry Fraser. Fraser told me that he was recognized at a few arenas around the junior circuit, but he couldn't get into the Northlands Coliseum once because he had forgotten his pass and couldn't convince security that he worked for the organization. "Guys on the fourth line were getting waved by and here I was standing there," Fraser said. "Slats [his boss, Glen Sather] was standing there laughing about it."

Soon I could see a hierarchy among the scouts. At the top were scouting directors, who had the ears of the general managers. Reporting to them were full-time regional scouts. Below them, part-timers—"bird dogs" who were either looking to break into the game or easing gently into retirement. The top dogs criss-crossed the continent a few times every winter and went to Europe for major tournaments, while the bird dogs never strayed too far from the home base.

Yet job titles alone didn't establish the pecking order. No, some of those with corner offices at the team offices didn't command the respect granted some regional scouts or even part-timers. Among his peers, a scout was judged on his track record and his work ethic. The first count was simply the success of the players he spotted—such was the case with Fraser. The latter was not simply how many games a scout logged over the course of a season, but also how far he'd go to find a player and get the inside dope. Marshall Johnston was a classic case. Johnston was scouting for the New Jersey Devils when I was starting out on the hockey beat, and he was considered the ultimate grinder—not someone who simply filed reports, but one who worked a network of contacts across North America and Europe. Some scouts were satisfied with getting to the games and filing their player reports, but Johnston wanted to get the backstory, what was going on behind the scenes.

Others were taken far more lightly.

For some, it was tied to personal style. Tom Renney was a textbook case. Renney is obviously a good hockey man with a good record as a coach, most recently with the New York Rangers. But before he went behind the Rangers' bench, Renney scouted for the same outfit and never won over his peers during that stint. I couldn't put my finger on a reason, so I asked a scout, one of the regulars, what he thought of Renney, and his scouting report was concise. Two words: "Silk scarf." I took a good look and, yes, Renney was wearing a scarf that looked like it was worth as much as all the clothes a typical scout took on a ten-day road trip. Which is to say, Renney appeared to be more concerned with style than practicality, a notion the average scout couldn't get his mind around.

For others it came down to the organizations they worked for. When I first tried to make my way into the circle, one scout was the butt of more one-liners than anybody else: Don Murdoch, a.k.a. Murder. Colourful he was. The only scout who was ever linked romantically to Margaret Trudeau, Murdoch was a natural scorer and legendary party boy when he broke in with the Rangers, but it all went south quickly after he was busted with cocaine on a team flight to Toronto. Just on reputation he seemed like the last guy an organization would recruit as a scout, but that's what the Tampa Bay Lightning did—the Lightning then being the worst team in the league and arguably the worst-run organization in all of professional sports. Murdoch was hired by probably the only general manager who'd give him the time of day, Phil Esposito, a former teammate of Murdoch's in New York and an executive who would always find a job for a blood relative or crony.

In between the legends and the laughingstocks were scores of other scouts of various stripes. Young ones trying to make a name for themselves, doing little to conceal their ambitions. Veterans making the most of sinecures with an organization they used to play for. Several were second-generation scouts—like Craig and Tod Button, the sons of the late Jack Button, a Hall of Famer who founded the NHL's Central Scouting Bureau. Many, like Shawn Simpson and Archie Henderson, were members of Jack Button's scouting family—scouts he mentored. The good, the bad, the indifferent, they all had stories and knew hundreds more about the game, enough to launch a thousand libel suits. I heard all about friendships and grudges, about great finds and brutal mistakes, about players who went on to greatness and those whose hearts were broken.

I had seen them in good times. When I saw them scouting Sidney Crosby a few years back, the scouts were in an altered state, something approaching religious ecstasy. They went out of their way to drive out to Rimouski, a small town on the St. Lawrence where Crosby played in the Quebec league. For them, Rimouski was like Lourdes—if ever their enthusiasm for their job sagged, they were energized by this teenager from Halifax. Baby Jesus, some called him. He gave them faith. The scouts also made pilgrimages to Crosby's games in far-flung Chicoutimi and Shawinigan and Val d'Or. They went back time and again, when one viewing told them all they needed to know. "I made sure that I saw his first Quebec league game and I went back lots of times," Boston scout Daniel Doré said. "You don't get a chance to see a player like that too often. You go when you get a chance."

I had seen them despair, the times when all their work—a season's worth of reports, hundreds of games, thousands of reports, whole days behind the steering wheel in awful weather—went for naught. None was sadder than the sight of Earl Ingarfield at the New York Islanders' table at the 2001 draft. Ingarfield, a former NHL journeyman forward, was one of the Islanders' regional scouts in western Canada. A quiet, gentlemanly sort, Ingarfield had toiled away over the years, helping the Islanders staff establish an excellent record in rating talent—only to have general manager Mike Milbury, a.k.a. Mad Mike, turn around and trade a succession of young All-Stars in the making, including Roberto Luongo and Eric Brewer.

There might not have been a more frustrating job in all of hockey than working for the Islanders under Milbury, so it wasn't a surprise that once past age sixty Ingarfield decided he'd put in only one more year of scouting before retiring. It was going to be one last shot at having a long-term impact on the franchise's fortunes. Sure enough, after a full year's worth of work, he watched Milbury deal the team's first pick, second overall, to Ottawa to acquire sullen superstar Alexei Yashin on the eve of the draft. Milbury also managed to trade away the Islanders' other picks in the next three rounds. In Earl Ingarfield's last season of scouting, he sat at the Islanders' table on the first day of the draft with nothing to do—he might as well have pulled out a deck of cards and played solitaire all day. What kept him at the table, I couldn't figure out.

If there's a common thread running through the scouting profession, I've never found it. There's no one way they go about their work. Paul Henry, who used to scout for Florida and Phoenix, took down notes furiously all game long but never looked away from the action on the ice, never looked down at the page on his clipboard. It seemed like he was afraid to blink at the risk of missing something. Others watch the game for twenty minutes or more with no change of expression, no motion whatsoever, like champion poker players concealing any tells. Only when they're off by themselves in intermissions will they jot down a few lines in their notebook. Though you might sit next to a scout in any section and not have know it, they always favour seats in the corners of rinks, at least ten rows up, more if possible—a better vantage point than rail seats, where they might be screened out on a play. Some prefer to sit and work alone. Most sit in pairs or in a small group, giving them a chance to banter when play stops.

Home base is only rarely the city where their employers are based. Most are scattered randomly across the fruited plain. A large number have set themselves up in Ann Arbor, Michigan; the old saw about location, location and location applies. From Ann Arbor, the scouts have easy access to all levels of the game: major junior (the Ontario Hockey League has franchises in Plymouth, Saginaw and Windsor); NCAA (the University of Michigan is the school that made Ann Arbor famous, and Michigan State and several other schools are an easy drive away); and USA Hockey (the national over-seer of the game has based its development program for the top under-18 players in Ann Arbor). But when scouts would go home, they would usually head off in all directions, across Canada, across the U.S. The last few years he scouted for the Oilers, Barry Fraser's home was in Mexico.

Like I say, I was a neophyte. Someone who had covered hockey as Red Fisher had in Montreal, someone who had put in whole decades and worked thousands of games: that would be an expert. I was simply looking to learn about the game. And I looked to the scouts for that. Samuel Johnson wasn't a hockey man, but he filed the defining scouting report on what passes for knowledge: "Knowledge is of two kinds: we know a subject ourselves, or we know where we can find information upon it." The scouts were my way to knowledge about hockey. I didn't even need to ask them questions. It would be an education through immersion—I figured if I loitered in the rooms reserved for them at junior rinks I could eavesdrop. If I sat behind them at games I could look at their notes over their shoulders. If I knocked back a beer with them after a game I could sound them out casually—to find out what they saw that I missed. And to try to get to know them better, I would have to spend a season in those corner seats, trying to do what they do—trying to put together files on players.

That's not to say that the scouts were an entirely welcoming bunch. Few have much time for the fans sitting next to them in the stands. Most are suspicious of the media, even hostile. Most avoid reporters as a reflex and will knock any of their peers who bother to talk to representatives of the fourth estate.

Maybe it was to be expected. It's a matter of security, not insecu-rity. "Knowledge is power," Francis Bacon wrote. Information is the

currency of the scouts' trade. They're only as good as their own opinions. They're reluctant to show their hole cards to anyone else, never
mind to someone who's going to broadcast them. They can't patent
their scouting reports, the information they glean through their
knowledge of the game; all they can do is protect it. And I know one
scout who ended up on the chopping block a few years back because
his bosses thought he gave his knowledge a little too freely to *The
Hockey News* for its draft preview. Whenever I've been brushed off,
I've tried not to take it personally. I couldn't blame them if they
observed a hockey version of *omerta*, if talking too freely really
would put their jobs at stake.

Earning even the limited trust of the scouts isn't easy. Maybe
another reporter would come up with a time-effective method.
Maybe another reporter could impress them with his knowledge.
Maybe he could invoke credentials earned by playing junior or college hockey. All I could do is show up at games and hope to get
marks for attendance. Not just the ones in my backyard, but in the
backwaters too. That is, maybe I could get a modicum of respect—
not as a peer, just an amateur—if I could show something approaching their passion and commitment. Not an investment of a few
games or even a season, but something that was going to take years,
the bulk of my somewhat accidental career.

These days, scouting has unprecedented cachet in the sports world.
The scouts would be the last ones to use the word, but lately they're
sexy. The public seems to crave the stuff of the scouts' work. All
kinds of scouting services have bubbled up—outfits that peddle
player rankings and other dope to recruiters from U.S. colleges and
rubbernecking fans alike. When new-media types cooked up a sub-
scription sports-information website, they named it scouts.com.
Newspapers eschew labelling a set-up for a game as a preview—
they go for *scouting report* instead. Magazines like *Sports Illustrated*
and *ESPN The Magazine* will offer as a regular feature reports on
players and teams from anonymous scouts in the full range of
sports. *USA Today* gave a regular hockey column to Kyle Woodlief,

a former scout with the Nashville Predators and editor of the *Red Line Report*, which offers scouting reports on all levels of the game, ostensibly for NHL scouting departments. Scouts, more than the voices of play-by-play, more than the writers of columns, offer up the authoritative take. Their opinions are viewed as more credible because an NHL franchise once paid for them.

I started to look longingly upon the work of hockey scouts. I wanted to be one of them. Not that I wanted to stamp myself as an authority. Anything but. That notion—*"The league is only as good as we are"*—that's what I wanted a hand in. To contribute to the game by filing reports on young players who could feed the game's insatiable hunger for talent. As a writer and reporter I always felt like an unnecessary accessory to the game—as a scout I could at least be in the weave.

Right-minded people would regard mine as a fool's ambition. There are many scouts who never played in the NHL, but those who didn't play pro at least played junior or college. That void alone would seem enough to kill my credibility. Still, I thought—or at least hoped—that I could offer skills developed in a couple of decades in the journalism biz, as well as whatever knowledge I might have soaked up running with the scouts.

Maybe other businesses would be open to approach from mere wannabes; and maybe, say, the marketing and public-relations departments of a NHL team would hold open a couple of spots for student interns. It's hard to imagine an NHL scouting staff open-ing its doors to a guy walking in off the street. You couldn't blame a scouting director if it wouldn't be worth the time and bother to read the reports of an amateur, of someone who wants to learn to be a scout. For a team executive you'd presume that the only opin-ion that would matter is one he'd pay for: the essence of profession-alism. Yet I've met scouts who started out just that way, as unpaid volunteers. Not many, mind you, but even some big names got their starts by cold-calling organizations and pitching them on fil-ing reports from the field.

Jimmy Devellano, the vice president of the Detroit Red Wings, is probably the best-known to have walked in off the street and into the game. Devellano was working for the federal government back in the '6os and his administrative job took him on the road all over Ontario. To kill time on the road, Devellano would catch games at the nearest major junior arena. When the NHL expanded to twelve teams in 1967, Devellano saw an opportunity to turn his pastime into a profession. He contacted the St. Louis Blues and made them an offer too cheap to refuse: he'd work on spec. "I told them that I'd file reports from as many games as I could make it out to, and let them judge for themselves whether it was useful or not," Devellano said. "I didn't have the reputation as a former player or a coach. I was just an ardent follower of the game, and from watching it enough over the years I had my own sense of those who could play and those who couldn't. And, really, as complicated as you can make scouting out to be, it's nothing more than that. Just because you played the game doesn't mean that you can scout— conversely, just because you didn't doesn't mean you can't scout."

In time Devellano went from the Blues to the New York Islanders and played a key role in assembling talent for a franchise that ran off four consecutive Stanley Cup championships. He later moved on to the Detroit Red Wings, where he has collected three more Cup rings.

Bob Tindall got his start with the Boston Bruins in much the same way: a day job that put him on the road, a passion for the game, chutzpah to approach an organization with an offer that cost it nothing to accept. Tindall ended up being a lieutenant to Harry Sinden for almost four decades. "It might be that someone like Jimmy and me would not only do a job as good as a lot of the others inside the game, but maybe even better," Tindall said. "After all, we're doing it because we want to, not because we have to. And starting out we had to work hard to prove ourselves."

I wasn't alone in wanting to be a NHL scout. A U.S. college has started a non-credit course in hockey scouting. From the online calendar:

The Hockey General Manager and Scouting Course is a fully accredited 8 **week online course** that offers cutting-edge

theories on how to develop a career in professional or colle-
giate hockey. The Hockey General Manager and Scouting
Course will cover issues including hockey operations, team
management, scouting talent, player personnel, cutting-edge
ways of scouting, NL traditional scouting techniques, statistical analysis and other essential tools . . .

The calendar suggested that the course was suited for those who
"want to pursue a career in professional hockey" in a wide variety of
capacities—everything from "NHL agent" to "NHL Game
Operations," from "NHL Sports Marketing" to "NHL Media &
Community Relations." And, of course, "NHL Management," "NHL
Front Office" and, most of all, "NHL Scout."

At the rink, I started to see unfamiliar names on sign-in lists in the
media-and-scouts' rooms. And an unfamiliar acronym under the
heading of "affiliation": ISS—International Scouting Service, the
folks who set up the Hockey General Manager and Scouting
Course. In its online literature, ISS claims to be "on a mission to be
the leader in hockey information worldwide." ISS wasn't alone. No,
now there were other outfits—how credible or widespread they
were, I could only guess. It seemed as though a scout could be anyone with a business card and a clipboard.

On press row at a recent NHL draft I made the acquaintance of
one such ISS scout: a blonde woman with an Australian accent that
was thought to have died with the Crocodile Hunter and a ring that
featured a diamond the size of a glass doorknob. From what I could
tell, she was based out west, either in Portland or Seattle, and whenever a Western Hockey League player's name was called she would
announce for the benefit of the media sitting around her: "I saw
him, yes, I did." As if somehow her seeing the player put him on the
fast track for selection at the draft. I would have asked her a few questions about her work, but she spent the entire draft on the phone to
her party planner and caterers.

If I'd had the chance, I would have asked her how she'd got her
start in scouting. I'd have to figure out my way on my own.

PART ONE

MY PLACE IN THE WAR ROOM

I'VE ALWAYS BEEN FASCINATED BY DRAFTS. It doesn't matter which sport, which pro league, I just pore over previews and forecasts and lists for hours at a time. It goes back to high school. I remember picking up a *Sport Magazine* and reading an analysis of the San Diego Chargers' draft one season back in the '70s. In the twelfth round, the Chargers selected John Van Reennen. He was designated a defensive lineman by the club even though he had never set foot on a football field—he was a six-foot-seven discus thrower from South Africa. I still remember the comment attached: "That's the Chargers' draft—the Sahara Desert." The geography was wonky, but the allusion appropriate: It was as hopeless a flyer as ever was. That I can still remember this more than thirty years later tells you how much I care about drafts: too much to be socially acceptable. Yes, obsessing about drafts could be a symptom of career bachelorhood, or a root cause—early on, I learned not to bring it up on first dates.

I've tried to figure out why drafts intrigue me and can only take an educated guess: caring about a game or a team is an emotional exercise, while caring about drafts is much closer to an academic one. The latter is how I lean. Drafts lend themselves both to history and statistics. Fans of sport will sit around and talk about the great teams of the past—I'll want to talk about the great drafts. (First in my heart: the Pittsburgh Steelers in '74 netted four Hall of Famers; in all, five starters on four Super Bowl–winning teams.) They'll talk about great players—I'll want to talk about how they were landed. (How good was the guy the Philadelphia Phillies took in the first round, if they waited till the second round to take Mike Schmidt?) Or I'll want to talk about how they were missed. (I've gone to the wall defending Houston's selection of Akeem Olajuwon at No. 1 over Michael Jordan, but Portland's bypassing of His Airness for brittle-boned Sam Bowie is unconscionable then, unconscionable now.)

Long before I started on the hockey beat I studied the NHL draft—not just memorizing names and draft slots, but actually studying, looking for trends, looking for patterns. I could have told you that historically and on average there's a greater difference between a player selected first through tenth and another selected eleventh through twentieth than shows up between a second- and fourth-rounder. (Seven out of the top ten draftees will play 400 games, compared to three to four of the second ten. In the latter instance, the difference is marginal, somewhere in the range of 15 out of 100 second-rounders reaching the 400-game benchmark while 11 or 12 of 100 fourth-rounders will get that far.) Some people sit down with crosswords and come up with solutions; I sit down with old draft lists and look for patterns, trends, systems.[1] Though there's more sports gambling than society can reasonably bear, the aspect of pro sports that runs closest to horse-race handicapping is the draft. And if NHL scouts ever reminded me of fixtures in another sport, it would be the railbirds at the racetrack.

It sounds dead goofy (but it shouldn't surprise you at this point): I was more excited about covering my first draft than I was about

---

1. My systematic approach: If I were a team with a second-rounder, I would attempt to trade it for two fourth-rounders, which would give me a better shot at landing a prospect who would go on to play 400 NHL games. And if I were a team with a first-round pick in slots eleven through twenty, I'd be prepared to trade that pick and my second-rounder to move up into the top ten—probably not the top three picks, but even picks seven through ten provide a far greater return than, say, No. 15. NHL general managers might laugh in my face but I could show them the work-ups. I'm not claiming that those are trades that are easy or even possible to make, but I'd be in there swinging.

covering my first Stanley Cup. I've reported from a dozen NHL drafts over the years. The first was in Edmonton back in 1995. That was the draft in the wake of the lockout-shortened season. The Stanley Cup playoffs extended into late June, so the 1995 draft was the first to be staged in July. Ottawa had the first pick in the draft and opted for Bryan Berard; the Islanders, going second, tapped Wade Redden. A season later, before either played in the NHL, the two franchises swapped one for the other. Not the oddest thing that ever issued out of a draft, mind you. That would be the second draft to be undertaken in July, the Sidney Crosby draft of 2005.

It was another draft put together after a lockout, the one that made the 2004–05 season something like a war year. The draft had been scheduled for Ottawa that year, but, lacking a collective agreement, the league scuttled its plans to hold it out at the Senators' home arena in Kanata. When the league and players' association finally patched together a deal, the draft was the first item on the agenda—that is, if you don't count the league-wide lottery, a televised spectacle that had thirty general managers and team governors sitting around waiting to hear their franchise's name called. If that was silly, it was no more so than the draft, which was staged in a conference room at the Westin instead of a proper arena venue. Only a dozen or so invited players were allowed to attend, and they had to wait together in a green room until their names were called. The league came up with all kinds of reasons for going small with this momentous event, but everyone was convinced that it was done this way to spare Commissioner Gary Bettman the longest, loudest booing in the annals of sport.

I had covered the drafts, as others do in the sportswriting dodge. The reporters were always on one side of a chest-high fence, the management and scouting staffs of the thirty teams on the other. I can only presume that the board of governors narrowly rejected Lou Lamoriello's proposal to line the fence with razor wire. At various times during the draft-day proceedings, a general manager or coach would stand by the fence to drop a few quotes in the reporters' notebooks. Maybe a few reporters had cozied up to a source who occasionally offered a little inside stuff on background. Other than that, the vast majority of stuff on the floor never made it up to the fence. What went on at the tables and in the days leading up to the draft was not for publication. It was, in a way, like court coverage that offered only verdicts, and no opinions or accounts of the deliberations.

In the spring of 2006 I set about trying to get to the other side of the fence. I set about getting access to a team's war room leading up to the draft. I had no expectation of success. Nothing like this had ever been done. Oh, a few years back the Carolina Hurricanes allowed a camera into their conference room at a combine, but only a short clip made it to air. And Leafs TV, the digital cable channel owned and operated by Maple Leaf Sports and Entertainment, had a more extensive "inside" look at a scouting staff in conference. It was nothing more than a showcase for Barry Trapp, a blustering forty-year veteran of pro hockey and the Leafs' head amateur scout at the time. The Leafs had control over the editing of the feature, so the team got out there only what it was happy to make public. These two limited exceptions notwithstanding, what happens on one side of the fence stays on that side of the fence—even more so than the old line about what goes on in a locker room.

I made calls, left messages and fired off emails saying: "Dear Lou/Bob/Darcy/Ken, etc., Could you see it in your heart to allow me into your meetings before the draft, so I can show the public exactly how you go about your business? And if there's anything at all confidential, I won't tell anybody. You can trust me. After all, I'm a reporter. Best to the wife and kids, Gare."

For a couple of weeks I didn't get so much as a returned call. Not from organizations and executives I knew only in passing, not from general managers that I've known for years. The first—and, as it turned out, the second-last—response came from Doug Armstrong, the general manager of the Dallas Stars. Looking back on it now, I think Doug wrote back to me simply because he was concerned about my mental health. He emailed a message saying that he was going to refer me to Tim Bernhardt, a former Maple Leaf goaltender who has worked for the Stars for a good, long stretch. I thought that this might be promising; I was on good terms with Tim, and he's an interesting and shrewd guy. When Tim and I finally spoke, I told him that I wanted to be inside the team's room at the Central Scouting combine and sit on interviews with the draft's top prospects. Sure, Tim said, but there's one problem — Dallas doesn't interview players at the combine. The Stars bring in a few players for interviews with a sports psychologist, but not at the combine. When I asked about sitting in on meetings where the scouts were going to go over their lists, Bernhardt told me that was one door the Stars weren't about to open. "We just don't do that crap," he reassured me.

Yeah, pretty soon I was resigned to the fact that no team was going to do "that crap." Then one day I got an email from Doug MacLean, the general manager of the Columbus Blue Jackets. All it said was, "Let me talk to Don Boyd about it."

Hope. Doug MacLean has always been the NHL's most media-friendly executive. It seems like he does two or three radio or television hits every day. He figures one of a general manager's jobs is to sell the game, not surprising given the two markets where he's worked the last ten years (Florida, then Columbus). Well outside the hockey mainstream. I first met him when the Florida Panthers brought him in as coach during the franchise's third season and MacLean took a team loaded with journeymen and other people's leftovers to the Stanley Cup final. That bought him a couple of more seasons in Florida and later a chance to build the Blue Jackets from the ground up. Some execs can claim to be with a club since Day One, but MacLean was uniquely positioned — he was general manager of the Blue Jackets for two seasons before they actually had a team on the ice. Not just there for the birth but also the gestation period.

As personable as MacLean is, the Blue Jackets don't get many hockey fans' pulses racing — and casual sports fans might be surprised that there's an NHL team in the capital of Ohio at all. The Blue Jackets are overshadowed in their own division by the always-powerful Detroit Red Wings and the emerging Nashville Predators. And the Blue Jackets are overshadowed in Columbus by the Ohio State University Buckeyes' basketball and football teams, perennial contenders for Big Ten and national titles. Going into their sixth season, MacLean's team had yet to make the playoffs. They had assembled a few interesting players, particularly a towering and tough winger named Rick Nash, the No. 1–overall selection in the 2002 draft. But most of the Blue Jackets were, like the team itself, not quite even middle of the pack.

Going behind the scenes with the Blue Jackets might not have seemed like much of an opportunity. Frankly, not many people were all that wound up about the team that's in plain sight. Maybe if the Detroit Red Wings had signed on, I could go into the fact that their staff had landed great late-round finds like Pavel Datsyuk and Henrik Zetterberg. Maybe if the Buffalo Sabres had signed on, I could explain how they've managed to draft more players currently playing in the NHL than has any other franchise (almost all of them with more scouts and more money). But as Donald Rumsfeld decreed: "You don't go to war with the army you want. You go to war with the army you have."

Columbus would give me a chance to see the staff of a losing team working under pressure to turn the corner. The Blue Jackets' owner, John H. McConnell, made his fortune in steel, but there was nothing cast-iron about the executives' and scouts' security. After all, McConnell hadn't originally planned to be the Blue Jackets' proprietor. He came aboard with another sporting industrialist, Lamar Hunt, when the NHL was casting about for expansion franchises in the late '90s. When Hunt bailed out—a plan for community financial support fell though—McConnell stepped into the breach out of community spirit. That was how McConnell portrayed it when he and Hunt went to court to settle their accounts. With the stock price of McConnell's company tumbling, the owner's patience with the Blue Jackets had to be running out. This added nice dramatic elements to the Columbus war room (though I suspect MacLean and his staff could do with a lot less drama).

I told a friend in the scouting trade that Columbus might give me a peek inside their operation, and he was unimpressed. "They did okay getting Nash, but pretty well everybody had him that high."[2]

Eventually, MacLean passed along the phone number of Don Boyd, the team's amateur scouting director, and told me to set something up with him. I had no idea how much access the Blue Jackets would grant me. In fact, I wasn't even sure they'd grant me any at all. As it turned out, I sat in their meetings and interviews for about—a modest estimate here—eighty hours over the next three weeks, during which I was granted absolutely unfettered access. Though I was in and out of the conference room, interviewing prospects and team executives, I sat in on more interviews with prospects than many teams conducted. The Jackets asked me to clam up about a trade that was in the works, and they asked that I keep my mouth zipped until after the draft—to simply abide by the same rules as their own scouts. What happens on this side of the fence stays on this side of the fence . . . for a while, anyway. Later on, a few guys in the hockey media would ask me how I managed to get on the other side of the fence, and they smirked disbelievingly when I told them I had just asked politely.

---

2. A bit of historical revisionism. The name atop many scouts' lists that year was Jay Bouwmeester, a sky-high defenceman who played for the Medicine Hat Tigers and was the youngest player to make the Canadian roster at the world under-20 tournament. The Florida Panthers ended up selecting Bouwmeester with the third-overall pick, behind Nash and Finnish goaltender Kari Lehtonen, who was scooped up by Atlanta. Bouwmeester never made the Western Hockey League playoffs in Medicine Hat, and in his NHL career so far he has yet to make it to the postseason. Bouwmeester was outstanding for Canada in the World Cup in 2004. The jury is out on him to an extent. "You wonder about his personality," one general manger told me. "He's a total blank. You want a kid who's good around people, someone you enjoy being around. Didn't see that with Bouwmeester."

May 29, 2006, conference room, Renaissance Hotel, Toronto

"Johnson," Don Boyd reads out.

The List begins. It's all about The List. All the teams have their lists—lists at mid-season, lists at the end of the season. All the scouts on all the teams have their own lists—lists of players in their region, lists of goaltenders, lists of kids they just have a feeling about, good and bad. And out of all these lists comes one list. *The* List, the one that Don Boyd will pass to his boss, Doug MacLean, on the morning of the NHL draft.

Every team's list, every scout's list, every page of every scouting report starts as blank as the wall-sized erasable board that John Williams stands beside with a black marker. This is how the Columbus Blue Jackets' List begins. Small printing: 1-J-O-H-N-S-O-N. All the scouts sitting at the tables circling the board don't even look up from the screens of their laptops.

John Williams moves over the column marked +.

"Johnson . . . size, skating, strength, shot," Boyd says. Agreement all around. Williams moves over to the column marked –. "What are his minuses?" Boyd asks.

Dead quiet for a few seconds. Williams tries to lighten things up and move things along.

"Lack of experience in the NHL," he offers.

Nervous laughter.

The Blue Jackets' scouting staff nosh on Doritos and peanuts. That's how it will be for whole days. The staff met in the same room for eight hours on Sunday. Call that the agree-to-disagree day, the day that every scout gets his list out, the day when one guy's first-rounder is another guy's fourth-rounder, when one guy's can't-miss is another's can't-play. The ability to sign the names in play here is not an issue, not with the collective agreement's salary cap for rookies. The operating presumption: Everybody will come for a price dictated by his slot. The readiest to come are those playing in the Canadian junior leagues—draft them and they'll be in your pro training camp at summer's end. Those in U.S. colleges may require down the line, but the scouts themselves have all the security one-year contracts can offer.

Maybe Boyd is a little more secure than his staff—he just sold the family home in London and he and his missus, empty-nesters with the kids off to college, are in the process of moving into a condo in Columbus just a walk from arena. A leap of faith, faith in the Blue Jackets' ability to turn around their fortunes and get into the playoffs for the first time, faith in his former assistant's ability to remain the only general manager in the franchise's history.

If you just wandered into the conference room, you wouldn't know at first that this was sports business going on. Most of the time, companies book these rooms to talk about sales targets or corporate strategies. On the face of it—with the walls papered with lists of names divided up by regions, by position, by one category or another—the room looks exactly like that. No PowerPoint, which maybe suggests sessions that are a little more free-form, more loosely planned. But otherwise it looks like just another day at the Renaissance. It could be Amway in this room. It could be Century 21.

Look harder and you'd see the telltale signs that this is something out of the ordinary. If this room had been reserved by a real-estate company, a retail chain or a Fortune 500 outfit, a certain species of executive would be in charge of the room. A well-manicured guy in a suit would be talking about team-building and motivation while those in his audience, dressed to impress, tried to look attentive and say what they thought he wanted to hear. But Don Boyd, who's clearly in charge, is in jeans and a t-shirt, gritting his teeth while peering over his glasses at his computer screen or nervously pacing—stalking—around the back of the room. Boyd is a lumpenprole-looking kind of guy—short, stocky, balding. No silk scarves here. He has a weakness for junk food. He fractures syntax and drops malapropisms into conversation on a regular basis. Yet there's more to him than the plain picture. You'd never guess he went to Bowling Green State University on a hockey scholarship. Or that he rides a Harley. He was a street fighter in his time back in Dryden, Ontario. He is almost a wait because they have to stay away from the pro camp to retain their NCAA eligibility. Those in Europe, particularly Russia, may have complicating issues, usually a contract with a club, but maybe some to-and-fro with agents. And at this point the Russian federation is threatening to use its top prospects as human shields in negotiating an agreement with the International Ice Hockey Federation. But, again, Boyd maintains, while drawing up The List, the presumption is that everybody will come.

"Lack of experience in the NHL, that would be about it," Williams says. Maybe, Williams figures, they need a laugh to open things up—frayed nerves on the second day. Not Don Boyd. He was no cheerleader when he was a coach and general manager of the London Knights in the Ontario Hockey League. Back in London he hired a young guy from Prince Edward Island who was attending teacher's college, and that guy is now his boss, Doug MacLean. No, Don Boyd was never a cheerleader. He was a pusher, a hard-ass's hard-ass. That's the default mode. He's in the board room now, but he's exactly the same as he'd be behind a bench. He wants this crew to be ready for business from the first shift on—they shouldn't need to warm up for the work at hand. He dips his head and peers out over the frame of his glasses. His jaw slips into joint. Barely a minute in and he's already lost his patience.

"Can we get to work?" he growls, an order by way of a question. He figures they shouldn't need anything more than the understanding that, by the end of business today, there will be 100 or more names on that board, divided into Top Tens, First-Rounders, Early Seconds, Late Seconds, Thirds and Fourths, plus a goaltenders' list. The farther down the board you go, the farther from the NHL you get: that's how it's supposed to work when you spend a couple of million dollars in salaries and expenses putting The List together. Check that—that's how The List had better work, because they all might be out of jobs if it doesn't. Boyd and his staff have been together for six drafts, the Blue Jackets' entire history, and the team has yet to make the playoffs. All scouts live from draft to draft, List to List. They project players three or four seasons defiantly small-townish. He would be insulted if accused of going big-city and slick. That condo in Columbus? He would say that it just cuts down the commute to the office. He is tough, and tough-minded. He would be a grind in a college class.

Boyd sets the standard for style—or lack thereof. Style just doesn't matter here. Williams is in a t-shirt, shorts and bare feet. Golf shirts are as dressy as it gets. This isn't about looking good . . . it's about *getting* good. It's all about substance and results. The scouts don't feel a need to try to impress Boyd with appearances. Butt-kissing and apple-polishing don't matter. *Don't tell me about how hard you work, just be right about that list.* That's what he expects when he sends his scouts to a couple of hundred games a season everywhere from Siberia to Spokane, from Ivy League games in New England to mining towns like Val d'Or in Quebec. That's a couple of hundred games *each*. Every working winter night. Sometimes two games in a day. Sometimes three. The scouts file five player assessments from some games, ten from others, and at international tournaments, forty. Four thousand player reports for the year is not out of line—four thousand *each*.[3] And these reports better be right, not just because Boyd will see every player who matters, but because general manager Doug MacLean and his lieutenant, Jim Clark, will see the players who really matter, the players near the top of the list.

The scouts believe they're right. They all come from inside the game. Milan Tichy, the Czech scout, went the farthest as a player, getting in a couple of seasons with the New York Islanders and, at a lanky six-foot-three, he looks like he can still play. Artem Telepin didn't make it to North America but played several seasons in the first and second divisions in Russia in the '90s. The European head

---

3. This represents a single viewing of a player of interest. For example, from Canadian junior games a scout might file ten player reports, maybe a dozen. At the international under-18 tournaments, where almost every player on the ice is draft-eligible and of potential interest, the scout will file an assessment of thirty-eight players, presuming the backup goaltenders don't play.

scout, Kjell Larsson, has coached Swedish national teams. Sam McMaster is a hockey lifer—he was general manager in the Soo when the Greyhounds had a young phenom named Wayne Gretzky, and general manager of the Los Angeles Kings when No. 99 set NHL records every time he racked a goal or an assist. John Williams, who works the west, is a second-generation scout, his father having worked for the Florida Panthers. Wayne Smith, the Ottawa-based scout, was considered a top junior back in the late '80s and early '90s but lacked pro size. Paul Castron, the Blue Jackets' scout based in Ann Arbor, is a Sudbury native who played NCAA hockey and went on to work for the Ottawa Senators before signing on with Columbus. And Boyd, well, he was already a career junior coach when he hired Doug MacLean in London, Ontario.

They came by their bona fides in different ways and in different places, but they're all hockey men. I'm not—I mentioned it before, but it's worth mentioning again. Never was. Never will be. So, going into this, I expect that the scouts will be reluctant to open up in front of me, never mind *to* me. I expect that any question I may ask will be met with derision. And so, for the first day, I sit in the room and say nothing. I'll also do that for the second day. And the next. I'll lie in wait for the right time.

Knowing the game is just the first part of putting together The List. It only starts with the thousands of hours in arenas. After all those reports and games and miles and expense accounts, the scouts begin in the same place, on the same page: they agree on the Top Ten players. There is something approaching consensus on the pool of elite prospects. Not who will be in the first ten picks chosen at the draft in Vancouver in a couple of weeks' time. No, for Boyd and his staff, a Top Ten is a brand, a type. Top Ten is shorthand for *an eighteen-year-old who should develop into a first-line NHL player, maybe an All-Star, definitely someone who can contribute to a winning team.*

The Columbus scouts figure there are only seven Top Ten players on The List. In other years there have been a dozen. The 2003 draft was particularly deep—there might have been fifteen Top Tens.[4]

Maybe even more. But there are just seven this year, and that means it's an indifferent year. Not as deep. Not as high-end.

The Blue Jackets can take some consolation in the fact that they draft sixth overall. By their reckoning, that means that they'll get a player they figure is a Top Ten. That means they'll have to choose between two players when it comes to their pick—maybe three if there's a draft-day surprise.[5]

Three players on The List aren't going to be there at No. 6:

Erik Johnson, a tall, powerful defenceman with the U.S. under-18 program in Ann Arbor, logged more ice time than any other blue-liner on the US under-20 team. Johnson's game grew playing on the

---

4. Most of the players from the first twenty picks have already made the NHL and will be franchise cornerstones: 1. Pittsburgh (from Florida), Marc-Andre Fleury, G, Cape Breton (QMJHL); 2. Carolina, Eric Staal, C, Peterborough (OHL); 3. Florida (from Pittsburgh), Nathan Horton, C, Oshawa (OHL); 4. Columbus, Nikolai Zherdev, RW, Russia; 5. Buffalo, Thomas Vanek, LW, Univ. of Minnesota (NCAA); 6. San Jose, Milan Michalek, RW, Czech Republic; 7. Nashville, Ryan Suter, D, U.S. National Under-18 (NTDP); 8. Atlanta, Braydon Coburn, D, Portland (WHL); 9. Calgary, Dion Phaneuf, D, Red Deer (WHL); 10. Montreal, Andrei Kastitsyn, C/W, Belarus; 11. Philadelphia (from Phoenix), Jeff Carter, C, Sault Ste. Marie (OHL); 12. New York Rangers, Hugh Jessiman, RW, Dartmouth College (NCAA); 13. Los Angeles, Dustin Brown, RW, Guelph (OHL); 14. Chicago, Brent Seabrook, D, Lethbridge (WHL); 15. New York Islanders, Robert Nilsson, C, Sweden; 16. San Jose (from Boston), Steve Bernier, RW, Moncton (QMJHL); 17. New Jersey (from Edmonton), Zach Parise, C, Univ. of North Dakota (NCAA); 18. Washington, Eric Fehr, RW, Brandon (WHL); 19. Anaheim, Ryan Getzlaf, C, Calgary (WHL); 20. Minnesota, Brent Burns, RW, Brampton (OHL).

5. In 2005 the Blue Jackets got a draft-day present of this sort, when the Montreal Canadiens, seemingly set in goal for several years with the emergence of Jose Theodore, drafted a goaltender, Carey Price, with the fifth-overall pick instead of centre Gilbert Brule, who was snapped up by Columbus.

Minnesota 88s, a team of local kids born in that year. The group stayed together from fifth-grade through their mid-teens, and several of them are projected to be high draft choices. Johnson has signed a letter of intent with the University of Minnesota.

Jordan Staal starred with Peterborough Petes, like his older brother Eric, the franchise forward with the Carolina Hurricanes and the second pick overall in the 2003 draft. Jordan's numbers and his team's performance (an Ontario Hockey League championship) outstripped his older brother's. This is all the more impressive because Eric was a late birthday (meaning he turned eighteen early in the hockey season prior to his draft) and Jordan is still seventeen (he won't turn eighteen until just before his first NHL training camp). When Jordan Staal's name comes up, Wayne Smith notes that Staal *père* told another scout that this year's edition is physically stronger than Eric. Boyd asks if the father meant that Jordan is stronger at eighteen than Eric was at the same age. "No," Smith says. "His father says Jordan's stronger than Eric *right now.*" Head shakes and looks of astonishment all around. Behind only Sidney Crosby and Alexander Ovechkin, Eric Staal is arguably the breakout star of the 2005–06 NHL season. *What the hell is Staal 3.0 going to be like?*

Jonathan Toews, a centre out of the University of North Dakota, was born and raised in Winnipeg and played a year at Shattuck–St. Mary's, the Minnesota high school that Sidney Crosby attended before going to the Quebec junior league.[6] Toews led the

---

6. In fact, Crosby's teammate and best friend at Shattuck, defenceman Jack Johnson, was the third-overall pick in the 2005 draft. Other Shattuck alumni who have been selected in the first round of the draft include Zach Parise of the New Jersey Devils and Drew Stafford of the Buffalo Sabres. Kyle Okposo, another projected high first-rounder in the 2006 draft, played alongside Toews at Shattuck. So did Angelo Esposito, who played last season for the Memorial Cup champion Quebec Remparts and is the pre-season favourite of many scouts to be the first-overall pick in the 2007 draft.

Canadian team to the under-18 World Cup the previous summer. Scouts rated his performance in the tournament as being as dominant as those of Rick Nash and Vincent Lecavalier, the first-overall picks in 2002 and 1998 drafts respectively. Toews took a regular shift with the under-20 team that won the world junior title a few months later. He has already stated that he intends to be back at UND next season.

Any of them could go first, though St. Louis is supposedly leaning toward taking Johnson, who brings back memories of Chris Pronger, the Blues' former franchise player. Any of them could go third. Everybody has a minus. They have holes. The holes and minuses get aired out in the room. For Johnson, it's "doesn't have a killer instinct" and "won't back down but isn't mean." For Staal, it's "first couple of steps" and "faded in the Memorial Cup, didn't have an impact at the end of the season." The knock on Toews: "not a game-breaker." But the minuses don't go beyond that. They end right there, and so do Columbus's hopes of seeing them slide to sixth.

The way Don Boyd and his staff see it, four Top Ten players could be there at No. 6. Phil Kessel. Derick Brassard. Nicklas Backstrom. Peter Mueller. That's the list within The List. They spend more time debating their pluses and minuses.

Kessel first.

The brainstorming starts with the storyline. Kessel's talent is a known quantity. All the North American scouts in Columbus's and every other organization have seen him. Kessel starred for the U.S. team at the 2005 world under-20 tournament as a seventeen-year-old. Scouts can still see him darting down the right wing and scoring a hat trick in a tournament game. The European scouts know all about him, too. Kessel was the best player on the U.S. team that won the world under-18s in April 2005—in just six games he racked up nine goals and seven assists. And he's the rare draft-eligible player who has experience playing beside and against NHL pros: only a couple of weeks before, he was on the roster of the U.S. team at the world championships.

Kessel would have been the No. 2 pick behind Sidney Crosby in last year's draft if he'd been eligible.[7] With a birthday in October '87, he only missed being eligible by a few weeks. So scouts and Kessel had to wait until this spring. And in the interim, his stock has plunged.

"Strengths?" Boyd asks. "Speed, scoring . . ."

None of Boyd's staff jumps in. It's easy to imagine that, twelve months earlier, they would have been crowding each other to get in their two cents about Kessel's strengths. But Kessel's stock has crashed over the course of a season. First, there were rumbles about character. Kids who grew up playing beside Kessel in Madison, Wisconsin, had nothing good to say about him (maybe a predictable and envy-ridden by-product of Kessel's scoring 176 goals in a season as a fourteen-year-old). Same with players who were in USA Hockey's development program. Kessel's parents supposedly rubbed people the wrong way. But even with the character issue aside, a lot of the gloss had come off Kessel's performance at the 2005 under-20s. The U.S. team had been favoured to win the 2006 juniors, and Kessel was supposed to lead them, but the team crashed to a fourth-place finish and Kessel had little impact. He enrolled at the University of Minnesota and was expected to tear up the U.S. college ranks; by the end of the season he was dropped to the third line of a team that made it through only one round of the NCAAs. That would have been bad enough, but then Kessel was caught in a

---

7. It has been reported that some scouts, maybe as many as half the scouting staffs of NHL teams, favoured Kessel over Sidney Crosby last year. This isn't just pie-in-the-sky stuff, but rather a question that scouts had to sort out all season long. The NHL has always operated with a draft class comprising players born between September 15 of one year and September 14 of the next. Training camp was the reason for this—NHL teams want to bring their draftees to training camp as soon as possible, but bringing a kid in under the age of eighteen opens up issues of liability in the case of injury. In the back-and-forth of collective bargaining, one item on the agenda was the draft, and the NHL was contemplating

Minneapolis television news team's sting of a bar serving underage varsity athletes.

When it comes to listing Kessel's minuses, Boyd yields the floor to Brian Bates, the Blue Jackets' scout based in Minneapolis and the one who saw more NCAA games than anyone else the past winter.

Bates sticks to Kessel's skill set. Questions of character aren't going to be floated in this meeting. "I wonder about his game awareness sometimes," Bates says. It might not sound so damning, but it's a significant black mark to scouts and executives.

This gets nods all around the table. Agreed. "There might be some selfish play there sometimes," Boyd says.

Williams prints B-R-A-S-S-A-R-D on the board. A forward with Drummondville in the Quebec league who has moved ahead of Kessel in the rankings of a lot of teams, as well as those of the NHL's Central Scouting Service. Derick Brassard started off well behind Kessel. On the team Canada sent to the world under-18 the previous August, the team that Toews led to a gold medal, Brassard was a third-liner, a role player. But over the season, Brassard emerged as a player. He was transformed from one season (25 goals and 76 points in 68 games) to the next (44 goals and 116 points in just 58 games). His stock shot up at the same time Kessel's plunged.

"Speed," Williams says.

"Creativity, hands," Boyd dictates. Boyd doesn't try to keep a poker face here. No point. The scouts know that he's high on

---

going to a draft based on the calendar year. It was lost in the paper shuffle in the final days of the bargaining agreement, not enough of a priority to let negotiations drag out another day. However, if a calendar-year draft had been put into place, Kessel, who was born in October 1987, would have been eligible for the 2005 draft, not the 2006 draft. It's hard to find many scouts who'll 'fess up to a previously held opinion that Kessel was a prospect even close to Crosby, never mind ahead of him. I tracked Crosby throughout his junior career and talked to dozens of scouts in the months before the 2005 draft. I never met one who saw a hole in his game, not even a loose thread on his sweater.

Brassard. They know that he called MacLean from a game in mid-season and told the general manager, "I've just seen Joe Sakic." They know his story, and they've read Boyd's scouting reports.

Then he asks. "Game-breaker?"

Wayne Smith wants to jump in, but he's holding his cards tight. He has seen Brassard dozens of times over the past two years. He's *on* him. But he doesn't want to take over.

Neither does Sam McMaster. He'll make his pitch on Brassard later. He has him at No. 2, higher than everybody else.

No show of hands, but no objections.

"Has real good hockey sense," Paul Caston says.

One knock: size. "What is he, a buck-70?," Wayne Smith asks.

"Not going to be a big forward," Williams says.

On to Nicklas Backstrom. Not coming to the combine, no interview, no testing, says Williams. No surprise, says Boyd, not after Backstrom took a regular shift beside NHLers on Sweden's team at the world championships. The combine is regarded as nuisance, an inconvenience, but one that most prospects will submit to because passing it up will adversely affect their draft stock. Even Sidney Crosby, a player with absolutely nothing to prove, a player who knew he was going to be selected No. 1 overall, came out to the combine just days after a physically punishing run to the Memorial Cup final.[8] But Backstrom believes that he showed the NHL scouts everything they needed to know at the world championships, where he became the youngest player ever to play for the Swedish national team. It's one thing to show your skills at the world juniors or the Memorial Cup, another to do it at the world championships.

The floor is yielded to Kjell Larsson, the head of European scouting for Columbus and a former coach of the Swedish national

---

8. One scout at the combine said: "We didn't interview him. He interviewed us." Crosby even took part in some of the physical testing, though he begged off any lower-body testing because of knocks and bruises suffered at the Memorial Cup.

team. The North American scouts rib Larsson for always pushing for Swedes.

"Two little marks [below] what you said about Brassard, two little marks," Larsson says.

Williams marks dittoes under all Brassard's strengths.

Boyd asks: "What about speed? Brassard is an NHL skater right now."

Williams asks: "Is he a game-breaker?"

Larsson's not budging. "I think so. He's not a goal scorer now— he's in the elite league, playing against pros. But a goal scorer, I think he will become that."

The Columbus scouts usually give Larsson a hard time, and Larsson almost invites their shots. It's not that he only comes up to their armpits. No, it's the fact that he sees the world through blue-and-gold-tinted glasses—all things Swedish are good. He'd probably tell you that a fleet of Volvos would sweep Formula One races if they bothered to line up. And Larsson reflexively gets his back up at the suggestion that anything Swedish is anything less than excellent. Still, on the subject of Backstrom, the Blue Jackets' scouts listen intently. Yes, they know that Larsson's *on* Backstrom. He has had the most views of him. He's dialled in.

Of all the players in the Top Ten category, nobody's stock in this draft has climbed like Backstrom's. By the reckoning of scouts I had talked to outside the Columbus room, Backstrom would have been selected late in the first round if the draft had been conducted back at Christmas. Just on his play in the last three months of the regular season in the Swedish elite league and at the world championships, he's up near the top of the board.

"I was watching tape of him playing with Henrik Zetterberg, at the worlds, and sometimes I couldn't tell which was which," Boyd says. "Let's see if we can get him to come in to Columbus next week, Kjell. Otherwise, let's make sure we arrange to talk to him in Vancouver."

Next up: Peter Mueller, a forward with the Everett Silvertips in the Western league. Lots of crosstalk. Size is listed as an asset, but Williams says he looks smaller because he sits down on his skates. Shot is listed as a strength, his willingness to use it as a weakness.

"Not going to carry your team," Wayne Smith says.

"Best passer in the Western league," Williams says.

"He's from Minnesota," Boyd says, "so why did he go play junior rather than go to college?"

The question hangs out there. No answer. In Minnesota, kids don't talk about growing up to play in the NHL—they talk about becoming a Gopher, a member of the University of Minnesota Golden Gophers. That's the route Erik Johnson is taking. That's the route Kessel opted for, even though he had overtures from the Ontario Hockey League.[9] The conventional wisdom is that Mueller didn't have the grades. "We'll ask him in the interview."

Right now, in the early going, it looks as if Mueller will be in seventh on the Columbus list—just outside the mix. Of course, he could be the first to move up into the mix if something comes out of the combine testing and interviews.

Four names. It will come down to a choice out of two, maybe three.

That choice will be based on games, games that these four teenagers have played over the last four years while the scouts were taking notes in the stands.

Surf through the Blue Jackets' database. The scouts have seen all four in international tournaments. Use your imagination when you read the reports. You can see Backstrom in games against pros in Swedish league last winter. Mueller and Kessel in high-school play

---

9. Kessel was drafted by Saginaw of the Ontario Hockey League, but he told the team he had no interest in playing there. Nobody could blame him: Saginaw was the league's worst team the season before, and even with Kessel, it wouldn't have been much better. But if Kessel had signed off on the idea of playing in the OHL—which is to say, if he had named a price for his services, which could have been in the neighbourhood of $150,000, strictly off the books—then Saginaw could have at least traded his rights and received players in return. Evidently, teams at least inquired about Kessel coming to the OHL, but the matter never got as far as hard negotiations.

in the Midwest three years ago. Brassard going from a too-small kid to a dominant player across three years in small-town Quebec. The reports are usually in point form, sometimes tough to read, often with uncorrected typos. Columbus's Quebec scout often leaves out the f when he types "shift."

Search for reports filed on the four in play: 70 for Kessel, 50 for Brassard, 61 for Mueller, 41 for Backstrom. Those are just the reports everyone can access. Those numbers don't include the views of MacLean, Clark or Boyd. Not that the greater number of views translates into a more definitive read on a player. With this four prospects, it's the most-viewed Kessel who has the Blue Jackets scratching their heads.

Boyd and the staff will spend six more hours this afternoon and evening roughing out Nos. 8 through 100. The first set of names that come up for discussion after the Top Ten are First-Rounders. Just as there aren't ten players who fit the top category, so are there not quite enough First-Rounders to fill out the thirty first-round selections at the draft.

In contrast to the Top Ten, there are now too many moving parts for the scouts to be near consensus. I can detect a couple of trends.

Tichy and Telepin don't wave their respective flags like Larsson. Tichy soft-sells the Czech players, Jiri Tlusty and Michael Frolik, while Telepin is critical of the Russian players on the list. My gut tells me that Telepin doesn't want to end up "owning" a high pick who underachieves. The Blue Jackets may also be reluctant to draft a Russian prospect because of their experience with 2003 first-rounder Nikolai Zherdev. At that draft, MacLean boldly announced that the Blue Jackets had Zherdev ranked No. 1 on their list—a statement he must rue now. Getting Zherdev to play in Columbus was an ordeal. MacLean signed him in the fall of 2003 but CSKA, the Moscow Red Army team, took the Blue Jackets to court, claiming that Zherdev was still under contract to them. They also claimed that Zherdev was obliged to perform military service, a standard negotiating ruse among Russian clubs. It was messy, and Russian officials likely still hold a grudge towards the Columbus team. Zherdev seemed to have made a break-through last season, scoring 27 goals, including a couple of highlight-reel numbers that were as pretty as anything Sidney Crosby pulled off. But even though Zherdev left CSKA on bad terms, he's threatening to play in Russia next season because he's unhappy with his contract negotiations with the Blue Jackets. Add to that the fact that the Russian federation is spoiling for a fight with the International Ice Hockey Federation and the NHL over player transfer fees, and the drafting of another Russian seems, if not a high risk, then at least a potential headache.

The scouts will spend two more full days going back and forth on players who aren't Top Tens. They raced through Nos. 1 through 7, the list within The List. That doesn't mean it's final today, tomorrow, or even when the team and the players named here make it to Vancouver. It won't be until the draft is hours away. And even on the floor of the arena, with Columbus on the clock and five minutes to call out a name, the list within The List might be reopened.[10]

At the end of the day I cross-checked The List with NHL Central Scouting's rankings. The NHL Central Scouting Service was founded back in the 1970s by former Washington Capitals exec Jack Button as a tool for NHL clubs' amateur scouting departments. (Scouts employed by NHL clubs simply refer to it as "Central.") These days Central is headed up by E.J. Maguire, a longtime coach in the pro and junior ranks, and Jim Gregory, who was general manager of the

---

10. The Blue Jackets didn't dwell on goaltending for very long at all. Management was banking on Pascal Leclaire as the team's goaltender of the immediate present and future. By the first day of the meetings, MacLean was putting the finishing touches on a trade that would send his No. 1 goaltender last season, Marc Denis, to Tampa for Fredrik Modin, a winger who played a large role in the Lightning's run to the Stanley Cup in 2004. Both Denis and Modin were entering the last year of contracts and would be free agents if not signed to extensions.

Toronto Maple Leafs in the '70s and prior to that a mover and shaker in junior hockey with the Toronto Marlboros. Going into the 2006 draft, Maguire and Gregory had nine full-time and six part-time scouts in North America and six full-time scouts in Europe, along with European scouting director Goran Stubb. Central is where a lot of former players get their start in the scouting trade—as much as amateur scouting is key to keeping up the talent level of the league, so is Central crucial to the development of scouts. Jack Button seems to have mentored an entire generation of scouts, while a younger crew learned the business from Jim Gregory and Frank Bonello.

Central's rankings are not comprehensive but rather segregated—that is, the rankings are divided into North America on one side, Europe on the other. And within the region, players are further divided into the two categories of skaters and goaltenders. Central offers up a preliminary shout-out in the fall, essentially listing players to watch, and then in December it publishes a set of midseason rankings. Near the end of the junior season, Central issues its final rankings.

The way Boyd explains it, Central's preliminary and midseason lists are probably of more use to his scouts. "It's like a road map for us," Boyd says. That is, a list to cherry-pick from—names to chase down and see. The final list is useful for the media and the fans, but by the time it's issued NHL teams are more concerned about the lists offered up by their own scouts in the field.[11]

---

11. One criticism of Central's list is that there's a built-in geographical bias— that players who are closest to Toronto or other centres where Central's full-timers are based get significant larger numbers of views. As a result, players from certain teams see their value skewed up. It's a criticism I heard from several scouts, but they're reluctant to attach their names to it because they don't want to offend Maguire, Gregory and the rest. Said one scout for a Western Conference team: "The fact is, they do the best they can with the resources the league gives them. They give us a guide, not a definitive breakdown. If it was definitive, there'd be a lot of guys out of jobs."

Here is how Columbus's list looks next to Central's:

COLUMBUS
1.   Johnson
2.   Staal
3.   Toews
4.   Kessel
5.   Brassard
6.   Mueller
?   Backstrom

CENTRAL
1.   Johnson
2.   Staal
3.   Toews
4.   Brassard
5.   Kessel
6.   Mueller

There's only one difference—the placement of Kessel and Brassard—and one wild card: the slotting of the Europeans on the main grid. Both have immense implications for the Blue Jackets. And if one team ahead of Columbus goes for the goalkeeper, then a whole bunch of names will be in play.[12]

As I go down the list, though, the names and rankings jumble wildly. For instance, the tenth-ranked player according to Central Scouting, Cory Emmerton of Kingston, sits outside the top 50 on the Blue Jackets' board. Some fall off it entirely. David Fischer, a defenceman who played for his high school team in Apple Valley,

---

12. *Red Line Report*'s lists are at much greater variance. This is *Red Line*'s midseason list: 1. Kessel 2. Toews 3. Johnson 4. Frolik 5. Staal 6. Mueller 7. Bryan Little 8. Nigel Williams 9. James Sheppard, Cape Breton. 10. Michael Forney, F, Thief River Falls.

Minnesota, is ranked No. 29 by Central Scouting, a projected second rounder. Columbus wouldn't have him if he cost a buck. When his name comes up he's ranked ND—no draft.

Some players shoot up in Columbus's rankings. Ben Maxwell, a centre with Kootenay in the Western Hockey League, is 44th among North American skaters according to Central Scouting. The Blue Jackets, though, have him in their top twenty, including all of Europe. Likewise, Eric Gryba, a defenceman with the Green Bay Gamblers in the USHL, is 66th on Central's list but in Columbus's top thirty.

I look for trends on Columbus's master list—a bias favouring players from certain leagues, perhaps, or size being a determinant of variance from Central Scouting's rankings. I study it like Fibonacci studied the limbs of trees, like Newton studied the falling apple, and I can't pick up a thing other than eyestrain. Whenever I think zig, it zags. No unified theory. No logic.

Nigel Williams, a big defenceman with the USA Hockey Development Team, is 13th-ranked by Central Scouting but only No. 33 on Columbus's board—just two spots ahead of his teammate in Ann Arbor, Michael Ratchuk, another blueliner who's six inches shorter and 50 pounds lighter. By Central Scouting's reckoning Ratchuk is the 81st North American skater.

For players to swing twenty, thirty, even forty slots in one direction or another is routine: after the top ten only a handful of players fall into approximately the same slots in the two lists. Reasonable people will disagree about the value of a player, but the degree of their disagreement is striking in these cases and many others. I've always known that I watch one game and the scouts watch another, one rich in subtleties I miss.

May 31, 2006, conference room, Park Plaza Toronto Airport

Day one of four days of prospect interviews. For all the NHL teams here, the first two days of interviews focus on the European players only. Out in the lobby, clusters of Russian players are briefed by one agent, while a bunch of Finns and Swedes gather around another. The Czechs have control of the couches. All are comparing notes from their interviews.

Artem Telepin is working overtime. First he's in the Columbus room, translating for Boyd and the others when Artem Anisimov, the sixth-ranked European skater according to Central Scouting, comes into the room. Clearly the teenager is on the cusp of the business, but he doesn't get the business. He volunteers that he "hopes there's an agreement" between the NHL and the Russian league—right now an impasse is threatening to stall the release of many young players in Russia. Then Boyd asks him if he has a contract with his club back in Moscow. Telepin does the translation, and his eyebrows shoot upward reflexively when he hears the reply. "Yes, he has a contract . . . five years." Boyd grimaces. The scouts red-flag that fact in their notes. They project him possibly being available when their second-round pick rolls around . . . he might even be the name highest on their list. A tough situation, maybe Zherdev redux.

A few minutes later, Telepin is out in the lobby with an agent who represents Andrei Plekhanov, a defenceman selected in the third round, No. 71 overall, by Columbus in 2003. The Blue Jackets tried to get Plekhanov to come to North America right after they drafted him—their plan was to bring him to training camp and have him play a couple of years of junior with the Sarnia Sting. It didn't quite work out. He made it to Sarnia only briefly before returning to Russia to play for Nizhnekamsk Neftekhimik. He has made it made it back to North America only for a couple of weeks as part of a touring Russian all-star team. To this point, Columbus hasn't signed Plekhanov, and the Blue Jackets are now worried that they have seen the last of him. Even if he does come now, they believe crucial years in his development have been lost—most European players have an advantage if they get a taste of play in North America early on.

Telepin is in the hallway with Paul Castron, helping make their case to Plekhanov's agent. Clearly the agent learned his English early on—he goes back and forth between Russian with Telepin and almost lawyerly English with Castron.

"He needs to come here," Artem says.

"There's no question he has to get away," Castron says.

"Artem, you are preaching to the converted," the agent says.

"He is a damn good player," Artem says. "They don't use him enough with Neftekhimik. You can explain to him that he needs to come here."

"I agree wholeheartedly," the agent says. "One year he lost altogether. The clock is ticking for him. He didn't go to Sarnia. Whatever happened happened."

Paul Castron takes a posture on reconciliation. "It's over," he says. "Don't worry about that."

The Jackets and the agent *are* worrying about it, though. Artem mentions Alexander Radulov, a Nashville pick who came over to play junior in the Canadian junior league, led the Quebec Remparts to a Memorial Cup and watched his stock rise as if it was filled with helium. Artem doesn't have to run through the what-ifs; he leaves it to the agent to connect the dots: if Plekhanov had stayed in Sarnia, his story likely wouldn't have mirrored Radulov's, but things would look better than now. The meter is running.

The agent asks Artem if he talked to the coach and manager in Neftekhimik about the player. Artem says he didn't because he wanted to talk to the agent first—to keep the protocol in line, to avoid being seen as trying to influence player or team unduly.

"Paul, Artem, I'm on your side in this," the agent says. "We're on the side of the angels. We're in this together. He wants to come. It's the best thing for him. He just wants to know that he's going to get to play."

What Plekhanov is looking for—or, at least, what his agent is pressing Castron and Telepin for—are guarantees. A guarantee that the young Russian will get a serious look at the Blue Jackets' training camp. A guarantee of significant ice time—twenty minutes a game—if he's assigned to their American Hockey League affiliate in Syracuse. For his part, the agent claims that he can get Plekhanov out of his contract with his Russian league club—given the surliness of owners and managers in the Russian league, the agent is making a promise that Vladimir Putin would have a hard time keeping.

This discussion goes back and forth, to no good conclusion. All the agent's reassurances aside, the angels are coming up just short.

Boyd later tells me that the team didn't expect to be able to close a deal on Plekhanov here and now—the Blue Jackets were simply looking for progress. "If we could just get him over here for a summer to work out with us, we could find a way to keep him over here," Boyd says. Just as you need puck possession to score, so too would possession of the prospect give Columbus some leverage. At the end of this day, though, it's just another exercise in frustration, and Plekhanov's name is another on a list of other Columbus draftees who aren't in the NHL—nobody asks why; nothing mitigates the cold hard fact.

Boyd is emphatic about signability not being a factor when drawing up The List. Still, the frustrations with Plekhanov, the challenges with Zherdev and the lack of an agreement between the Russian federation and the IIHF would have to weigh on the minds of the Columbus scouts. The fact that the top Russian on Columbus's list, Yuri Alexandrov, didn't show for the combine doesn't help. If they were on the clock at the draft and a Russian teenager was the highest-ranked available player on The List, MacLean or Boyd would probably take a little extra time to clear their throat before calling out his name.

June 1, 2006, Park Plaza Toronto Airport

The Blue Jackets don't seem to be in the market for goaltenders—discussion about them has taken up precious little time here—but they interview all the European netminders who have made it to Toronto. They're a useful study in the contrasting personalities of the prospects who come to the combine. You might presume that all elite teenage athletes are of a particular type—maybe assertive, maybe aggressive, confident to the point of arrogance. Yet they seem to span the full range of personalities, no differently than if you were to yank kids at random out of a high-school class. A Finnish

goaltender, Riku Helenius, is silent, stiff and bolt upright while his feet bounce nervously under the table, out of the sight of the scouts. Another goaltender, Reto Berra from Switzerland, drops off his chair to his knees during the interview when asked what type of goaltender he is. Berra gets a big laugh when Boyd asks him if he goes to school. "Not much," he replies, but when the laughter dies down he explains that he's working in a bank, part of a job-placement program with the hope of earning a business or finance degree.

Most come in freshly fitted suits. Some of the East Europeans are more casual simply because they don't own anything dressy except a military uniform: Semen Varlamov is the best teenage goaltender in Russia, but he doesn't have a suit to bring to the combine. He's wearing jeans and a soccer jersey, accessorized by a thick gold chain. With his close-cropped blond hair he's a ringer for Eminem, and like you'd expect of a Slim Shady wannabe, Varlamov is the most phlegmatic interview—he goes through the session with feigned boredom, never makes eye contact, looks down at the floor and then at the ceiling distractedly, and speaks in Russian to Telepin in a low mumble. Varlamov could pass for a gang member being interrogated in a precinct office. Afterwards, Telepin explains that Varlamov isn't "just another goalie acting strange." Telepin says that Varlamov (and probably a lot of other Russian players here) have been badgered by authorities—"maybe police, maybe school, maybe hockey"—who tried to intimidate. "He thinks he has to show that he's not afraid," Telepin says.

Lingering in the hallway between interviews, I bump into a couple of scouts from other organizations. They ask me if I've heard that Barry Trapp is out with the Leafs.

Trapp had been around the game since Original Six days. Not that he had a NHL career as a player. No, he was a minor leaguer, playing with Al Arbour on a Leaf farm team in Rochester back in the early '60s that could have given the Bruins and Rangers of the day a good game. He had worked as a coach in the Western Hockey League and as a scout here and there. In the '90s he signed on with Hockey Canada as its head scout, in charge of putting together the world junior and under-18 teams. It seemed like a comfortable niche for him. When the Canadian team won the 1997 under-20 tournament, he was weeping. "In all my years, it's the first time I ever won anything," he said.

But putting together a world junior team proved easier than piecing together the Maple Leafs' draft lists. While he was in charge of the Leafs' amateur scouting, they drafted a host of kids from the Canadian teams that went to the world juniors—and none of them truly broke out. Matt Stajan has stuck with the big club and Kyle Wellwood was looking like he should. But the jury was out on a bunch of defencemen: Ian White, Brendan Bell and Jay Harrison. Expectations were low. There was no chance that any would develop into a star—whether they could even contribute in a limited role for a winning team was the pressing question. Other players selected on Trapp's watch were outright busts. Since he had joined the Leafs, Trapp had had one clear win: about ten grand in a 50–50 draw at the 2003 world juniors in Halifax.

"They're not renewing him?" I ask.

"No, it's effective immediately," one of the scouts says. "He won't be here for the combine and they won't bring him in for the draft."

It might have come out of the blue to those outside the scouting ranks, but his firing didn't surprise the scouts here. No, Trapp had been a hire of Pat Quinn, then the general manager of the Toronto Maple Leafs. The new general manager, John Ferguson Jr., wanted his own people in place in the organization. Ferguson Jr. had been a scout for St. Louis, and his father, John Sr., had long been a scout for the San Jose Sharks. Ferguson Jr. recognized that Trapp's position was a critical one to the franchise—no less a critical one to his keeping his own job. He wanted someone he knew well and trusted to be in place.

At the combine and interviews, the rumoured trades are outnumbered by the rumours of scouts on the chopping block or on the move to another organization. The Columbus room is no exception: Word has it that Wayne Smith will go over to the Boston staff because his friend Peter Chiarelli has just been hired as the Bruins' general manager and because Chiarelli will let him scout the Ontario league rather than Quebec, which is his main assignment with Columbus. Word also has it that the Blue Jackets will replace Smith with another Ottawa-based scout, John Stanton, who has been out of the business for a season after being let go by the Los Angeles Kings. Then again, it might be Stanton, unofficial social convener for the scouts on the road, who started the rumour, thinking wishfully.

June 2, 2006, conference room, Park Plaza Toronto Airport

Day three of four days of interviewing prospects. The Blue Jackets will have seen 109 teenagers by the end of business Saturday; every kid who was invited to the NHL Central Scouting Bureau's combine, plus a few kids who weren't but happen to be within driving distance. They come through the doors, one every twenty minutes. Blake Geoffrion from the U.S. under-18 program works the room like a stand-up comic and introduces himself as "grandson of Hall of Famer Bernie Geoffrion, great-grandson of Hall of Famer Howie Morenz."[13]

I had heard players from previous drafts tell horror stories about other teams' approaches to the combine interview, and maybe Varlamov was acting the way he did because he'd heard them too. One goaltender drafted back in the late '90s told me that a scout for an Eastern Conference team had him strip down to his underwear and show them how he dropped down into butterfly position — which sounds more like hazing than scouting. "He was a complete freak," the goaltender told me.[14] And I heard that a few scouts get

---

13. At the start of every interview, I introduced myself to the player and asked permission to sit in on their session, offering the right to decline. I also advised them that anything they said might be published. No players at the draft exercised their right to ask me to leave.

14. I'm not naming the team here because the scout who demanded that the player strip is no longer with the organization.

into the faces of the prospects, acting more like drill sergeants trying
to break a recruit than hockey men looking for talent. I don't see any
of this with Columbus through dozens of interviews.

Rather than badgering players, the Columbus scouts seem to be
trying to piece together stories on players—not much different than
my lot in sportswriting. It is a player *profile* that they're working
toward. One example is instructive: Claude Giroux, a skilled forward with the Gatineau Olympiques who is ranked 38th in North
America by Central Scouting. Wayne Smith has Giroux's name circled on his schedule of the interviews. He doesn't want to be out of
the room when Giroux comes in—in fact, when he does arrive,
Smith takes charge. "I watched you play lots of times," Wayne
Smith says to Claude Giroux. "You played great pretty well every
time I saw you . . . on a good team, too. You're going to play in the
NHL . . . but where did you come from?"

Giroux understands what Smith means. Giroux had to go to the
Quebec junior league because twenty Ontario league junior teams
passed on him through twenty rounds. Not one of the 400 best
players in Ontario, yet one season later the Columbus scouts figure he won't be available when their second-round pick comes up.
"I was small and I came from a small town, Hearst," he says. "I knew
I could play. I just needed a chance to play."[15]

Trevor Lewis is the same sort of story. Another player Columbus
has projected to play in the first round, Lewis, who played for Des
Moines in the United States Hockey League[16] the last two seasons,
was eligible for the 2005 NHL draft. Two hundred and thirty names

---

15. Of those 400 players drafted by twenty OHL teams that spring, only four
would end up being selected ahead of Giroux.

16. The USHL is not considered up to the quality of the three Canadian major
junior leagues. Some top talents do land there because a prospect can play in
the USHL and retain his NCAA eligibility. If the same player dresses for only a
couple of CHL games, he loses any NCAA eligibility.

were called that draft day in Ottawa, but not Lewis's. The scouts wanted to know how the OHL scouts missed Giroux, but Boyd thinks it's more relevant to figure out how Lewis flew under the radar. Lewis explains he wasn't hiding—he scored just 10 goals in 56 games one season and 35 in 59 the next. "I'm a late bloomer, I guess," Lewis says. "I grew and got a bit stronger. It wasn't that I wasn't trying that first season."

Lewis's name wasn't called at last year's draft, but rather was among the hundreds of names filed and discarded on the basis of a single comment—"no prospect." The kiss of death in almost every other instance save this one. If just one of the scouts could have seen past that label, maybe the Blue Jackets could have landed a late-round pick that they could dine out on for a good long time. As it stands now, though, Lewis should be gone by the time the Blue Jackets' second pick rolls around. There's no hope the Blue Jackets will land him.

Some kids are polished. Jonathan Toews literally looks like he's buffed to a shine—not a hair out of place, not a wrinkle in his suit, his fair skin as unblemished as finest porcelain. It's not just looks, though. Toews has his interview prep work down, too. He has all the right answers. Asked about being named captain of Canada's team at the summer under-18 tournament, Toews says: "As soon as I knew that I was going to have a chance to play for Canada I started getting prepared. When there had to be something said in the room, I got up and said it. I'm comfortable in that role." Toews does everything but write the scouts' reports for them. Completely self-possessed. If they wanted him to do the interview in French, he could accommodate them—an honours student who came up through a French-immersion program. Only one possible stain on his record: the Tri-City Americans, a franchise owned by Anaheim general manager Brian Burke, selected Toews first overall in the Western Hockey League draft. The Blue Jackets' scouts have to believe that the Americans wouldn't have drafted Toews in that slot unless there had been discussions with the player and his parents. That would just be standard procedure—looking for a commitment before spending the draft pick.

"Were there any promises? A deal?" Boyd says, staring him straight in the eye.

"No, there was no promise," Toews says. The closest thing to a crack in the porcelain.

Toews doesn't look worried when Boyd presses, and the fact is, he has no need to. He knows what his status is, that he's top-four at the worst.

Some of the prospects come across more scripted than others. My heart goes out to one completely unaffected. And some kids *are* unaffected. The scouts almost seem sympathetic when they ask Bud Holloway, a centre from the Seattle Thunderbirds, how many interviews he has lined up. "Three," he says, embarrassed that the demand is so slight, especially when the top kids will talk to practically every club. It would be even worse if Holloway knew that Columbus has faint interest in him.

They're all asked what they have to work on to be NHLers, and the one answer that they all give—that they all *must* give—is that they have to get stronger. And so the scouts ask them what they'll do to get stronger. Some kids talk about working out this summer with personal trainers and skating coaches. Then there's Holloway, a projected late second-rounder from Wapella, Saskatchewan, population 200, off in the middle of the Prairies, not far from the Montana border. What can you do in your hometown with no gym to get stronger? Boyd asks him. "I bought a set of weights at Wal-Mart," Holloway says. "My little brother will spot me."

Some are almost courtesy interviews. Some are conducted to cover tracks, to keep the Blue Jackets' draft interests a mystery. Only a handful are meaningful.

Mueller's the first up. He seems subdued. His voice, deep, throaty, never rises. A couple of times the scouts ask him to speak up. Boyd asks him directly: Was it your marks that kept you out of college? "No," he says. "I just want to play hockey, and junior is what prepares you best for the pros."

Brassard's next. "I am nervous . . . about my English," he tells the scouts. Wayne Smith tries to put Brassard at ease. Smith says he'll do the translating if the kid needs it. "My father is a bus driver and my mu'dder is . . . administration, administrator." The Blue Jackets hold their cards tight. They don't do overly enthusiastic, not at this juncture.

Sam McMaster plays the skeptic. He asks about a wrist injury that kept Brassard out of the lineup at the start of last year. "I wanted to get back in time to play All-Stars against the Russians," he says.

Boyd asks him to explain why seventeen players were taken ahead of him in the Quebec league's draft of fifteen-year-olds back in 2003. "I was . . . small," he says. "Four inches . . ." He moves his hand to eyebrow level. " . . . And it was Sidney Crosby's draft."

The scouts sit through all 109 interviews, dozens of them with kids not in the Blue Jackets' top fifty, some not in the top hundred. Williams dutifully loads notes from all 109 interviews into Columbus's scouting database, but none is more important to the Blue Jackets than Kessel.

And of all the prospects making the rounds of the clubs, no prospect has more to win or lose than Kessel. Stuff to answer for. Stuff to put to rest.

Kessel walks into the room at 1 p.m. In half an hour, he has to go through a battery of tests for the combine. The Blue Jackets are the first interview on his schedule. More than twenty clubs will end up talking to him here.

Kessel is barely in his seat before he's pressed, before he is sweated.

"Teammates," Boyd prompts.

Silence.

"Do you know what I'm talking about?"

"No," Kessel says.

How couldn't he? Everyone in the game knows what Boyd is talking about. Kessel has a reputation for being disliked by his teammates wherever he has played.

And, clearly, Kessel *does* know what Boyd is talking about. At the end of a few seconds of uncomfortable silence, a few seconds while the clock was ticking, more loudly for Kessel than the team, he starts talking.

Sputtering.

"I don't have a problem with my teammates."

Another uncomfortable silence.

"I don't have a problem with Jack Johnson."

Another uncomfortable silence.

"I had lunch with him [Jack Johnson] practically every day."

Kessel is cracking. Now it's not answers. It's explanations. And rationalizations. And excuses. Hard to imagine it going worse.

What about the television story about a bar serving underage students, including players on the Golden Gopher hockey team? "It happens everywhere . . . who'd think they'd have cameras in their lapels?" Only 18 goals last season, when you were compared to Sidney Crosby the year before? "I was on the third line . . . we rolled four lines."

Kessel's shaken at the end. He knows it hasn't gone well. He walks out the door.

"He's not going back to school," Castron says, unconvinced by Kessel's claims that he finished with a 3.2 grade point average after missing weeks of school at the world championships.

Boyd doesn't seem to hear Castron. He says to no one in particular, "Kessel's a helluva talent." As if replaying that highlight reel from the world juniors a couple of seasons back.

June 2, 2006, basement, Park Plaza Toronto Airport

The NHL Central Scouting Service organizes the annual combine. Central tracks players as a service for the league's teams, sending its scouts to evaluate draft-eligible prospects across North America and Europe. Central's pre-season ranking of prospects is a tool that teams use as a guide for sending their own scouts out into the field. Central's final rankings are a good measure of whether a prospect's stock is rising or dropping. The service invites its top 100 players to Toronto for a combine that gives them a last chance to make a good impression.

The basement of the hotel is the locker where the meat gets inspected. The players are given physicals and undergo fitness testing. It goes from basic stuff like the bench press to aerobic and anaerobic stuff. Like prospects heading to the NFL combine, a lot of the draft-eligibles who show up in Toronto have spent weeks training specifically for the CSB's fitness testing.

Brassard has tried to get ready. A couple of months before, Brassard couldn't do a single rep with the test weight, 150 pounds. He's barely shaving, still catching up to his growth spurt. He's only lately been able to pack on a few pounds. He has been working out on the bench and thinking about it. Dreading it. *Is it a breaker? Does it all come down to this?* He's down on the bench, and you can see his features sharpening. If looks could lift the bar, he'd get a few reps just on the basis of this stare. One, two . . . five, with arms shaking and spotters jumping in before the sixth falls on his chest.

Brassard knows his best friend, Mathieu Karle, a defenceman with Acadie-Bathurst in the Quebec league, did fifteen reps in the group that went through testing an hour before. Brassard knows five isn't good. Worse than he thinks. By the end of the day, his five reps will stand as the low total among all the forwards and defencemen tested. Bud Holloway, the kid with the Wal-Mart weights, manages twelve reps, a big number. A couple of seasons back, Andrew Ladd of the Carolina Hurricanes, a prospect who was about the same size as Brassard, knocked off twenty-two reps.

Brassard gets on the bike for the aerobic testing. His feet are taped to the pedals. A mouthpiece hooked to a tube. Testing staff shout at him. Top of their voices, drowning out conversation among the scouts. "Go. Come on. Go." The scouts see Brassard push. They see him strain. That much they like. Just the show of effort. Just the push. When they see the results later on, they'll like it even more. Nearly the best VO_2: 71.6. The workload number, 680 watts, will be the best at the combine. He goes harder and longer than anyone else. The test maxes out at fifteen minutes. That's the time limit. At fifteen minutes they tell Brassard to stop. He pedals ten seconds past it. "Okay, okay, okay," a member of the testing crew says, waving Brassard to a halt.

Boyd is in a crowd of almost 100 scouts and executives, watching the group go through an initiation by ordeal. For all the technology on site, for all the reams of data, Boyd believes that the scouts have to watch the prospects perform here, just as they have to go to games rather than look at a player's stats. Even here, in this den of sports science, Boyd says scouting is intuitive. Eyeballs and gut, not sensors and readouts. "You can always get a kid who's not in great condition to work on it," Boyd says. "What you get a look at here is just how willing the kids are to work on their own and what their work ethic is like."

The scouts know what they're looking for. They've seen it ever since they were the same age as these teenagers, sometimes when they looked across a dressing room, sometimes when they looked in the mirror. Some made the most of their opportunities and never cheated on effort, others went the other way.

Kessel comes in. He looks around nervously. Once he fills out the questionnaire—When was your last game? When was your last workout?—he moves to the fitness stations. Eyes are trained on his every move. The scouts' expressions repeat that question from the questionnaire: When *was* your last workout? He looks soft. Body fat. They can *see* that, they don't have to wait for the readout. Over 11 percent (compared to Brassard's and Holloway's eight percent and Plymouth centre John Armstrong at seven flat). The strength stuff is fine—eleven reps on the bench, decent vertical jump and standing-long jump. A different story on the bike, though. He looks gassed. His VO_2 at 53.4 is way back—maybe his weight room stuff should drop off but there's no aerobic base. Kessel cuts out at seven minutes. His wattage is 360, worst among forwards. "What was he doing at the world championships, playing his way out of shape?" one scout mutters.

Nine p.m., June 2, 2006, parking lot, Park Plaza Toronto Airport

Kessel meets up with Mueller and three other prospects who know each other from the U.S. development program to grab something to eat at a pizza place.

"How did it go?" Mueller asks Kessel, the roar of planes flying into the Toronto airport nearly drowning out conversation.

Kessel shrugs. No getting into the details from his testing. No getting into the interviews, especially the Columbus one. He knows the questions that were hanging out there, and he knows he hasn't put them to rest. He has to think, *It woulda been better if they could see this, woulda been better if you told them you were talking to me and going out with me for dinner.*

Nine a.m., June 3, 2006, lobby, Park Plaza Toronto Airport

Out in the lobby, Brassard is sitting on a couch across from Claude Giroux, the undrafted kid out of Hearst, and Francois Bouchard, a highly regarded forward with the Baie-Comeau Drakkar. They are immaculately turned out. The three of them could form a boy band—think of a Quebecois Menudo. They're comparing notes about the testing and interviews. It seems like nobody is a stranger in this game. Brassard and Giroux skate together in the summer and they've played with Bouchard in all-star games. They're all getting along—professional friendships rather than peer rivalries. That's how it feels—not just with them, but with other groups of prospects out there. Everybody knows somebody. Everybody gets along. At least in the absence of parents and agents.

I ask Brassard if I can have a word with him. I tell him that I hear his father, Pierre, was a great player—Tim Bernhardt, the Dallas scout, played with him in Cornwall and says that he was a natural scorer whose skating was not quite good enough for the pros. Pierre Brassard went on to play for Bryan Murray when he was coaching senior hockey in Pembroke.

"He always made sure that I worked on my skating," Brassard says. "He got on the ice with me. He can still play."

Brassard tells me that his father has only missed a few games in his career. "He's a bus driver in Gatineau and he gets shifts early if it's a long drive to a game," he says. "He drives for work and then drives all afternoon to games. Then all night to get home."

It's not the only story like this that I hear at the combine—when the agents are filling me in I'm half expecting a string chorus to break out. Still, it has the ring of the amateur. So many of the players come from privileged circumstances. So many come out of age-group programs that are run with a professionalism that would surpass that of a couple of NHL sad-sacks. I remember hearing about a player at an NCAA school whose father didn't miss a game across two years—flying to Alaska for one tournament, to Scandinavia and Russia for world juniors. There were lots of stories like that, both on the U.S. and Canadian sides—the game had seemed to go from the frozen pond to a game only country-clubbers could afford. A game for white-collar families. Yet here was a devoted, supporting father, practically living behind a steering wheel to make ends meet and to make it to his son's games. He didn't count on his son making it—he knew better than anyone that there were no guarantees going into Derick's junior career. Just hope, and maybe not that much of it when his son broke in with Drummondville.

Two p.m., June 3, 2006, conference room, Park Plaza Toronto Airport

After they've interviewed seventy prospects, no one could hold it against the Columbus scouts if they're growing weary of asking the standard questions. *Who's your agent? What's your strength? What do you have to work on? Have you ever been in trouble?* (Usually a leading question when a player has been in some sort of well-known jackpot with his team or authorities.) There's probably a dozen of the questions, pertaining to hockey and upbringing, that they ask every kid who walks through the door. And I suspect the players are somewhat weary of answering the same questions in every room (though a kid like Bud Holloway, with three interviews, wouldn't mind getting the third degree from a few more clubs).

Anyway, it's more out of the scouts' fatigue than the teenagers' that Don Boyd turns to me in the middle of an interrogation and asks, "Gare, do you have any questions?"

Interviews are booked for twenty minutes—that's the way it is for all teams and all players. This particular interview is flat-lining—a kid who isn't a going concern for Columbus, and maybe even less so after an indifferent interview. The standard questions get short, bored and boring replies. We're through the required elements in about twelve minutes. Boyd might be offering this up to me just to break the monotony. I ask a couple of questions about his family because I know a few scouts who've told me that scouting the parents can be as important as scouting the players.[17] Nothing memorable—a one-off, I figure.

But when the next player comes in, after ten minutes Boyd asks me again if I have any questions. And so I break out some standard ones that I'd use if I were writing a feature about a young player. *Which coaches influenced you most? What were the most important things they taught you?*

As the day goes on, I get a little more adventurous in my questioning. Consider this exchange with Ty Wishart, a six-foot-four defenceman with the Prince George Cougars, ranked No. 21 among North American skaters by CSS.

"In the guide it says you were born in Belleville . . . are your parents in the military?" (Kids whose parents are based at Camp Borden in Trenton are usually born at the hospital in Belleville.)

"My father was, and my mother still is. She was transferred to Victoria."

"What was the happiest day of your life?"

"My first game in the Dub [the WHL]."

"I doubt that. I suspect it was when you left Trenton for Victoria."

"I *liked* Trenton." The Blue Jackets' scouts laugh, but Wishart looks deadpan.

---

17. Parents have too often been the personal hell of Brian Kilrea, the only junior hockey coach in the Hall of Fame. I once told Kilrea of an encounter I had with one player's mother. "In all my years of coaching," Kilrea said, "all my best players were orphans."

"Nobody does. It says here that you are a provincial-level basketball player and baseball player. What positions do you play?"

"I'm a four in basketball, a pitcher in baseball."

"Which position suits your personality more?"

"I'm more comfortable on the court, I think."

Okay, it's not rocket science. It's not science at all. A pitcher has more decisions to make than a power forward. (Just as a point guard would have more decisions to make than a first baseman.) I figure we might glean a little insight into the character of the prospect—and in the process make a projection or two about his game. A point man on the power play is probably closer to pitcher than power forward.

I don't think too much about the questions and Wishart's answers—there's no doubt that his ability to play on provincial teams in basketball and baseball while rising to first-round status says a lot more about his athleticism than anything that comes out of my interrogation. But afterward Wayne Smith, Columbus's scout in Ottawa, tells me that I asked "good questions, useful questions."

By the end of the final day of interviews I'm more comfortable in my role in the mostly gentle inquisitions—truth be told, as a media type, I've never had the hammer with an NHLer or even a junior. Here I can demand answers, and players are motivated to play along. I wish I had jumped in earlier.

The crew packs up. The Euros and the regional scouts will go home until a few days before the draft in Vancouver.

Nine a.m., June 14, 2006, Blue Jackets offices, Nationwide Arena, Columbus

Don Boyd was hoping more players would come for the Blue Jackets' private testing and interviews with the GM. He sent out word to all the Top Tens, their agents or, with the college kids, their "family advisors." The team would cover the expenses for the juniors and Backstrom, but the college kids would have to pay their own airfare to keep their eligibility. (Once they made it to Columbus they'd have to bunk with one of the other Top Tens.) But Johnson passed. He had already paid his own way to St. Louis. Toews passed, too. They knew they weren't going to be there at No. 6. Backstrom sent his regrets. He's planning to come in two days before the draft in Vancouver—he'll do interviews at the draft, that's all. Kessel begged off, too. He paid his own way to St. Louis—maybe he hadn't got the word that it was either Johnson or Staal who had locked up the Blues' pick, first overall. Maybe he was still looking at last year's clippings. Maybe he was worried that a second interview with Columbus would go worse than the first.

And so it's Staal, Brassard and Mueller who make it to Columbus. Staal and Brassard were on *Hockey Night in Canada*, talking to Don Cherry on the Monday night broadcast of Game 4 of the Stanley Cup final. They spent much of the day before kicking around airports. Mueller had a direct flight in from Minneapolis.

Boyd isn't pissed that the others didn't come. That's their choice. But he thinks making the effort to come out says something about the character of the three players. Especially Staal, who knows it's a longshot to land in Columbus and who has lived out of his suitcase for more than three weeks.

"We got you a flight to Carolina for Game 5 tonight," Boyd tells him in the morning. "We'll get you out to the airport as quick as we can."

Jordan Staal seems unexcited by the prospect, even though his oldest brother Eric would have a chance to raise the Stanley Cup in Raleigh that night. "If it's okay with you, I'd rather stick around and watch the game on television with Brass and Mulls," he tells Boyd.

"You're joking," Boyd says.

"No, really," Staal says. "St. Louis was gonna fly me to Carolina early in the series, but I told them I'd rather just go to the Cards game with the other guys."

We came here . . . for what? That's the look on their faces when they watch the Blue Jackets' strength coach, Barry Brennan, set up two low standards with a string running between them. It looks like a high-jump bar for pre-schoolers. Brennan walks them through the exercise — it's a dainty exercise and a small comic turn, because Brennan is large even by the standards of pro sports strength trainers. His chest is as thick as a bank-vault door and he's leading the prospects through something like a dance step. Here's the drill: with feet together, right up against the string, lift one foot over the bar and touch your heel on the other side. It looks ridiculously easy. It is, in fact, impossibly hard. The trick is that the toes of your shoes are directly below the string. Maintaining your balance is one trick. Being flexible enough to do it without your knees or feet going offline is the other. Lose your balance — there might be issues as far as symmetry in muscle development is concerned. Get offline — there might be issues with the lower muscle core, a red flag for a player who might be at risk for abdominal muscle injuries, the type that cost players whole seasons — and teams millions of dollars.

Staal manages it smoothly. Brennan shakes his head. "This kid is a pure athlete," he says. "That is one hell of a genetic pool."

Brassard struggles. He even knocks over the standard at one point.

Mueller's feet turn out. A member of the training staff is recording the exercise with a Handicam. Brennan will go back and look at the video of that.

"A little tightness in the hips," Brennan notes at the end.

It's the type of red flag that goes up. In an exercise that looks like a sobriety test, just a foot turning a little, a matter of an inch or two, could hardly seem less significant. But no detail is too small — not when The List is riding on it. That tightness in the hip is just a blip now, but it's the tightness that can lead to groin injuries, abdominal stuff that gets chronic, stuff that can make the investment in a first-rounder go bad. Brennan says it goes down in his report to Boyd but that it's not so much a mark against a prospect, just something that will require work if he's drafted.

Brennan does a double-take when he sees Mueller do squats. In the warroom at the combine, at least one scout wondered about Mueller's strength. Not Brennan. "His quads," Brennan says. "He's got *rockets.*"

The three prospects have a down hour before lunch. Brennan opens the gym for them should they want to work out and gives them the run of the team room, steam bath and all. Castron brings down a sliding board good for practising stickhandling. He shows them a few drills. Castron's eyebrows rise. Mueller goes straight from basic moves into a figure-eight, Ginsu knife–sharp stickhandling, effortless. First time he's ever tried it, and Mueller goes straight to graduate-level stickhandling. *Noted: Hand-eye co-ordination.*

The last drill is a shuttle run around pylons set out on the floor of the arena. Again the players go through their paces. Staal's a quick study. Mueller, whose brother is an NCAA Division II football player, looks acquainted with the drill. Brassard, though, has never been asked to do anything like this and looks a little sheepish. The best that can be said at the end is that he pushed hard enough to dive across the line.

One p.m. June 14, 2006, Doug MacLean's office, Nationwide Arena, Columbus

Brassard's English is clipped, broken. He struggles often when asked a question. In the interview at the combine, Smith translated for him. No such luck here.

"Did you break curfew this year?" MacLean says.

"Yeah," Brassard says, laughing, not nervously. He has been prepped. Better to tell the truth than to be caught up in a lie.

"Why?" MacLean asks.

"A girl," Brassard says.

"Good," MacLean says. "If you're going to break curfew, it better be a girl and it better be worth it."

MacLean's trying to break the ice.

"What do you know about our team?" Doug MacLean asks Brassard.

"Everything," Brassard says without hesitation. Brassard goes through the lines. He talks about Rick Nash, Gilbert Brule. He struggles to pronounce "Zherdev."

"You don't know how good it is to hear someone come in here who knows about our team, who follows the game," MacLean says. "We like that. We think it's good when a player is interested in the game."

"Who are you like as a player?" MacLean asks.

"I like Scott Gomez," Brassard says.

"Are you like Joe Sakic?" MacLean asks. "I got a phone call one night and Don Boyd told me, 'I just saw Joe Sakic.'"

"Not Joe Sakic, not now."

"You're not old enough to remember Joe Sakic when he came into the league," MacLean says. Fact is, he was a year old when Sakic came into the league. He has no way of knowing that Sakic was about as slight at eighteen as he is. MacLean moves on. "What's your strongest asset?"

"Hockey sense," Brassard says—again, without hesitation.

"You're right," Jim Clark says. "That is your strength."

"You're what, six feet? One-seventy?" MacLean says, not waiting for an answer. "When I was in Detroit we had Steve Yzerman, and he was about that and he worked at the game. Are you going to work at the game?"

Brassard says he will, and of course he would say so. He probably even means it—they all do at this moment. But what MacLean is looking for is not something a questionnaire can tell you, not a line Brassard can fill in. Will he get along with people? Will he be intimidated by new situations? The answers aren't something that you can pick up definitely from what he says, only something you can guess at by how he says it. And, ultimately, how MacLean takes it: it can start here and it can end with a halfhearted handshake when twenty minutes are up.

And the twenty minutes do go by. Brassard's expression at the end of it reads: "C'est tout? Is that all there is?" Flying in from Edmonton, staying a couple of nights in a hotel, just so he can ask me about breaking curfew?

MacLean says it's not complicated. "I just want to look them in the eyes and see if they're engaged," he says.

Nine p.m., June 14, 2006, Champps Americana Restaurant, Columbus

The Blue Jackets take the players out for dinner out beside the hotel where they're staying. (The execs might be worried about them getting the wrong idea about Columbus, because an evangelical conference has soaked up every available room and conference hall downtown and the streets are lined with Bible-toting church ladies.) There are lots of four-star steakhouses available, but the Blue Jackets understand the players and opt instead for a sports bar. Staal, Brassard and Mueller are at one end of the table, woofing down nachos; MacLean, Castron, Boyd and Clark, at the other, go for better appetizers. Between courses the players go over to a basketball hoop and shoot around—Mueller has clearly played a lot more ball than Brassard, and Staal could be a player if he ever put his mind to it.

"How was it today, boys?" MacLean asks. "What did you do after the interviews?"

"We came back out to the mall here and went to Play World [games arcade]," Jordan Staal says. "I think Brassy fell in love with some girl out there this morning. He couldn't wait to get back."

Not to worry about the church-lady thing.

A question for Staal just in casual conversation: What was it like when he went to the drafts when his big brothers Eric and Mark were selected?

"I didn't go," he says. "When one of us is up for the draft, then our parents go with that one . . . this year, it's my turn; my brothers are gonna stay home."

"Good for your parents," MacLean says.

Boyd's eyebrows shoot up. Not that it's a matter of the parents' thrift, just a matter of devoting their attention to the son who's in the spotlight and under pressure at that moment—not that Jordan Staal seems like he could ever feel pressure. It might have been something the Staal parents carefully planned, or something they just happened on, but there's no doubt that their sons aren't merely well prepared for the NHL, but almost ridiculously well-adjusted.

The Hurricanes–Oilers game is on in high-definition screens in every corner of the room. Jordan's big brother Eric scores his second goal of the first period as Carolina jumps out to an early lead. The Blue Jackets' braintrust look for a reaction from Jordan. Nothing. Not even a glance up from his nachos. The average kid would look more excited if he was just a fan of the team. *Already a pro.*

By the time the game gets into overtime, the kids have gulped back all the pop their bladders can stand. They head back to their rooms and pack for early flights home. Jordan Staal expresses relief that he'll finally get a few nights in his own bed before it's time to head off to the draft.

"It surprises me every time, but the kids who come in seem to get along with each other," Boyd says. "Good kids, mostly. These ones seemed to strike up friendships pretty quick."

Yeah, it would have been nice to put Phil Kessel to that test.

Boyd asks me if I've heard who the Minnesota Wild hired as an assistant to general manager Doug Risebrough. I saw Risebrough at the combine and he hadn't mentioned that he was in the market for help. I tell Boyd that I don't have a clue.

"Chris Snow," Boyd says. "Know him?"

Yes, I know him. And I'm stunned. Snow is one of sportswriting's boy wonders. He's barely older than the soon-to-be millionaire teenagers who just excused themselves from our table. Snow went from the Syracuse University newspaper to the big daily in Minneapolis, the *Star-Tribune*, covering the Wild, then on to the *Boston Globe* covering the plum beat, the Red Sox, by age twenty-four. (At that age I was a mere copy boy at a miserable tabloid.) Yahoo was pitching him to sign on as a columnist on its emerging sports page. *Sports Illustrated* would be knocking. He was at the height of the business while he still had his baby teeth and *he did what?* Threw it all away to work in the front office of the Wild? If you're going to defect from media to sports, the Minnesota franchise seems an unlikely destination, especially for a rising star. It would be one thing if the Red Sox or the Patriots were to come calling. In the U.S., the NHL's profile is closer to the Arena Football League than the National Football League, and of its member franchises, the only one as anonymous as the Blue Jackets might be the Wild.

I met Snow once, just after he started at the *Star-Trib*—it might have been after the NHL awards, I'm not sure, but he was in a cluster of NHL writers. I had broken a story about a young prospect with the Mississauga Ice Dogs of the Ontario league, Patrick O'Sullivan, a kid who had been emotionally abused and eventually physically assaulted by his father. In fact, a court issued a restraining order against the father, forbidding him from entering hockey arenas—all around the league, teams were put on notice to report any sightings of O'Sullivan *père*. When Minnesota drafted O'Sullivan, Chris Snow followed up on the story. He seemed like a decent, ambitious kid. It always seemed that the most powerful person in the room was magnetically drawn to him, and, an aw-shucks or two later, he was under Snow's spell. A kinder, gentler Sammy Glick.

"A reporter, a young kid. That's thinking outside the box," MacLean said.

Risebrough, though, is no slave to convention. He brought his Minnesota team into the league at the same time as MacLean rolled out his Blue Jackets, and so far the Wild have been much more successful on the ice (making the Western Conference final in their third season) *and* off the ice (playing to capacity crowds all season, turning substantial profits). Risebrough got his franchise off to a much better start by salvaging players other organizations had given up on and drafting shrewdly. The one component that Risebrough has looked for—whether in a first-rounder or a journeyman free agent—is speed, and Chris Snow has overtaken everyone in the business on his way to the top.

The way Risebrough's record reads, I keep thinking that in another three years Snow will be president of the team—and league commissioner by age thirty. Then again, the move gives me faint hope of being able to cross over. That being in the media won't completely taint me. That some might look at my skills in the sportswriting dodge and see applications on the scouting side. Outside the box, but maybe not out of the question.

June 22, 2006, conference room, Marriott, Vancouver

Another meeting room, another pass at The List. Again, Boyd and the staff pick apart the Top Tens.

Johnson at one—that's a given.

Staal at two—trending up.

Picks three and four shuffle back and forth. Toews—a flag goes up when the scouts see two concussions marked beside his name on the combine physical. Backstrom—talent, but questions about size, and no interview.

Five and six are even more contentious. Kessel edges Brassard on the board, but there's no consensus. McMaster has Brassard No. 2 overall on his list. "Love this kid," he says. "Goes into corners and comes out with the puck like there's glue on his stick." Wayne Smith is pro-Brassard. "I know more about this kid than he does himself," he says.

MacLean watches. He doesn't say anything as the scouts go through the Top Tens, through the first-rounders and right through to No. 100. Looks like business is concluded after three hours. It isn't.

"Okay, Doug has something to ask you," Boyd says, giving his boss the floor.

The room goes dead silent.

"Offers are out there," he says. "Is it worth trading up to No. 2 for this year's No. 6, next year's No. 1 and maybe more?"

"No," says McMaster, who thinks that No. 2 on his list this season could be there at No. 6 on the floor.

"Yeah," Wayne Smith says. "If you have a chance to get a big, skilled centre like Staal you have to go for it. You don't get many chances. They don't come along every year."

The room divides. Columbus hosts the draft next year. No one mentions the worst-case scenario: what if Columbus were to trade next year's first-round pick and then fail to make the playoffs next spring? No one needs to mention it. The optics would be terrible. A lottery pick would be embarrassing enough. Lose the lottery and it could be the first overall. A nightmare at Nationwide Arena: their season ticket holders booing an announcement of a high pick that had been Columbus's going to

Pittsburgh, which already has Sidney Crosby and Evgeni Malkin. The ball is in MacLean's court, and he says the deal would be tough to close.

"Any point going to No. 3?" he asks without enthusiasm, anticipating the answer. Quick consensus: no, it wouldn't be a control situation. No either-ors, not up that high. Again, some think that No. 2 or 3 on their lists may be there at No. 6.

At the close of the meeting, Boyd and his staff know that The List is all but closed. How it will get used is still an open question.

One p.m., June 23, 2006, Doug MacLean's suite, Marriott, Vancouver

Kessel walks in with an empty plastic water bottle in his hands, as if he doesn't want points deducted for littering. He shakes hands with MacLean, Boyd and the rest, then sits stiffly on the couch, next to Clark, across from MacLean. He taps the bottle against his palm, a drum beat.

"Peter Mueller told me that you were good friends in the under-18 program," MacLean says.

"Me and Peter went to school together," Kessel says. "We went to lunch practically every day."

Kessel makes eye contact with MacLean, but it only lasts a moment or two before he pans the room and then the floor.

MacLean asks Kessel about all the teams he's played for, about all the coaches he's played for, and about teammates he might have had problems with. Or not. And then MacLean gets out of the past tense.

"How would you look with Nash?" he asks.

"I think I'd look pretty good."

"Do you dish the puck well enough to play with Nash?"

"I think I dish it pretty well."

"I'm not sure that you'd get it back."

An uncomfortable silence. Kessel sniffles, says he has a cold, worse with the flying he's done lately. That just reminds the Blue Jackets that he has flown to other places but not Columbus.

"Phil, I watched you test at the combine," Boyd says. "I don't have the book in front of me. How do you think you did?"

Kessel knew this one was coming. "I think I did pretty well," Kessel says. "It was tough. I just came back from the world championships. Didn't have that much chance to prepare for it."

"You walked around that room," Boyd says. "You saw the conditioning level of other guys in that room. You're smart enough to know what's goin' on around you. Where do you think your conditioning is? There's a lot of guys who look like they've been in the gym longer than you. I'm not talking about the last few weeks. I'm talking about the last year, year and a half."

"I doubt that."

"You train pretty hard?" Boyd says.

"Yeah. I mean, I didn't have a chance to work out for practically a month and a half," Kessel says.

Noted: Deflecting rather than accepting criticism.

The rhythm of questions: build up, tear down.

"Are you a rink rat?" MacLean asks.

"Yeah," Kessel says. "I like to be around the rink."

"Are you a hyper kid?"

"I'm nervous . . . in situations like this, yeah," he says. His face tenses and he makes an effort to exhale and slow down. "More relaxed this week than at the combine."

"Did you get to Roxy's?" MacLean asks. Roxy's is a club in Vancouver.

"No," Kessel says with a forced laugh.

Don Boyd makes it plain. "It's an inference of what happened at Minnesota," he says.

"You're not a big drinker," MacLean says.

"No, not at all," Kessel says.

"The odd pop," MacLean says.

"Gotta have fun sometime," Kessel says with a shrug. *Be believable.* That's the message Kessel got after his interview with Columbus at the combine.

The Blue Jackets want to diffuse the tension. "If you were in my shoes, you'd do it to keep your sanity," MacLean says.

When the laughter dies down, Boyd goes right to the scouting report. "How would you respond if someone said to me, 'a little bit immature . . .'"

Kessel grimaces and Boyd backs up.

"Listen to me . . . 'needs to work a little harder in the gym, practise a little harder, needs to learn some social skills, people skills' . . . we'll leave it at that."

Kessel's voice goes down to a whisper. "I'd say okay . . . yeah, a little bit . . . some of that stuff . . . it's a little hard . . . work on some of that stuff, I guess."

It's over soon after that. Kessel looks a little disheartened as he leaves the suite. He doesn't see that the Blue Jackets were actually trying to make him feel comfortable, to put his "issues" in a soft focus. He doesn't see that Columbus will almost certainly take him at No. 6 if he falls there. MacLean appears to feel sorry for him. "If what they're saying about this kid isn't true, it's criminal," MacLean says. "Because I don't know if I've ever heard the negative stuff like I have with this kid."

"It would be a tragedy," Boyd says.

Tragedy to mystery. Backstrom is next to come in. Kjell Larsson ushers him into the room and introduces him to MacLean. MacLean's expression registers surprise. *He's bigger and thicker than I thought. NHL size.*

Backstrom one-times his questions. Controlled. Short. Literal. Almost philosophical.

"Why were you the youngest player ever to play for Sweden in the world championships?" MacLean asks him, wanting to get Backstrom to describe his game.

Backstrom answers it literally. "The coach, Bengt Gustaffson, chose me," Backstrom says.

"Bengt is a really smart hockey man . . . the first player I ever had who was smarter than the coach," MacLean says. "I was the assistant coach."

It's MacLean's shtick. Once again he tries to defuse the tension with humour, but Backstrom misses it. It may be a language issue, or it may simply be the tension of the moment.

Backstrom looks uncomfortable with all the eyes in the room staring at him. He doesn't seem to know whom to make eye contact with. He sits as stiff as a mannequin on the couch, hands on his knees.

"Are you Forsberg?" Boyd asks.

"There is only one," Backstrom replies.

No hesitation. Complete respect. Perfect answer.

"How many teams will you talk to?" Boyd asks.

"Lots of them," Backstrom says cautiously.

"Tell them bad things, because we'd want you at six if you're there," MacLean says.

One bad thing—or at least one potentially bad thing—comes out. MacLean asks Backstrom when he'd like to play in the NHL. Not for at least one season, Backstrom says. He says he thinks he needs a year and wants to play again for Sweden. Not the answer MacLean wants to hear. No, he wants to hear a player who wants to get to the NHL right away or is happy to let the team decide. Backstrom goes the other way. "My option," he says.

After Backstrom leaves, Larsson stays to do damage control, to fight for the player he has near the top of his list. "Swedish kids are like that. Patience is important. He wants to come when he knows he can succeed. He doesn't want to fail. Almost all Swedish kids would say the same thing."

MacLean seems convinced about the talent and character—not convinced that he can get Backstrom to camp in September. He liked Backstrom's confidence, but is hardly confident himself that Backstrom will be there when the sixth pick comes up.

Four p.m., June 23, 2006, conference room, Marriott, Vancouver

The Blue Jackets have one last interview to squeeze in: Yuri Alexandrov, a Russian kid who is Central Scouting's top-ranked defenceman in Europe. Alexandrov didn't make it to the combine, and the Blue Jackets aren't high on him—and it's not just

Telepin bad-mouthing him. Still, it's a matter of due diligence, trying to figure out if he's hiding an injury, getting the lowdown on his contract status. As soon as Alexandrov walks into the room in jeans and a t-shirt, there seems to be a clear reason why he didn't make it to the combine. He's junkie-thin. It looks as if he might not have been able to do a single rep on the bench at the fitness testing. His agent would have been wise to have found him a suit with padded shoulders.

The interview goes poorly for Alexandrov.

"Why didn't you come to the combine?"

Alexandrov says he couldn't get the paperwork in order.

"All the others did. Why not you?"

A shrug.

If Varlamov wanted to show that he wasn't intimidated, that he'd been through worse, then Alexandrov is assuming that he's the precious goods here, that he's the valued commodity. And if Varlamov has been, like Telepin says, kicked around by hockey officials and coaches through his career, then Alexandrov represents another face of the touted prospects coming out of Eastern Europe these days. Russian (and to a lesser extent Czech) players jump from agent to agent, often before they're drafted, often before they're signed. "They like to date but not get married," a once-burned, forever-after-shy agent told me. "They get what they can from you and then wait for the next offer."

The privileged North American kids don't have a monopoly on entitlement.

An interview scheduled for twenty minutes is over in half that time. The Blue Jackets weren't planning on taking him beforehand—and now nothing's changed, except that they feel more confident in their decision. Boyd looks at him as if to say, "Don't let the door hit you on the way out."

This is the final, *final* pass at The List. Not everybody is going to be happy, but when John Williams puts Kessel's name on the board at No. 4, it causes a wince or two around the table. A couple of Blue

Jackets staffers clearly hope that Kessel's off the board when Columbus is on the clock. And others are either conflicted or worried at some level by the possibility that he might be still be there. The consensus: Kessel is the draft-eligible player most ready to step into the NHL next season. The consensus: He's also the draft-eligible player most likely to blow up, most likely to wear out coaches, and, yes, most likely to be a black mark on the record of the scouting staff.

It seems so critical a point in the building of a team that I'm amazed at how little the Blue Jackets know about Kessel. And how they came upon their scant knowledge. They have their scouting reports, ratings of performance. They have statistics. They have reports that made it to the press. But the rest . . . a bad interview in Toronto, a bad meeting with the general manager and his staff in Vancouver. It doesn't seem a lot. It doesn't seem much more than impressions. They do have second-hand information from other players and contacts around the game, but nothing organized, authoritative or definitive. It almost seems that the draft process is an exercise in high-priced window-shopping—I feel as if I've put as much thought into buying a car. Phil Kessel, with millions at stake, with the jobs of the general manager and his staff potentially on the line, and, possibly, with the fate of a franchise worth tens of millions in the balance, should be no mystery to Columbus. The way a chief executive should be no mystery to the corporation that recently headhunted him, the way a police officer should be no mystery to the department that just recruited him.

What do they know about Kessel? How you grade him in the interviews is a subjective matter. One thing is incontrovertible and, to me, overpowering. He declined to come to Columbus for an interview—it's not that he turned down all post-combine interviews—he made it to St. Louis, after all. But he didn't come to Columbus and pleaded poverty—to keep his NCAA eligibility, he would have had to buy his own ticket and pay his own way. *But he paid his own way to St. Louis.* No one in the Columbus room believed that he wanted to go back to Minnesota (and most people in hockey had concluded that the school was ambivalent about having him back). The Blue Jackets could only guess about his claims. They couldn't even be sure, beyond Kessel's own claim to be a 3.2 student, about his academic eligibility to play next season. They couldn't know whether going to Columbus would have been an expense his family couldn't afford or mere pocket change to his father. If it was a dodge, why? If it was a dodge, what does he not want the team to know? There seemed no good way to read it.

More than that, there seemed to be no good way to look at this hole in the Blue Jackets' research—the hole being the Kessels' financial wherewithal, or lack thereof. Kessel didn't come to Columbus, his representatives said, because of the price of a plane ticket. (The team would have had him room with one of the other players who came in for interviews and testing.) Privileged or hardscrabble? It seemed basic stuff to know about the player. A few calls to his coaches. A couple of questions for former teammates. Maybe even a call to a reporter at the newspaper back in Madison. Something that could be pieced together in an hour—no more. It would seem like due diligence given the stakes, the millions of dollars written into an entry-level contract. A lot of teams are second-guessed about their top picks—and more than a few scouts will second-guess themselves. The latter would be haunted less by the bad picks they made than by the extra mile they might have gone to avoid mistakes.

"Who do you feel strongly about?" Boyd asks. "Who are you passionate about? Who do you want as a Blue Jacket?"

I wonder who can be passionate about anything at the end of long weeks of tossing around hundreds of names, parsing every scouting report.

Sam McMaster pipes up first. "I really like that Sestito in Plymouth," McMaster says. Just saying the name makes him smile.

"You feel strongly about Sestito?" Boyd asks.

"I feel strongly about him," McMaster says. "A big, strong kid. I loved how he played when I saw him this season. He's a Blue Jacket."

Tom Sestito. I don't remember hearing the name at any of the meetings, don't remember it from the waves of prospects who walked through the door into Columbus's interview room at the combine, don't remember seeing it in any of the draft previews. I double-check. He wasn't invited to the combine. I look at Central Scouting's list. Sestito . . . a left winger. Final ranking: No. 112 in North America. Mid-term ranking: No. 180. He's listed at six foot four and 209 pounds. The Plymouth Whalers picked Sestito in the fifth round, 93rd overall, in the 2003 Ontario league draft. This season he scored 10 goals and 10 assists in 57 games. Dozens of forwards, maybe a hundred of them, have put up better scoring statistics, but the numbers that probably impress most are his height and weight. I saw Plymouth play last season and I can't place him at all. This is way out of the box—a player who might be drafted in the sixth round at best, maybe the seventh, and quite possibly not at all.

(I do a search on a newspaper database at the end of the day and the only hit on a Sestito with a Columbus connection is a tenuous one: an obituary in the *Columbus Dispatch* for one of the paper's retired press operators just a few months ago.)

Castron nods. Boyd's interest is piqued. By the end of this discussion Sestito moves up the Columbus list, all the way to No. 31.

When the second round comes around, I'll look for Columbus to call on Sestito, to the shock of other scouts on the floor.

Ten a.m., June 24, 2006, Mathieu Carle's room, Pan Pacific Hotel, Vancouver

Carle is checking out the suit he'll wear to GM Place in a few hours. Derick Brassard doesn't look up at him or at the draft preview playing on the TV. Brassard is sitting in a chair, writing down the teams in draft order and filling in spaces next to them on a paper napkin left over from breakfast. He's making his own list:

St. L Johnson
Pitt Staal
Chi Toews

Wash *peut-être* Backstrom
Boston
Columbus

Peut-être. Maybe. Just *peut-êtres* and maybes on his list.

Eleven thirty a.m., June 24, 2006, GM Place, Vancouver

The fence between the teams and the media is up on the arena floor. It's half an hour before the commissioner will open the draft proceedings, and the reporters already line the fence like crows on hydro wires. My unlimited access ends here. I've had breakfast with Boyd and the rest, but I have to stop at the fence. The NHL's long-standing decree is in place: access to the teams' tables is reserved for those employed by league teams (general managers, coaches, personnel directors, scouts) and those soon to be employed by league teams (the drafted players). My approach to NHL's media-relations department was like kissing a stone wall. I couldn't get an exception for my story. I couldn't get an exception for a photographer.

I catch an unexpected break, however. The Blue Jackets are assigned a table closest to the stands, just ten feet from players, their families, agents and the general public. The seats aren't assigned, and I'm lucky enough to get there early. MacLean, Boyd and the rest are all within earshot (though MacLean alone will leave the table to huddle with other general managers). If I stand up and lean over, I can flag the Blue Jackets over for a quick question.

This is the largest assembly of Blue Jackets staff to date. Everyone, from MacLean and the Blue Jackets' coach, Gerald Gallant, right down to the part-time scouts in Boston and Quebec, reports to the table promptly half an hour in advance. Each has a copy of The List—the *Final* List, 1 through 100. It's the Company List, the one Don Boyd has signed off on. The scouts will mark their copies with felt pens and highlighters. They'll use their own colour schemes, make their own notations.

They listen to the first three picks go down.

1. St. Louis — Eric Johnson
2. Pittsburgh — Jordan Staal
3. Chicago — Jonathan Toews

Now the intrigue.

Washington has Alexander Ovechkin announce their selection. He gets a standing ovation from the fans in GM Place. When he says Nicklas Backstrom's name, the scouts highlight another name on the list. Makes sense. Backstrom seems a better, more reliable fit with Ovechkin. Phil Kessel sits with his parents and brother in the stands. No change of expression. Derick Brassard sits with his parents, aunts, uncles and friends. They talk all the way through it.

Boston is up next. Some have been guessing Boston will go with Brassard because he grew up in Gatineau, the backyard of Daniel Doré, the scout who scored with the selection of Patrice Bergeron three years back. Others thought the Bruins couldn't pass on Kessel.

A couple of minutes go by. MacLean does his best to look matter of fact. *World War Three.* That's what MacLean thinks he'll have on his hands if Boston takes Brassard. Yeah, Kessel is there at five on the Blue Jackets' list. Most would want Kessel over Brassard. And all would want Kessel over Mueller — all except one: MacLean's assistant GM Jim Clark. As much as The List is definitive, Clark would make his case to pull a different trigger. He doesn't want Kessel.

And then, it's all clear.

Boston — P. Kessel goes up on the board.

Everybody is on the same page. Now Boyd is on the mike. First he invites everyone to come to Columbus for the 2007 NHL draft, and then he says, "With their first selection in the 2006 NHL draft, the Columbus Blue Jackets are pleased to select Derick Brassard of Drummondville."

Brassard stands up and hugs his father, Pierre, who is in his shirt-sleeves, his leather bomber jacket on his seat behind him. The teenager goes down the line—aunts, uncles, his agent and Mathieu Carle, and then up to the stage. He stands beside MacLean, Boyd, Castron, Clark and Smith. He puts on a Columbus Blue Jackets sweater and poses for photos. As he descends from the stage, a Quebec television crew stops him for a quick interview.

Derick Brassard passes through security and makes it over to the Blue Jackets' table. On the way he walks right through the path of Phil Kessel, who is wearing a Bruins sweater and being led to an interview area. Brassard shakes the hands of the scouts who had them on their lists. He pulls a crumpled paper napkin out of his pocket. On it is the list—*his* List—the one he worked on in Mathieu Carle's hotel room. He worked on it right up until he and his parents made their way to the arena. Now it reads:

Washington ~~peut-être~~ Backstrom
Boston Kessel
Columbus !![18]

He sits at the table. *He'd sit here through seven rounds if we let him,* the scouts think. *He's into it.* He told Doug MacLean that he knows "everything" about the Blue Jackets, but he doesn't know how he ended up a Blue Jacket. It's too long a story to tell, but here's how it started. Not with The List, but with this:

"Not big, was one of the best players offensively, skating is very good and show scoring [sic] touch if he get bigger should be a early pick"

---

18. Brassard's napkin edges out *Red Line Report*'s mock draft, which had Johnson going to St. Louis but Kessel to Pittsburgh at No. 2, Toews to Chicago at No. 3, Staal to Washington at No. 4, Backstrom to Boston at No. 5, Mueller to Columbus at No. 6 and Brassard to the New York Islanders at No. 7.

That's the first entry for Derick Brassard in Columbus's scouting database. No. 1 of 50. July 24, 2003.[19] Back before he ever played junior. Denis Leblanc, the part-time scout in Quebec, the one who spells "shift" without the f, filed the report when Brassard was playing with the Gatineau midgets and skated in a midget showcase. Today, Brassard is close to the NHL. Back then, he was a long way from The List. He was even a long way from the napkin.

Two hours pass before the Blue Jackets pick again. Boyd's not impressed by what's available there—that is, assuming that nobody else is on Sestito, that he'll be around in the third round. So MacLean deals away his second-rounder (No. 36 overall) to San Jose for the Sharks' third-rounder (No. 85), fourth-rounder (No. 113) and a second-round pick in the 2007 draft.

When the Blue Jackets' own third-rounder rolls around (No. 69), I'm expecting them to call Sestito, but even though they've taken little time to discuss goaltenders they select Steve Mason, a goalie with the

---

19. Here are the first reports filed by Blue Jackets scouts on the other four prospects in play for Columbus in the sixth slot.

Phil Kessel: February 9, 2003. Shattuck vs. Madison. "Pretty poised for a young guy, late 87, about two years away, not bad size for a player this young, skates well, will be looking for more over the years, player to follow, may try junior next year?"

Peter Mueller: January 18, 2003. "First look at this kid. Very skilled, he sees the ice so well, scored first goal on a good move, he is hard working, he works hard on his draws, unselfish with the puck, perhaps this game he should have kept it more, legitimate 6.00. He can come out of the corner with the puck, very good hand skills, player to watch for sure. I would think he would go to USA program, definitely a player to watch, very good right now."

Nicklas Backstrom: October 2, 2004. "Very good game from him . . . the best player on the ice. . . . smart and controlled everything. . . . sees his team mates and protects the puck, drives to the net and has a nose for the net. . . . player to watch for the draft–06."

London Knights. It's a surprising pick. Central Scouting ranks Mason No. 9 among North American goalies. Still, the dots are easy to connect. First, it's a pick right in the backyard of Don Boyd, a goaltender back in his day. It's also a pick based on the say-so of Columbus's goaltending coach, Rick Wamsley, who is based in Toronto and thus sees a lot of action in the OHL. Mason's regular-season numbers are about as limited as those of Sestito—only five wins and three losses in a backup role. But in the Ontario league playoffs Mason went 4–0, with a sparkling 2.66 goals-against average and a .931 save percentage. The pick starts to make even more sense when Wamsley tells me that he's a former teammate and roomie of London coach Dale Hunter—that Hunter has only good words for Mason. "Dale's tough on goaltenders," Wamsley says. "Mason's in a good program, with a good coach. He'll get a chance to step up next year."

There might be goaltenders who offer greater rewards and considerably more risk—there *might* be. But at some level Mason looks like a safe pick—just an unlikely one. That there was so little discussion on goaltenders in general, and on Mason in particular, suggests that the scouts recuse themselves—or at least step back and yield the floor to the former NHLer Wamsley—when talk winds its way around to the most specialized and technical position. *It takes one to know one.*

At No. 85 the waiting stops. Boyd reads out Sestito's name. There's no gasp from the crowd, no frantic shuffling along press row. But again, the selection *is* a significant break from Central Scouting. Smiles all around at the Columbus table. The player they would have liked to have taken at No. 36, they get forty-nine picks later— with Mason and a second-rounder next year tossed in. There's no popping of champagne corks yet. There's no calling it a victory. But MacLean and Boyd feel like they've maximized the value of their picks and position.

About ninety seconds pass before Los Angeles calls out the name of George Holloway—that would be the given name of Bud of Wapella, Saskatchewan. The kid with the Wal-Mart weights and no more than two meaningful interviews at the combine.

—

The draft has hours to go. I pore over my notes from the top of the draft. The scouts are at the table, taking down names on one list, scratching off names from another.

It looks like a convention for crossword buffs, and the names going up on the board behind the stage are like the solutions to the crossword puzzle that all the scouts have been trying to solve all season long.

The top picks are like the solutions to the Across clues,

7 Across: A forward who played for Shattuck–St. Mary's before going to Des Moines of the USHL and who's headed to the University of Minnesota. Central's eleventh-ranked American skater and son of a Nigerian immigrant. The Islanders select Kyle Okposo.

8 Across: "Rocket" thighs, tight hips and sharp hand-eye co-ordination. The Phoenix Coyotes select Peter Mueller.

Three of the top eight picks—Erik Johnson, Okposo and Mueller—were teammates for the first time back in fifth grade with the Minnesota 88s. These three also figure to play together again on the American team at the world junior tournament in Sweden next season.

More names to fill in.

10 Across: A skilled forward who plays for Kladno in the Czech league but is ticketed to play for Rimouski in the Quebec league. The Florida Panthers select Michael Frolik.

Milan Tuchy liked Frolik but didn't fight to shift him into the Top Ten category.

13 Across: Frolik's teammate in Kladno, who'll also be heading to North America in the fall. The Toronto Maple Leafs select Jiri Tlusty.

Another that Tuchy liked well enough, just not enough.

15 Across: The jittery Finnish goaltender who won't be in Tampa next year, but rather with his club team in Tampere. The Tampa Bay Lightning select Riku Helenius.

Helenius looks a little less nervous—but not a lot less—coming across the floor of the arena to the stage.

16 Across: The army-brat defenceman who answered my questions and was regarded as a "bad interview" by at least one scout in the Columbus room. The San Jose Sharks select Ty Wishart.

History repeating itself. Doug Wilson, the San Jose general manager, was a defenceman, an army brat and a first-round draft pick.

17 Across: They could have had this speedy forward from Utah last year in the last round of the draft. The Los Angeles Kings select Trevor Lewis. Lewis attracted no attention in his first year of eligibility in Des Moines, but is up on stage in Vancouver. Central's rankings had him at No. 30 in North America, Columbus at No. 22 on their master list.

20 Across: The 29th-ranked player according to Central Scouting, the pride of Apple Valley, Minnesota. The Montreal Canadiens select David Fischer.

The Canadiens disagree with Columbus to an even more extreme degree than did Central Scouting. Fischer is the player rated ND by the Blue Jackets. (From what I hear, a couple of other teams feel about him the same way Columbus does.)

22 Across: A skilled little winger who, like Trevor Lewis, knows what it's like to pass through a draft unnoticed. The Philadelphia Flyers select Claude Giroux.

In fact, Giroux almost goes unselected at No. 22 because Flyers general manager Bobby Clarke walks up to the stage and to the podium and promptly forgets Giroux's name. At the Columbus table the scouts put a stroke through the eleventh name on their list.

23 Across: A Russian goaltender who impassively mumbled his way through the Columbus interview. The Washington Capitals select Semen Varlamov.

34 Across: A Czech goaltender with Sparta Praha. The Washington Capitals select Michal Neuvirth.

The selections of Varlamov and Neuvirth have scouts flashing back to 1989, the last time the Capitals selected two goaltenders with consecutive first- and second-round picks. The Capitals first chose Olag Kolzig at nineteenth overall and then, after they took Byron Dafoe with the thirty-fifth pick, coach Bryan Murray cracked up nearby tables at the draft when he said, "What, did we give up on the other guy already?" Maybe the selection of Neuvirth will get Varlamov's attention.

36 Across: A gritty forward who played in the Memorial Cup as a sixteen-year-old. With the pick originally owned by Columbus, the San Jose Sharks select Jamie McGinn.

Another Doug Wilson connection is in play. Both McGinn and Wilson played junior hockey for Ottawa 67's coach Brian Kilrea.

37 Across: The top-ranked European defenceman, who did not make it to the combine. The Boston Bruins select Yuri Alexandrov from Cherepovec.

Neither being skinny nor absent from the combine scared off Boston, but some others, Don Boyd among them, weren't impressed.

41 Across: A smallish centre with the Kingston Frontenacs, scorer of 90 points in the regular season but just two in a fast fade from the play-offs. The Detroit Red Wings select Cory Emmerton. Emmerton's day must be tense and disappointing to him, having been Central Scouting's tenth-ranked North American skater. He lands much closer to his ranking with Columbus, the 52nd slot.

42 Across: A small, skilled defenceman from the U.S. under-18 team. The Philadelphia Flyers select Michael Ratchuk.

51 Across: A big, hard-hitting defenceman from the U.S. under-18 team. The Colorado Avalanche select Nigel Williams.

With their rankings of Williams at 33 and Ratchuk at 35, the Blue Jackets end up closer to the industry opinion—that both are second-round talents—than Central Scouting's, which had Williams as a projected first-rounder (13th ranked among North American skaters) and Ratchuk as a likely fourth-rounder (85th in the same North American rankings).

54 Across: He hopes there will be a deal between the NHL and the Russian federation, or else he's looking at five years in Yaroslavl. The New York Rangers select Artem Anisimov.

Anisimov may need all of Madison Square Garden's financial clout to get his five-year contract fed into the shredder.

56 Across: Grandson of Hall of Famer Bernie Geoffrion, great-grandson of Hall of Famer Howie Morenz, the player at the draft most ready to move right onto the banquet circuit. The Nashville Predators select Blake Geoffrion.

I'm expecting to read about Blake Geoffrion working comedy clubs in Nashville anytime soon.

The picks of Mason, Sestito and Holloway are tipping points. In the first round, teams use all their allotted ten minutes to make their picks, trying to close deals with other teams or fielding last-second offers. When the draft hits triple digits, in Round 4, the picks are made as quickly as bids at an auction. It becomes hard to keep up. It's the tipping point for the crossword, too. Now we've come to the Down clues.

106 Down: Not Yogi, not a catcher with the Yankees, but a goaltender and banker in Zurich. The St. Louis Blues select Reto Berra.

Berra probably drops to his knees when he hears his name called.

113 Down: The foremost defenceman from Foremost, Alberta. Columbus selects Ben Wright from the Lethbridge Broncos. A trend, or a coincidence? As it did with Mason, Columbus opts for a player who doesn't jump out in the regular season (five goals, 18 points, in 55 games), but closes fast in the playoffs (three goals and five assists in six games).

123 Down: Central's 25th-ranked North American skater, and thus projected by many in the media—and certainly his family and friends—to be a first-round pick. The Carolina Hurricanes, defending Stanley Cup champions, select Bobby Hughes.

Hughes is the last pick of the fourth round. Kingston's quick playoff exit hurt Hughes most.

At this point I focus on Columbus's picks, as the Blue Jackets attempt to find a gold nugget among the ashes. That would mean more to MacLean and Boyd and their peers than it would to their owner, who wouldn't appreciate the immense difficulty.

129 Down: Give one to Kjell Larsson. Easy to do with the player who stands at No. 48 on the Columbus list, two places ahead of Bobby Hughes. Columbus selects Robert Nyholm from Sweden. In something less than a nod to Larsson and a move consistent with the Blue Jackets' belief that Canadian junior hockey is the best venue for player development, Columbus will see to it that Nyholm lands with Kingston of the OHL in the fall.

136 Down: A forward from Toronto who passed up junior for college. Columbus selects Nick Sucharski, who played in 36 games for the Michigan State Spartans but scored only two goals as a freshman.

142 Down: A teammate of Derick Brassard with the Drummondville Voltigeurs, he didn't score a point last season. Columbus selects defenceman Maxime Frechette. Frechette's season lasted only 13 games because of injury.

159 Down: A defenceman in the Dub, he scored one goal in three seasons. Columbus selects defenceman Jesse Dudas. Dudas played only 24 games last year in a season divided between Lethbridge and Prince George.

189 Down: A Medicine Hat Tigers teammate of defenceman Kris Russell, the Blue Jackets' third-rounder in 2005. Columbus selects Derek Dorsett. Dorsett, a right winger, scored 25 goals with Medicine Hat last season. The scouts at the table have had a few more views of Dorsett than some other candidates in the sixth round because they had a particular interest in Russell's progress.

194 Down: A better playoff than a regular season, he was on the ice when the national junior championship was decided. Columbus selects left winger Matt Marquardt. Marquardt scored 16 regular-season goals and five more in the playoffs for a Moncton team that won the title in the Q, only to lose in front of the home crowd to Quebec in the Memorial Cup final.

Marquardt is Columbus's last pick. The crew packs up. Others are beating them to the door. They'll wait to read about the last picks—the final squares of the crossword—tomorrow.

213 Down: The very last entry in this entry draft; if you will, the bottom right-hand corner of the crossword. Born in Switzerland, plays in British Columbia, headed to upstate New York. The Carolina Hurricanes, the defending Stanley Cup champions, select Justin Krueger. The Swiss-born defenceman played last season for the Penticton Vees in the British Columbia Junior League, a Tier II loop below the Dub, and will enroll at Cornell University in the fall.

Krueger's name goes up on the board on the stage, as it would in the crossword, in the bottom right-hand corner. By the time Carolina selects Krueger, there are only a handful of scouts left on the floor, packing up their paperwork. The janitors are in the hallway. The draft commenced with the selection of Erik Johnson at 12:05. A scoreboard clock shows the time of Krueger's selection: 10:30.

I am certainly the only one who's sad that it's over.

June 25, 2006, Vancouver

The scouts hadn't even left the floor of the arena before the writers and broadcasters began ranking the draft's winners and losers. The routine in the newspaper trade is to give classroom grades or thumbs-up and thumbs-down ratings. With the advent of weblogs, assessments are made in real time—judgment is passed within minutes of a selection.

The NHL draft is one of the most unusual events in all of sports, and particularly sports journalism. Never is so much written and said about so many based on so little first-hand knowledge. Thousands of words are written about players who represent the future of the franchises, yet those doing the writing—and doing the ranking of winners and losers—are seeing most draftees for the first time at the draft. In their street clothes. The vast majority of writers haven't seen even video highlights of players. In fact, especially for the U.S. hockey media, the vast majority have never even been to a Canadian junior hockey game. I don't think I'm out of line by suggesting that some wouldn't have known which provinces Medicine Hat and Prince Albert are in.

This little snippet from Eric Duhatschek's blog for *The Globe and Mail* is instructive.

The Toronto Maple Leafs finally make their way to the draft table (where GM John Ferguson Jr. was booed mercilessly by the crowd in Vancouver) and select Czech 18-year-old Jiri Tlusty. Tlusty was expected to be drafted much higher than 13th position (The Hockey News *had him ranked 8th) so this is a similar bonus as when the Maple Leafs were able to snap up Finnish netminder Tuukka Rask 21st overall last year.*

The writer's take: Because *The Hockey News* had Tlusty higher in its projections, the Leafs come away with a "bonus." Ostensibly a good draft. Except that the scouts who viewed Tlusty didn't like him at No. 7, or No. 8, or No. 10 or even No. 12. No, if someone did, then the Leafs would not have had an opportunity to pick him at No. 13. It's that simple.

In the absence of inside information (access to scouts' individual lists or organizations' master lists) or first-hand knowledge (viewing the draft prospects in game action), the hockey writers use the very limited tools available to them—they look at NHL Central Scouting's rankings and *The Hockey News* projections. Even at that, they often draw the wrong conclusions. This blog entry is typical. The Maple Leafs might have landed an excellent prospect—for all anyone can know, he might turn out to one of the best players in this year's draft. But *The Hockey News*'s projections don't have anything to do with it, and neither do Central's rankings—they don't determine the value of prospects. No, their value is reflected by the slots where they're selected. Period. Couldn't be any simpler.

If the projections of one team or one media outlet or one scouting service were truly meaningful, then the Blue Jackets would regard as good picks Montreal's selection of Kootenay centre Ben Maxwell at No. 49 and Ottawa's plucking of Green Bay defenceman Gryba at No. 68. Columbus did have Maxwell in their top 20—No. 19—and Gryba as a late-first or early-second rounder as their 29th-ranked draft-eligible player. Ultimately, though, these players will constitute "bonuses" only if they actually play in the NHL and have an impact (or if they are viewed as valuable assets in trade). Likewise, Central Scouting and some other team probably figure that Columbus selected Tom Sestito far too high in this entry draft—that there were dozens of more highly ranked players still on the board. These might end up as good picks but it's too early to judge. It's what goes forward that starts to count—and where these players end up is the ultimate measure.

It's not just that judgments are passed on the basis of received wisdom and virtually no evidence. There may be a time to rank winners and losers, but the days after the draft are not it. Sometimes it takes years to figure out. The draft is a loud noise, but it's the echo that counts. At least once, those criticized are vindicated down the line, though maybe not in time to save their jobs.

The draft defies immediate evaluation even a year or two out because it's rare that any eighteen-year-old, even a top-five selection, skates immediately into a NHL lineup and survives, let alone excels. It was remarkable that Sidney Crosby was able to score 100 points as an eighteen-year-old, but it was almost as noteworthy that he made it through his first NHL season without injury. Most teenagers break down when they're rushed into the lineup, even physical studs like Rick Nash and Ilya Kovalchuk.

What scouts take real pride in—how they rank winners and losers—are the selections in later rounds who will have an impact in the league. Those selected outside the first round who play at all as eighteen-year-olds are the real diamonds. Good scouts go whole careers without finding one. The player who most recently pulled it off was Patrice Bergeron with the Boston Bruins, a 2003 second-round pick who wasn't even invited to the Canadian under-18 camp before the draft or the under-20 summer camp after it. Less than a year after Boston selected Bergeron in the second round, he not only had played the full season with the Bruins but also had collected a gold medal with the Canadian team at the world championships. You'd have to go all the way back to Luc Robitaille (171st pick in the 1984 draft, 668 career goals, three First All-Star Team selections) to find a match: someone selected after the first round who played in the NHL at eighteen and had immediate impact.

Second- and third-rounders who cause even a ripple a few years after their drafts are hard enough to come by. Fact is, Steve Mason and Tommy Sestito notwithstanding, the Columbus Blue Jackets are still looking for their first one. Their record in the second round has been no better than average, and some scouts would say a lot worse than average. Aaron Johnson, the second-rounder in 2001, has shuttled between Columbus and the Blue Jackets' AHL affiliate the last couple of seasons.[20] Dan Fritsche, a second-rounder in 2003, seems to be destined for a NHL career as a third-liner, no better than lower-middle of the NHL pack.

When it comes to the rush to judge winners and losers at a draft, the classic story is Don Murdoch and the Tampa Bay Lightning at the 1998 draft. "Murder" was teased and the Lightning ridiculed at the draft in Buffalo. The franchise owned the first-overall selection because the team was easily the league's worst, almost indescribably bad, and they all but clinched the top slot in the draft in January. The front office was in utter disarray. The general manager was Phil Esposito, a disaster as a hockey exec whose staff consisted entirely of cronies. Esposito didn't report to owners per se—the standard line in media reports was "Japanese mystery men," investors who never deigned to take in a game or even, apparently, set foot in Tampa. By 1998 the mystery men were set to sell the franchise to the owner of basketball's Detroit Pistons, Art Williams, a guy who had made his millions selling used cars. In advance of that, they cut the team's operating budget to the nubbins. The team had the first pick in the draft, but only four scouts on staff and a threadbare travel budget.

Murdoch made the best of a bad situation. He couldn't travel like other scouts—seeing twenty teams in ten towns in ten nights. He homed in on the two players who emerged as the prospective No. 1: Vincent Lecavalier in Rimouski and David Legwand with the Plymouth Whalers. "I basically parked in Rimouski for a week at a time," Murdoch told me.

Murdoch couldn't see as much of the players as he would have liked. When Lecavalier made the Canadian under-20 team, Phil Esposito decided not to send Murdoch to the world junior tournament in Finland but sent his own brother, Tony, instead. Tony's credentials as a goaltender were the stuff of legend, but as a hockey man he was the butt of jokes. Other scouts were convinced that he couldn't tell one player from another—that he couldn't put a name to a number—at games he worked. That became easier to believe when I saw him talking to Vincent Lecavalier's father, René, at our

20. Scouts will joke that Johnson's best asset is the fact that he's from Prince Edward Island, like MacLean, Clark and Gallant.

hotel one morning. Afterward I asked René Lecavalier if the scout was asking him about his son's desire to be the first-overall pick and his attitude about joining the troubled franchise. René Lecavalier said that was hardy the case. "He didn't know who I am," he said, "and I'm not sure that he knows Vince."

Few will admit it now, but scouts were divided about the No. 1 pick: most liked Lecavalier's skill and feel for the game, but some thought his skating would limit him in the NHL. Legwand was an explosive skater, and the Ontario league was presumed to provide better competition than Lecavalier saw in Rimouski. Murdoch had no doubts: on the basis of his scouting, the Lightning chose Lecavalier.

Few took note of it then, but the Lightning's next pick came in the third round, and Murdoch again took a player from Rimouski. That had other scouts smirking at their tables. They didn't have this Rimouski player anywhere close to 60th overall, the slot where Tampa Bay selected him. They put it down to Tampa's tight budget limiting Murdoch in the field. And maybe there was something to that. As it turned out, Brad Richards not only led Rimouski to the Memorial Cup in 2000 but also won a major NHL trophy before Lecavalier did. Yet by the time Richards hoisted the Stanley Cup and was handed the Conn Smythe Trophy, Murdoch was long, long gone from Tampa Bay—he was coaching in the low minors and would soon be out of hockey.

Maybe a few analysts had Tampa Bay as a winner at the 1998 draft, but it would have been on the selection of Lecavalier alone. Murdoch should have been able to dine out on the Richards selection for years—at the very least it should have bought him tenure with the Lightning. But, no, the sale of the franchise and the hiring of a new general manager (and then another and another) ensured that no one remembered who had pushed for Richards. Such cases of workplace amnesia are business as usual in the NHL.

The scouts have longer memories than their bosses. For all the excellent choices in his stints as a scout in Quebec and Ottawa and even Columbus that Don Boyd might attach himself to, there's one player who lingers in his thoughts around the time of the draft.

Not a player he drafted, mind you, but one he coached; one who should have made it but didn't.

A few names are always mentioned when conversation turns to the biggest busts in the history of the NHL draft. They're like commercial products marketed as the next big thing that flop with consumers. They're like movies developed to be blockbusters that end up unwatchable. They're like politicians hyped and fast-tracked to office who utterly lack substance. These bad ideas are fascinating because they're not one man's mistake but the product of what passed for collective wisdom.

Well, Jason Bonsignore is like Stockwell Day in a theatre watching *Ishtar* while drinking a New Coke.

Other names will get mentioned as the draft's biggest busts. Most frequently nominated is Brian Lawton, chosen by the Minnesota North Stars with the first pick of the 1983 draft.

As it turned out, Minnesota's general manager, Lou Nanne was wrong about a kid from down the street—Lawton played for Mount St. Charles High School in Minneapolis. Nanne misjudged three future Hall of Fame players who were among the next eight picks (Pat LaFontaine, Steve Yzerman and Cam Neely). But worst of all, he portrayed himself as the smartest guy in the room. In the early '80s, Nanne came up with a test for top prospects. He insisted it wasn't a psychological test. "We've spent a lot of time and money developing it, so I'm being deliberately vague about it," he told the *Globe and Mail*'s Neil Campbell in 1982. "I can tell you we've found it to be extremely accurate." Lawton proved that the test was only *fairly* accurate. And after a couple of seasons Nanne wasn't talking about the North Stars' top-secret testing anymore.[21] Lawton's career pales next to LaFontaine's, Yzerman's and Neely's, and in fact the rest of the players in the top ten went on to more

---

21. According to one player who took the Stars' secret test, there "wasn't much to it at all . . . just a bunch of questions like any other personality test. I did it over the phone in a couple of hours."

significant careers than the first pick's. But at least Lawton had a career—he played just under 500 NHL games and scored 112 goals, including 21 in 66 games as a 21-year-old. Lawton's story isn't that of a bad draft pick but of a hyped prospect who was rushed to the NHL and ruined by it.

No, the most magnificent bust has to be Jason Bonsignore. At the start of his draft season, 1993–94, the Central Scouting Service ranked him No. 1 overall among North American skaters. He struggled, dropped a couple of notches by the time the draft rolled around, but some still compared him to Mario Lemieux. Bonsignore always dismissed the comparisons—but then again, he made a point of wearing a black turtleneck under his sweater just like No. 66. Born and raised in Rochester, New York, Bonsignore didn't seem to mind the idea of being the American Mario.

"He did have a lot of talent," says Boyd, who was Bonsignore's coach with the Newmarket Royals, Bonsignore's team in the Ontario Hockey League. "He could step over the boards in a close game and score at will, just like Mario."

The key words are "at will." Bonsignore was anything but driven. In fact, he seemed less interested in hockey than in go-kart driving. "That's all he talked about," Boyd says. "His father had been a car racer. He told everyone he was going to take his NHL bonus and open a racetrack."

Grant Sonier, an assistant coach for Boyd in Newmarket and these days a scout for the Los Angeles Kings, came up with a brain teaser about player evaluation: If you had three categories—talent, hockey sense, and character—and only six chips to place in those slots, how would you distribute them? Discussions about this over beers on the road are the nearest scouts get to Socratic inquiry. I asked Sonier how he'd spread those chips if he were scouting—in retrospect—Jason Bonsignore. His reply was quick and to the point: "Six on talent, none for hockey sense, none for character."

In retrospect it seems obvious, but at the time most missed that critical point: Jason Bonsignore had a talent for hockey but almost no interest in it, beyond what it could do for him.

The old line stands true: players make the best scouts, and Boyd's players were way ahead of Central Scouting, the NHL scouts and even their coach. "He was a nice kid, good-looking, had everything going for him," Boyd says, "but they just hated him." Grant Sonier reckons "hated" doesn't overstate the case. "He came back from the world juniors and hung his U.S. sweater and sweats in his stall," Sonier says. "The players took them to the middle of the dressing room and burned them."

Boyd doesn't claim to have spotted the red flags when he traded Bonsignore to Niagara Falls in that 1993–94 season. Still, Bonsignore's stock was high enough for him to be drafted fourth overall by the Edmonton Oilers, and they weren't poor-mouthing him as a prospect.

Glen Sather, Edmonton's general manager, put the pressure on his scouting staff to come up with a player—not a star, but a safe bet. The Oilers had two high picks, No. 4 and No. 6, in the 1994 draft. "I told our scouts Sunday night that the two picks we get have to be able to play," Sather said. "Maybe not this year, but sometime. You can't make any mistakes. It would be wonderful if we could get two impact players like Jason [Arnott], but that's a little optimistic. They can't be any worse than third-line players." The scouting staff hyped Bonsignore—there was no talk about him being a role player or a third-liner. "For what we're looking for, he's the whole package," said Kevin Prendergast, the Oilers' director of hockey administration.

Edmonton's scouting staff was much cooler about the second pick in that draft—some scouts liked Ryan Smyth, some preferred other names. Smyth went on to become the heart and face of the franchise for more than a decade. Smyth was a native son and was playing in the Oilers' backyard, but some couldn't see him as a player—and certainly not one who'd go on to collect an Olympic gold medal and lead the Oilers to a Stanley Cup final.

Jason Bonsignore proved to be something less than the whole package:

Season	Team	League	—Regular Season—					—Playoffs—				
			GP	G	A	Pts	PIM	GP	G	A	Pts	PIM
1992–93	Newmarket Royals	OHL	66	22	20	42	6	7	0	3	3	0
1993–94	Newmarket Royals	OHL	17	7	17	24	22	—	—	—	—	—
1993–94	Niagara Falls Thunder	OHL	41	15	47	62	41	—	—	—	—	—
1994–95	Niagara Falls Thunder	OHL	26	12	21	33	51	—	—	—	—	—
1994–95	Sudbury Wolves	OHL	23	15	14	29	45	17	13	10	23	12
1994–95	**Edmonton Oilers**	**NHL**	1	1	0	1	0	—	—	—	—	—
1995–96	Sudbury Wolves	OHL	18	10	16	26	37	—	—	—	—	—
1995–96	Cape Breton Oilers	AHL	12	1	4	5	12	—	—	—	—	—
1995–96	**Edmonton Oilers**	**NHL**	20	0	2	2	4	—	—	—	—	—
1996–97	Hamilton Bulldogs	AHL	78	21	33	54	78	7	0	0	0	4
1997–98	Hamilton Bulldogs	AHL	8	0	2	2	14	—	—	—	—	—
1997–98	**Tampa Bay Lightning**	**NHL**	35	2	8	10	22	—	—	—	—	—
1997–98	San Antonio Dragons	IHL	22	3	8	11	34	—	—	—	—	—
1997–98	Cleveland Lumberjacks	IHL	6	4	0	4	32	8	1	1	2	20
1998–99	**Tampa Bay Lightning**	**NHL**	23	0	3	3	8	—	—	—	—	—
1998–99	Cleveland Lumberjacks	IHL	48	14	19	33	68	—	—	—	—	—
1999–00	St. John's Maple Leafs	AHL	29	6	13	19	30	—	—	—	—	—
2000–01	DID NOT PLAY											
2001–02	DID NOT PLAY											
2002–03	Springfield Falcons	AHL	37	9	12	21	39	—	—	—	—	—
2002–03	Lowell Lock Monsters	AHL	12	1	4	5	8	—	—	—	—	—
2003–04	South Carolina Stingrays	ECHL	5	2	5	7	2	—	—	—	—	—
2003–04	EHC Biel	Swiss-B	9	9	3	12	6					
2004–05	South Carolina Stingrays	ECHL	1	0	0	0	0	—	—	—	—	—
2004–05	Las Vegas Wranglers	ECHL	18	4	8	12	51	—	—	—	—	—
2005–06	Pelicans (Lahti)	FNL	7	4	1	5	18	—	—	—	—	—
2005–06	Ilves Tampere	FNL	4	0	1	1	6	—	—	—	—	—
	NHL Totals		79	3	13	16	34					

In all, Jason Bonsignore played in 79 NHL games and scored three goals. Bonsignore is back in Rochester, but I have no luck getting in touch with him. I leave messages with the racetrack and go-kart operation he runs there, but no one calls back.

July 1, 2006, Toronto

I get a call from a friend in the scouting ranks. For most scouts in the biz, yesterday was Day 365 of their one-year contracts with their clubs, the day when a lot of business cards become obsolete.

The biggest news is sending a chill through the trade: the Buffalo Sabres, a team that came within one game of the Stanley Cup final last year despite a toll of injuries usually associated with trench warfare, have axed a bunch of their scouting staff. Among those cut loose were two respected veterans: amateur scouting director Jim Benning and Don Luce, who had been employed by the Sabres, first as a player and then as a scout, for more than thirty years. The Sabres had done better in the draft than any other squad in the league. Not only did drafted players form the nucleus of the squad that made a surprising run to the brink of the Stanley Cup, but, more broadly, there were more players drafted by the Buffalo Sabres playing in the NHL than draftees of any other team. When it came to the idea that the league is only as good as the scouts, well, the league owed more to Benning, Luce and other former Sabres employees than any crew of scouts.

The big media haven't reported the house cleaning and the Buffalo *News* barely mentions it. The Sabres' timing is impeccable: they gassed the scouts in and around the time that the team is heading into arbitration hearings with Daniel Briere and J.P. Dumont. These, of course, are the stories the beat reporters focus on. Further, if the axing of the scouts was noticed at all, the suits in the front office had a made-to-measure fallback position: This small-market team was pressed to make ends meet, what with an arbitrator handing their asses to them.

Benning won't be out of work for long. The Boston Bruins are making him an offer. Luce, though, is still looking for a soft spot to land.

As the story goes, though, this isn't simply a change in scouting personnel. It's a deeper philosophical change. The Sabres have long felt a tight financial squeeze—at various points in recent years they have wondered whether their cheques would clear, white-knuckled their way through a bankruptcy filing and watched their one-time patron, John Rigas, do the perp walk after being indicted for bank, wire and securities fraud. Benning, Luce and the Sabres' scouting staff managed to be among the NHL's best all the while, working with ever-diminishing resources. Their travel budget was a fraction of that of the big-market clubs. The Sabres' scouts just made do with less. But with their top scouts being shown the door, the Sabres are changing strategy. They are stripping the scouting staff down to a skeleton crew. Word is that they plan to rely on video for scouting. For scouts, this is an unthinkable compromise. Video offers them only a partial picture of players—for them, it's like reviewing movies based on trailers.

Sabres owner Tom Golisano was probably influenced by other owners, or maybe even executives within the league. Golisano was claiming hardship, even though his team enjoyed a long playoff run and hit its threshold of season-ticket subscriptions. What kind of savings will he net from the slashing of the scouting budget? Likely around $750,000—the price tag of a garden-variety fourth-liner. That, or the base salary of a first-round draft pick who doesn't work out because he was poorly scouted. It has the look of a classic case of being penny-wise and pound-foolish. Then again, pound-foolish is Golisano's track record. Three times he entered the gubernatorial race in the state of New York as the candidate of the Independence Party. He didn't mind pouring his own millions—probably up to eight figures in all—into three quixotic campaigns where he topped out at 14 percent in the polls.

Few in scouting would ever be found rooting for the opposition, but no outfit will be less popular this season than Buffalo, and not just because of the poor treatment of well-liked industry regulars. For Buffalo fans, Golisano played the role of white knight, throwing his vaultfuls behind the franchise when it was on the verge of folding. To scouts, though, Golisano is nothing less than the prince of darkness. "We better hope the Sabres screw up and fast, or we'll all be out of jobs," my friend says.

I've known Buffalo's general manager, Darcy Regier, since he stepped in as general manager of the team back in 1997. We were always on good terms. I wondered why he didn't get back to me when I emailed around, looking for a team to follow through a draft—it was an idea that I first broached with him about a year or two after he joined the Sabres. If he knew that he had to strip down his staff, there was no way he'd entertain my request for access. Some scouts believe that he should have gone to the wall, not just in support of Benning and Luce, but also the role of scouts in an NHL operation. Still, I can't imagine that Regier was happy to let his top scouts go. He knows exactly how his team, a legitimate Stanley Cup contender, was built. He knows the Sabres' scouts did a good job, uncovering top picks like Thomas Vanek (fifth overall in 2003) and Drew Stafford (thirteenth overall in 2004). He also knows that in his first year the Sabres landed Maxim Afinegenov with the sixty-ninth pick in the entry draft, as well as emerging all-star defenceman Brian Campbell at No 156. And that two years later the scouts plucked his franchise goaltender Ryan Miller with the 138th pick overall.

PART TWO

THE VIEW FROM THE CORNER SEATS

MY FATHER TOOK ME TO SEE WHAT TURNED OUT TO be the last game of Bobby Orr's junior career. Orr's Oshawa Generals were playing the Edmonton Oil Kings at Maple Leaf Gardens. I was not quite ten, but even at that point I understood that Orr was a marvel, unlike the other players I saw playing junior hockey at the Gardens. Even in fourth grade I was a fixture in the cheap seats of Toronto Marlies games on Sunday afternoons and, though I cheered Brit Selby and Mike Byers and the rest of the Marlies, the guy in the gold and black with the buzzcut was simply a player of another sort.

My recollections of the 1966 Memorial Cup are vague at best. I remember it was the last game I went to, an Oshawa loss that gave Edmonton the championship. That I'm sure of. I remember that I was disappointed that my program contained a glossy photo of an Oil King and not Orr. And I remember that a woman sitting behind my father and me was an Edmonton fan who traded with me for the photo in her program—Orr's, of course. And I remember thinking that the Oil Kings all looked like they were ten years older than Orr and the other Generals.

Something else I remember was an observation by my best friend's father, a guy who grew up playing hockey on frozen ponds on Manitoulin Island. Ivan McAnsh was a policeman in Toronto's mounted division and a mountainous defenceman on the Toronto police hockey team. When he hit his forties he served as both player and coach. That was no small accomplishment in those days, because the police force competed with the American Hockey

League for Junior A players—and frequently won, because the pay was better.

Ivan was not as impressed as his son and I were by Orr's play. When we gushed about Orr, Ivan would shake his head and tell us our hero worship was misplaced. We protested and said that he was the next great player. "Maybe," he said, "but skating that bowlegged his knees are going to go. He's not gonna last like Doug Harvey."

It was a remarkably prescient observation, well in advance of the worst of Orr's injuries. We were watching how *fast* Orr was skating; Ivan was watching *how* he was skating. Ivan also understood the risk attached to the way Orr skated. He picked up on both the nuance and the consequence. It was no lucky guess, and I'm thankful that he never suggested that I might have knee troubles. I was reminded of Ivan's prediction when Bobby Orr couldn't play in the 1972 Summit Series because of knee surgery, when he gutted out the 1976 Canada Cup a diminished player, and when he was finally driven out of the game after his ill-fated stint in Chicago. I learned a crucial lesson that served me well in my professional life: Those who play and those who played see a different game than even the most dedicated spectator. The lesson was reinforced for me at the combine and the draft once again. It is proven every year.

If Ivan McAnsh were around today, maybe an NHL team would tap him as a bird dog or give him a full-time scouting job, just as his players might have had opportunities to make a buck from the game rather than join the force. Then again, if playing jobs were scarce back in the '60s, scouting jobs were even more so. That was something that hit home for me when I struck up a conversation with one of NHL scouting's elder statesmen, Ted Hampson, who worked for the St. Louis Blues for several years before joining the Colorado Avalanche.

Hampson was first signed by the New York Rangers in 1957. A forward more gritty and canny than skilled or gifted, over the next decade he spent more time in the minors than the NHL. When the league went from six teams to twelve in 1967, Hampson was assured of a full-time job in the big leagues. In the end, he logged

nearly a thousand games in the NHL and WHA and was in his
mid-forties when he last played for a buck in the minor pros.
Hampson is as sharp a hockey man as you'll find, but even at that
it should come as no surprise that details about events five decades
ago might get a little sketchy. I was poring through old microfilm
of bygone newspapers one day and came across the story of the
scout who claimed to discover Ted Hampson. Now, Hampson has
told me that another Rangers scout signed him to a C-form with
the team—and this is true, as far as it goes. But according to newspaper accounts dating back to a simpler time, the scout did this on
the instruction of Al Ritchie, the longtime Rangers scout in western Canada. And, with regard to the scarcity of NHL scouting jobs
back in the old days, it should be noted that for many years Ritchie
was the Rangers' *only* scout. Fact is, he discovered and signed
almost the entire roster of the New York Rangers' 1940 Stanley
Cup team. Even more remarkably, he worked many years without
drawing a salary or commission.

Al Ritchie's name wasn't kicked around in the sports pages in
his day, and he didn't enter the game's lore—he came along
decades before scouts became part of the conversation. He was
both a junior hockey coach—taking the Regina Pats to the two
Memorial Cup championships—and a football coach who led the
Regina Roughriders to four Grey Cup games. Yet for most of his
career Ritchie was (brace yourself for an outdated colloquialism) a
simon-pure amateur. He didn't draw a paycheque coaching either
hockey or football. He even worked for the Rangers pro bono when
he was the scout for the best team in hockey. Many years later, the
Rangers started sending a Christmas bonus, and after that a small
retainer. Still, Ritchie said money wasn't the compensation he was
looking for.

"I got my pay when I heard Foster Hewitt talk about my boys on
Saturday night hockey broadcasts," Ritchie once told a newspaper
reporter.

It's not that the idea is now quaint—it was hopelessly naïve even
then. As it turns out, Ritchie didn't have much use for the Rangers'

money. He had a day job with the federal government's customs and excise department, and he also had a gift for investments. He lost $75,000 in the crash of 1929, but made it all back and more: by the time he retired from his job with the feds he owned twelve houses in Regina along with various other properties. And he lived within his means. Ritchie never married and lived with his sister into his dotage.

Al Ritchie has a place in the Saskatchewan Sports Hall of Fame, and there's a park named after him in Regina (I couldn't determine whether he ever owned the property). But Ritchie came within a stroke of a pen of having a more prominent place in history.

Ritchie made a trip out to Saskatoon in the spring of 1942 to scout a junior hockey team and found himself with a couple of hours to spare. To kill the time, Ritchie took in an industrial league game at the rink. Most of the players in the game were in their thirties, so Ritchie didn't pay close attention—until one player caught his eye. "I figured this fellow must have been a good player at one time, so I asked someone where he had played when he was younger. He told me the player's name was Gordie Howe and he was only fourteen. I couldn't believe it because I've never before, or since, seen a fourteen-year-old with the moves of this kid."

Ritchie tracked down the Howe family and was desperate to lock him up for the Rangers. Mrs. Howe advised the scout that Gordie couldn't be signed until he finished Grade 8. Eventually, Howe was brought to the Rangers' junior camp. Over the years the story has been told in several versions; according to the best known, Howe failed to impress Lester Patrick, the general manager of the Rangers, and was cut loose. The way Ritchie told it, Howe was impressive but the Rangers didn't have room for him on their list of protected players—they hoped he wouldn't sign with anyone in the meantime. The Red Wings got wind of the phenom and the rest—as they said even back in Al Ritchie's day—is history.

Howe was just one of the Hall of Famers Ritchie discovered and lost. The Bentley brothers, Doug and Max, were two others Ritchie desperately wanted. Every scout has a fish story, but none have had a bigger one get away. Sometimes scouts have been fired for not fighting hard enough for a future star they wanted. The Rangers weren't in a position to fire a scout they weren't paying.

August 8, 2006, Zimny Stadion, Breclav, Czech Republic

Ivan Hlinka Memorial, preliminary round
USA 3 Finland 2
Russia 7 Czech Republic 1

The winter game seems to go on twelve months a year, but really it's only the business side that grinds through July. Hockey makes news in the seventh month when free agents are locked up and coaches and general managers are let go or hired. The players whose seasons have ended in spring—as early as March, as late as June—hang up their skates, rest and heal from a winter's worth of battering.

So the Ivan Hlinka Memorial in midsummer represents hockey coming out of its hibernation. The tourney started back in 1991 and was originally called the Pacific Cup. For its first three years the under-18 tournament was staged in that fabled hockey hotbed, Japan. The inaugural event featured four teams: the hosts, Canada, the U.S. and the Soviet Union. Though the Canadian team featured future NHL all-stars Paul Kariya and Chris Pronger, the Soviets came away with the gold. The summer tournament shifted around during the mid-90s, moving from Japan to Mexico and on to British Columbia, before settling down in the Czech Republic and Slovakia. Maybe they weren't the most attractive places to stage a tournament, but they were the cheapest. Officials changed the name of the event to the Under-18 World Cup, but it was hardly global in scope. By 1997 the field had been whittled down to three teams, the Czechs, the Slovaks and the Canadians, all the other hockey nations having decided to dedicate their resources to the IIHF world under-18 championships in the spring.

The World Cup continued mostly at Hockey Canada's behest. Hockey Canada believed that its under-20 team would be operating at a disadvantage at the world juniors if its players couldn't play together in any event in seasons leading up to the under-20s. Other national programs played in the mid-season invitational under-18 tournaments and the IIHF world under-18s in the spring. Hockey Canada officials believed they couldn't send a team to the IIHF event because it conflicted with the major junior playoffs. The little summer gathering wasn't ideal—there are only so many games you can play in a three-team tournament. Still, for Hockey Canada's purposes, it rounded up the players projected to be on the under-20 team at some future point and gave them a chance to show their stuff and develop some chemistry.

In the last few years, though, the landscape has shifted dramatically on a couple of fronts. Since 2002, Hockey Canada has sent a team to the IIHF under-18 world championships, taking the best players whose teams have been eliminated early from the CHL playoffs. I showed up at Canada's debut in the spring tournament; it was a debacle—and, fittingly, the site of the tournament was Piestany, Slovakia, where in 1987 the Canadian and Soviet teams were tossed out of the world under-20s for brawling. At the 2002 under-18s the Canadian roster featured a single player who would go on to NHL stardom: Eric Staal of the Carolina Hurricanes. The rest of the lineup consisted of serviceable juniors but only a couple of players with a prospect of playing professionally above the East Coast Hockey League. That inaugural Canadian team was life and death to beat Norway by a goal and lost to a hardworking but hardly talented squad from Belarus. Worst of all, the U.S. squad, the under-18 team that trains and plays together all season in Ann Arbor, Michigan, dealt Canada a crushing defeat, 10–3, and took home the gold. With the sixth-place finish, Hockey Canada had to wonder whether it could ever compete with a patchwork squad. The next year, though, the Canadians ended up as tournament champions, and a couple of years later lost narrowly to the U.S. in the final. Hockey Canada has accepted that the spring tournament is a hit-and-miss proposition—though it can still work in the service of the under-20 program, even with a diluted roster.

Likewise, the summer under-18 tournament has evolved over the years. The tournament was renamed the Ivan Hlinka Memorial in 2005, a year after the former Czech hockey star and beloved coach of the 1998 Olympic champions was killed in a car accident. But the most significant change has been substantive: the tournament has become a World Cup in all but name. By 2003 all the major hockey powers had joined or rejoined the field for the August tournament: Canada, the Czech Republic, Finland, Russia, Slovakia, Sweden, Switzerland and the U.S.

It's like summer school for hockey's honour students. In fact, because the roster of the Canadian team here isn't limited by the CHL playoffs, you could make a case that the talent on show at the Ivan Hlinka Memorial is better than at the spring tournament.

I hitch a ride from Prague to Breclav, a three-hour drive, with a few scouts from the Calgary Flames. When I first came to this tournament in 2003, it fell in the middle of the worst heat wave in modern European history—the temperature outside the arena was 42 degrees Celsius on the first day, and attendance was driven by locals looking for a way to get out of the heat. Today, though, it's damp and cool. It could be October. It could be April. That it's hockey season fully registers when we pull into the parking lot. There the Finnish team is warming up, kicking a soccer ball around by the back door of the arena. The soundtrack is provided by the DJs on the U.S. team, what with Metallica booming out of the speakers set up near the open windows of their dressing room.

The U.S.'s record in recent under-18 tournaments is an impressive one. They won the summer tournament in 2003 and the spring tournaments in 2002 and 2006. The scouts are anxious to get a look at the American team that will face the Finns in the tournament opener, but the roster is less than the Americans' best. USA Hockey is hoping for the best with less than best. For Americans, this is a strategy rather than necessity. Their priority is the IIHF tournament, and the bulk of that team will be drawn from the ranks of USA Hockey's development team that will convene in Ann Arbor this fall. The organization invests millions in the care and feeding of those elite prospects, and its staff will have a full eyeful of the players enrolled there.[1] What USA Hockey wants from this summer tournament is something more than a glimpse of the top players who won't be heading to Ann Arbor; rather, it wants to get a book on players who might work their way into the plans of the world junior team a couple of years down the line. The coaches will look at prospects who'll play high school hockey this winter. For instance, defenceman Tommy Cross plays for Westminster High in Connecticut in a league that doesn't challenge him, a league that's a big step down from, say, the game in the Boston area or in Minneapolis or Detroit. Fact is, Cross is only in his junior year—as it stands, he's looking at two more seasons at Westminster. USA Hockey can get a far better read of his skills here against international squads than it can when he plays against kids who wouldn't have a shot at making the varsity at Shattuck or one of the high school hockey powers.

The USA Hockey staff will also dope out players who are headed to the junior United States Hockey League. Defenceman Nick Petrecki is the prospect of greatest interest in this category. Petrecki was getting attention from college recruiters when he was an oversized fourteen-year-old playing Junior B in upstate New York against nineteen- and twenty-year-olds. Even though the Plymouth Whalers of the Ontario junior league drafted him eighth overall in the midget draft, Petrecki chose to play last season for the Omaha Gamblers and will be heading back there again this fall, intent on enrolling at Boston College in the fall of 2007. The *Red Line Report* is already touting him as the top defenceman in any league eligible

---

1. According to NHL Central Scouting's early list of players to watch, the USA under-18 development team features four players projected as first- or second-round picks in next June's draft, and seven more skaters and two goaltenders who are rated as likely selections in the first five rounds.

for the 2007 NHL entry draft. There are also lesser prospects ticketed for the USHL, like David Brownschidle, who'll play for the Lincoln Storm in the coming season. Again, the quality of the USHL isn't quite up there with major junior or the development team—it's closer to the better Tier II leagues in Canada. Conditions may not be ideal for viewing these prospects in Breclav—it is, after all, the middle of summer, and players have only been on skates for a short time, timing and conditioning being far from midseason levels. Still, in terms of putting a challenge in front of them, this will be the best the USHL players will see all year.

What works for USA Hockey works for the scouts, too. The best reads they can get on Cross and Petrecki are right here at the summer under-18s—the only chance for better viewing would be if USA Hockey were to have them back for the spring tournament, which is no sure thing.

The Americans don't have a gift in the first game. The Finns beat them out for the bronze at this tournament two years ago. It doesn't look as though they have a marquee prospect among their '89 birthdays, but they are always a patient, disciplined, nettlesome opponent. Because the pool of talent in Finland is small, the players in any one year seem to benefit from playing together on a regular basis. What they lack in high-end talent and depth, they make up for with chemistry. And recently they've had a nasty habit of coming up with an elite goaltender in every age group—now Finland stands as the Quebec of Europe. Riku Helenius, that nervous, toe-tapping goaltender from Columbus's interviews at the combine, was named the top goaltender at the 2006 IIHF under-18s, where the Finns finished second.

Though the U.S. would be favoured in this matchup, they get off to a slow start. The Americans' timing is off because it's the off-season, and they're still a little legless from the travel and time change. And you'd count on the Finns to grind away, keeping the game close. That's exactly how the game unfolds. The Americans control the puck on the cycle against the smaller Finns, but struggle to finish off scoring chances. Twice the U.S. takes a one-goal lead;

twice Finland comes back to tie, the second time with less than four minutes to go. Just as overtime looms, Jimmy Hayes, a big winger from Dorchester, Massachusetts, scores his second goal of the game to give the U.S. a hard-earned but deserved victory. Hayes is arguably the most impressive player—at six foot three and 210 pounds, he's the most physically imposing here—but because he was born in November of '89, he's a late birthday and not eligible until the 2008 draft. Of players of interest, Petrecki doesn't look like the best defenceman on his team, never mind the best eighteen-year-old in the world. Meanwhile, Tommy Cross, the Connecticut high schooler, fits in seamlessly on the U.S. blueline. His stock rises with every scribble of the scouts' game notes.

After the U.S. game my notebook is a complete mess. Fact is, there was no one player I could focus on the way I would if I were just writing a newspaper or magazine story. No, I was trying to look at the game as a scout would. I was trying to keep track of prospects for the 2007 NHL entry draft. That eliminated only Hayes and a few other players by reason of late birthdays, the backup goaltenders and, from what I can tell, Eddie Olczyk Jr., son of the former NHLer whose invitation to the tournament must have been a condition of his father's commitment to coach here.[2] The few deletions helped, but I still felt like a baggage handler who was sent upstairs to fill in for an air traffic controller. It was information overload.

I spot the Boston Bruins' scout Daniel Doré in the stands and ask him how he manages to walk into a building in August and keep

---

2. I'm not really clear why USA Hockey sought out Olczyk Sr. It can't be on the basis of his record as coach of the Pittsburgh Penguins, who won 31 of 103 games he worked despite the presence of Sidney Crosby *and* Mario Lemieux in the lineup for some stretches. Prior to going behind the Penguins' bench, his work experience after his playing career had been strictly in the broadcast booth. It's hard to imagine that he was the most qualified candidate to coach the Americans at this tournament.

track of everything in front of him. After all, he's getting a first look at many of the players. And there are others he might seen once or twice before, but has never made them priorities for viewing.

Doré tells me it's better to narrow my focus at a tournament like this. "Just pick a player or two on a shift—say, how a winger works against a defenceman and vice versa," he says. "Look for who wins matchups. You can't do all twelve players all at once. Better to give your attention to a couple out there at a time. Change it around every few minutes. Really, all you're looking to get is impressions— not to get a perfect read on a player, more like trying to figure out what players to watch down the line. But believe me, this tournament is tougher for us to work than a junior game back home when each team will have two or three draft-eligibles that you can watch each and every shift."

A relief, because I don't have a clue off my notes.

The second game of the doubleheader pits the Russians against the host Czechs. Though the U.S.–Finland game was played in front of a hundred scouts and a couple of dozen American parents wearing starred and striped sweatshirts, the night game will draw a few thousand local fans. To guarantee gate receipts, the tournament is always set up to have the Czechs playing in Breclav and the Slovaks across the border in Piestany. Over the last six tournaments, that bit of home cooking has contributed to the Czechs landing on the podium five times: four silver medals and one bronze. This year they also have the top-ranked European player among the '89 birthdays: Jakub Voracek, a skilled winger, who was the first-overall pick in the Canadian Hockey League's European import draft. He'll be headed to Nova Scotia next week to play for the Halifax Mooseheads.

If the Finns are the epitome of team play, then the Russians have too often been the antithesis. Too many of their top players are written up (and, to an extent, written off) with a line usually found on kindergarten report cards: *Does not play well with others.* The first spring under-18 tournament I attended featured, among others, Alexander Ovechkin, who showed some awareness of his teammates, and Nikolai Zherdev, who was a pure soloist—I don't recall him ever passing the puck, though I vaguely remember another Russian poke-checking it away from him once. Zherdev was the most conspicuous puck hog and grandstander, but not the only one. The Russians approached most of the worlds as their own private skills competition. Many scouts seemed thankful that the U.S. knocked off the Russians in the final of that tournament, viewing it as a triumph of the game's old-fashioned virtues over the Russian *divos*. Those with a longer historical view regarded it as bitter irony: the Soviet teams that battled the NHL's best back in the 1970s and '80s were steeped in a team-first ethic. One frequent criticism levelled against Soviet teams of that era was that they too often passed up a chance to score in search of a pretty pass.

The recent stereotype is turned inside out three or four shifts into the Czech Republic–Russia game. Voracek doesn't have an impact, but he can hardly be faulted. The Russian teens, they throw the puck around with uncanny precision—sequences of four, five, even six tape-to-tape passes leading to easily finished scoring chances. The crowd is so awed and quieted that I can hear the puck hitting the blades of the sticks. It's hard to imagine that any coach these days could sell a bunch of Russian kids on the message of team play, but even harder to imagine that they could work so well together in the middle of the summer. At the end of the first period, the Russians lead 5–0. The official scoring shows that the Russians have only ten shots on goal in the opening twenty minutes, but I'm sure that they've had at least five more golden scoring chances that they didn't put away. So dominant are the Russians that they can afford a little mercy, easing up on the Czechs en route to a 7–1 victory (after leading 7–0 midway through the second period).

Alexander Vasiliev, a skilled little winger, racks up a hat trick and an assist for the Russians and Evgeni Dadonov adds a pair of goals, but they aren't the players who catch my eye as much as Alexei Cherepanov, Sergei Korostin and Alexander Karamnov. Cherepanov generated chances every time he touched the puck, without ever seeming to work too hard. Korostin and Karamnov were the other side of the coin—skilled enough, but intensely competitive. It's only 120 minutes into the season but it's a game that will stick in my memory through the winter and into the spring.

August 9, 2006, Zimny Stadion, Piestany, Slovakia

IVAN HLINKA MEMORIAL, PRELIMINARY ROUND
CANADA 4 SWEDEN 1
SWITZERLAND 2 SLOVAKIA 1

The expected level of talent to be showcased at the Ivan Hlinka Memorial took a hit a week ago, when the most heralded player outside the NHL went down with a knee injury at the Canadian under-18 team's tryouts in Calgary. John Tavares, who played in the world under-18s as a fifteen-year-old in the spring, suffered a sprain that was going to keep him from making the trip. Tavares, a centre with the Oshawa Generals, isn't eligible for the NHL draft until 2009, but scouts were eager to see him in the tournament. Tavares was not just the youngest player in the Canadian junior leagues last year—he was only fourteen at the beginning of the Generals' season—but also the Canadian Hockey League's rookie of year, scoring 45 goals in 65 games. When the scouts got word of the injury, it was like hearing that the star of a Broadway show had the sniffles and they had bought tickets to see an understudy in the lead role.

Tavares's injury, along with an another to Ottawa 67's centre Logan Couture on the final shift of the final scrimmage prior to the selection of team, moved the spotlight to Angelo Esposito, a centre with the Quebec Remparts. Three years ago, when he was a scoring sensation in Quebec's midget leagues, Esposito (no relation to Phil and Tony) was first touted as the likely first-overall pick in the 2007 draft. Casting around for new challenges, Esposito enrolled at Shattuck–St. Mary's, the Minnesota high school *cum* hockey factory. At Shattuck, Esposito skated alongside Jonathan Toews and Kyle Okposo and planned to follow them to a U.S. college. If peer pressure was a factor, it was no match for the psychic pull of Patrick Roy, a crooked-nosed Quebecois deity in a goaltender's mask. Roy raised Stanley Cups in Esposito's hometown of Montreal, then bought the Quebec Remparts junior club after his playing days in Colorado wound down. Roy selected Esposito in the first round of the Quebec league draft and sold his family on the virtues of the junior game.

Tavares's injury has cleared the way for Esposito to be *la vedette* of a team for the first time since he was playing AAA hockey in Montreal. Esposito was just another face in a crowd of NHL prospects at Shattuck–St. Mary's, the youngest member of the Future NHL Millionaire Boys' Club. In Quebec there wasn't the same calibre of ensemble, but Esposito still played a supporting role. And even though Esposito's numbers (39 goals and 59 assists in 57 games) were impressive and comparable to Tavares's, the Remparts' indisputable star was Alexander Radulov, a Russian forward whose numbers (61 goals and 91 assists in 62 games) left Esposito well in the wake. In the playoffs, the separation between Radulov (21 goals and 34 assists in 23 games) and Esposito (6 goals and 5 assists in 23 games) was all the more plain. It was Radulov, not Esposito, who was named the most valuable player in Quebec's victory at the Memorial Cup. The Nashville Predators drafted Radulov fifteenth overall in the 2004 draft and reasonably expect him to move right into their lineup in the fall.

And while Sidney Crosby's star shot up without a pause through the junior ranks, Esposito has already been dealt a setback: he was an early cut from the Canadian squad that won the world junior title in Vancouver in January. Esposito led Quebec to a narrow victory over the U.S. team in the gold-medal game at the under-17 challenge in Regina a few weeks later. Even then, Esposito was overshadowed by Tavares, who ran away with the tournament scoring title and made the all-star team along with American forward James van Riemsdyk.

When the under-18 team broke camp a few days ago, Hockey Canada named Esposito the team's captain, possibly an expression of faith as much as a reflection of his leadership skills. The Canadians are in the express line to the final—the other side of the draw in Breclav is much stronger than the group in Piestany. And the Canadians beat Switzerland 5–3 in their tournament opener, with Esposito picking up a pair of goals. But in his first few shifts against Sweden, Esposito isn't effective. It's a game that's best played in the moment, instinctively, intuitively, and Esposito's struggles seem to stem from trying to impress, trying to do too much.

Though the Swedes captured two golds in the last four Olympic tournaments, they've struggled in under-20 and under-18 championships. Too often they seem listless and intimidated against Canada, the U.S. and Russia. At this tournament, though, expectations are higher. They're icing a team with more solid prospects than any since the Sedin twins came through in the late '90s, including two who'll be high first-round picks next June: forwards Mikael Backlund of Vasteras and Oscar Moller, who plays for Chilliwack in the Western league.[3]

Early on, the Swedes take the game to the Canadians. Moller scores on a power play early on to give Sweden a 1–0 lead after seven minutes. With every game of the opening round pivotal—there is no semifinal; only the winners of the two groups advance to the final—the Canadians have to stanch the bleeding. Four minutes later, Tyler Ennis, an industrious forward with the Medicine Hat Tigers, works a drop pass, setting up Kyle Turris, a skinny forward from Burnaby, British Columbia. Turris, the only member of the Canadian team who'll play in Tier II this year, wires a wrist shot past Swedish goal-tender Mark Owuya to tie the game.

The score remains tied into the second period, and Esposito has yet to make his mark on the game. Far more influential is a rough-and-tumble forward, Brett Sonne. Other players here posted gaudy numbers in major junior last season, while Sonne

---

3. Twelve Swedish players have been selected in the first round of the last seven drafts.

scored only 12 goals with the Calgary Hitmen in 57 games. He was slotted to be an energy player and penalty killer, a fourth-liner. Yet in this limited role he turns the game against Sweden in the Canadians' favour and clinches their berth in the tournament final. Sonne's moment comes when Canada looks to be in dire straits: defenceman John Negrin takes a major penalty and a game misconduct for running a Swedish forward from behind midway through the second period. Sonne rolls over the boards when Olivier Fortier, one half of the first penalty-killing unit, makes it to the bench. Sonne reads the play, sees that the Swedes are in the middle of a line change and chases a defenceman who's handling the puck a little too casually in the neutral zone. Sonne forces a turnover and then just about carries the defenceman on his back as he drives to the net. Sonne's goal energizes his teammates and deflates the Swedes.

In the third period, the Canadians pour it on. Angelo Esposito's play picks up a bit; he draws assists on goals by Nick Ross of the Regina Pats and Colton Gillies of the Saskatoon Blades. Nothing spectacular, mind you, just decent plays. It comes back to expectations, I suppose. I was hoping to be blown away. In the end, I'm disappointed in Esposito. I wanted something like a breakout performance from the biggest name—or from anyone else, for that matter.

I tried to look at the game the way that Daniel Doré described—isolating two players on opposing teams in a matchup—but it was hit and mostly miss. Too often, those I focused on wound up on the periphery of play. Oh, it would have been hard to miss the intense competitiveness and nasty edge that Brandon Sutter played with, even if he didn't have his breeding (son of Brent Sutter, nephew of five other former NHLers). There was no missing the face washes and slashes he administered after every whistle, though that background noise might have made it easy to overlook how effective he was. Though I could claim forty "views," I only came away with any useful read on a select few. For instance, I bookmarked a defenceman named Mark Katic, who had been selected to the tournament all-star team at the under-17s last winter. My interest was piqued when the team's trainer told me that Katic had posted the second-fastest time ever in a skating drill that Hockey Canada has used at its tryouts the last ten years or so. Katic, though, ended up doing most of his skating in the warmups. Once the game started, he hardly saw the ice. I put it down to the fact that Katic plays for Sarnia in the Ontario league, and the coaching staff is entirely drawn from the west: head coach Cory Clouston is the coach in Kootenay; one assistant, Jeff Truit, is the head coach in Kelowna, while the other, Dave Hunchak, is an assistant in Swift Current. The coaches lean on players from the WHL not as a matter of loyalty to the Dub, but out of a coaching reflex: they go with the players they know best. I can't help but think this puts some players from Quebec and Ontario in the margins.

Before the second game, Switzerland vs. Slovakia, I head down to the dressing room to talk to the Canadian coach, Cory Clouston. "Espo's been good for us," Clouston says. I try to keep an open mind—he did, after all, score a pair in the opening game here, and he showed enough to earn the captaincy at the tryout camp. "The kids do look up to him. For him to have played on a Mem Cup champion and an under-17 champion—the players can respect that. We don't have a really loud group, but Angelo is a mature young man, well-spoken, respected by his teammates."

Clouston, though, makes it plain that awarding Esposito the captaincy was a way of throwing down the gantlet to him. "This tournament is an opportunity for Angelo to step up in every department," Clouston says. "That what were looking for."

When I ask him about Brett Sonne, Clouston says he didn't see his breakout performance coming. "To be honest, Sonne didn't have the best camp for us," he says. "He was a bit of a disappointment. But it's so hard for these kids to hit the ground running in the middle of the summer. He didn't disappoint us at all today. He was one of our best out there."

Milan Tichy, Columbus's Czech-based scout, and Kjell Larsson, the Blue Jackets' Swedish scout, are going over their notes in the

Jaromir Jagr Bar inside the Piestany arena.[4] Most of the scouts who've come out for the tournament are over in Breclav, which they regard as the stronger of the two pools. Tichy and Larsson have come to Piestany because this tournament might be their only chance to see some of the Canadian under-18s. As I'd expect, Larsson, the fierce patriot, looks crestfallen after Sweden's loss to Canada, while Tichy appears to be amused by his co-worker's looking at the game through blue-and-gold-coloured glasses.

I ask them about Esposito and say that I didn't think it was a good game at all for him.

"It's okay," Tichy says. "He'll be a player. You can see the tools he has. He will get stronger when he gets older. His skating is good, maybe not with a burst, but technically good. He should get more speed when he gets stronger. Look at this game to see what progress he makes later in the season. Look at it to see what his strengths are. Don't make it too complicated. It's early."

"Maybe a player," says Larsson, who then starts talking about Backlund and Moller, matters nearer and dearer.

It's all I can do to stay awake during the game between the Swiss and the Slovaks, and not just because of jet lag. My scouting report on the Swiss would be the same one I could have filed from the dozens of games I've seen their young teams play over the years: They're big enough and skate well enough, but have no finish. Switzerland beats the Slovaks, and Tichy is disgusted. "Very poor for the Slovaks. They should be embarrassed playing like that at home," he says. The result assures Canada a berth in the gold-medal game. It also assures that Canada will face an upgrade in competition, that Esposito and the rest will have to get over something more than their own nervousness.

---

4. It has always struck me as odd that a Czech player would have an ownership interest in a bar in a town in Slovakia. It's a little like Peter Forsberg being the proprietor of an establishment in Turku. Or Don Cherry opening an establishment in Rimouski.

The most exciting thing about the Switzerland–Slovak game is the update on the results from the other side of the draw in Breclav. The U.S. defeats Russia 4–2, staving off a third-period rally that saw the Americans outshot 21–7. I didn't see that coming — not after the U.S.'s narrow win over the Finns and Russia's electrifying performance against the Czechs. That sets the stage for a Canada–U.S. final.

August 10, 2006, Zimny Stadion, Piestany

Ivan Hlinka Memorial, preliminary round
Sweden 5 Switzerland 3
Canada 4 Slovakia 1

Against Sweden, Esposito and his teammates seemed to be tense. Against Slovakia, with nothing at stake, they can afford to play fast and loose and run the host team out of the rink. It's a good measure of the stifling effect that pressure can have on the teenage psyche: the Canadians didn't muster twenty shots on the Swedish net in their second game here, but they fire twenty-three shots in the first period alone against Slovak goaltender Matus Andreanin. The final score, 4–1 for Canada, flatters Slovakia. Brett Sonne again impresses, opening the scoring with five minutes to go in the first period, again more through will than skill. Others were effective for Canada. Logan MacMillan, projected by NHL Central Scouting to be a third- to fifth-round draft pick, catches my eye. He looks like he might end up being a better player than his father, Bob MacMillan, who had a journeyman's career in the NHL and WHA, a twenty-goal man in an era of fifty-goal scorers, save one magic season in Atlanta when he scored 37 goals and racked up more than 100 points. The younger MacMillan scored only nine last season for the Halifax Mooseheads but he makes one heady play after another, not having a bad shift all game. Mark Katic got a bit more ice time, but seemed overeager, running frantically around his own end. Still, he set up Bryan Cameron of the Belleville Bulls for Canada's third goal, the back-breaker, midway through the second period.

And Angelo Esposito—well, again, he's in and around the play but never fully takes charge. It seems as if his skills would serve him well on the Olympic ice surface, but he doesn't show a first step or change of pace that will separate him from checkers. On this count, Milan Tichy's read seems accurate: Esposito's a good skater in the sense that he's smooth, just not explosive. I can't decide where Esposito falls: he seems equidistant from Milan Tichy's declaration ("He'll be a player") and Kjell Larsson's equivocation ("Maybe a player"). I guess that middle ground is that he *should* be a player.

August 11, 2006, Hotel Satellit, Piestany

I've arranged with the Canadian team's management to interview Esposito after practice on the day before the gold-medal game. Team officials asked if I just wanted to interview Esposito over the phone, but I held out to do it in person—just about the only chance to get more than a rote answer. It's not as if the Blue Jackets or any other NHL club would settle for talking to a prospect over the phone. So I set about watching him in unguarded moments around the team's hotel and with teammates as they walk around town in their free time.

All I ever needed to know about Sidney Crosby I learned from watching him at this tournament—not on the ice, but playing Ping Pong and pool with his teammates at the team's hotel. He didn't just compete. He was consumed by competition. And when he was up against a far better player in one of those games—the backup goaltender, Devan Dubnyk, could hustle table tennis— Crosby demanded rematch after rematch, sputtering mad. I don't claim that the Blue Jackets can learn everything they need to know about Phil Kessel, Derick Brassard or Angelo Esposito by handing them a Ping Pong paddle or a cue, but there has to be some value in viewing a prospect in an unguarded moment, *in situ*, in his natural habitat. It has to be as valuable as anything that he might say in an interview (where he's likely to say what he thinks is expected of him).

I spy Esposito walking around Piestany with a small cluster of team-mates. The players are easy to pick out. Maybe in another European summer spot they'd blend in with backpacking youth, but Piestany is a spa town, a spot favoured by the old and infirm—hordes of German retirees come here to go to the hot springs, which are supposed to cure all. Among a group of Canadian juniors, Esposito is in the middle of the front row—leading, not following, engaged, not going through the motions.

It's the same dynamic at the team lunch. Esposito goes from table to table, language to language, making an effort to engage his teammates the way a politician would work a room. For some politicians, it would come naturally; for Esposito it feels a little forced. Then again, few eighteen-year-olds would qualify as fully formed leaders. At least he's taking the notion of being a captain to heart. Others would look at the "C" as a responsibility that starts in the dressing room and means the most on the ice.

After the meal I sit down with Esposito in the lobby of the Hotel Satellit, named as a tribute to the Soviets' Sputnik program. The hotel's boxy furniture hasn't been much updated since the height of the Cold War, and Esposito struggles to get comfortable on a couch that's all right angles.

In my years covering junior hockey I've met a mix of extroverts and introverts, just as you would plucking kids from any Grade 12 class. Esposito falls between categories. He's soft-spoken, and almost every answer he gives comes only after a thoughtful pause. I get a sense early on that he won't give an easy answer if a harder one is the truth.

Here's his backstory, as he lays it out to me—snippets to piece together:

"My grandparents came from Italy. My parents were born in Montreal . . . they own a chain of grocery stores . . . I've got an older

sister who goes to school in Montreal and a younger brother, fourteen, who's going to be a good player. I used to do figure skating. It
started with my mother taking my sister to the rink, and I just went
along. When I was ten I decided to stick to hockey. My parents
moved several times so that I'd be eligible to play for teams in certain areas. It wasn't easy, moving just for me. They've done everything for me. If I wasn't working hard, they let me know, but so long
as I worked hard they were there for me."

I ask Esposito about the players he saw growing up, about those
who succeeded and those who fell by the wayside.

"I saw cases of guys who should have been better but weren't—
it might have been that they didn't work hard enough or didn't
want it or had bad breaks. Unfortunate for them. It's hard,
because you also see guys on your team and you respect them for
how hard they work, but you know that they just don't have the
talent to make it."

I ask him about going to Shattuck–St. Mary's.

"I was fortunate going to Shattuck because it took a lot of attention off me. I think there would have been more attention playing
closer to home. Down at Shattuck I could just concentrate on the
game without distractions. I was one of the younger guys, a couple
of years younger than most. I looked up to a lot of my teammates.
When I was at Shattuck, my plan was to go to college—either
University of New Hampshire or Boston U. My mother wanted me
to go to college; my father just wanted whatever was best for me and
my game. But a couple of weeks after the Quebec draft, I went to
visit the team and Patrick [Roy] and I realized that hockey is the
most important thing for me now."

I ask him about getting cut by the world junior team. He's
unusually candid.

"I had the skills and the talent to be there. That was the most disappointing moment for me. It was the first time I had been cut from
a team since I tried out for the Montreal Hurricanes atom AA—I
was three or four years younger than everyone else. I think I may
not have been strong enough [to compete with the under-20s]. And

as much as I wanted to play in the world juniors, I wouldn't say that [the decision] was the wrong one."

I ask him about the biggest influence other than his parents or his coaches. He stays on hockey. He mentions Vincent Lecavalier of the Tampa Bay Lightning, a former first-overall draft pick and leader of the team that won the Stanley Cup in 2004. I tell Esposito that I went out to Rimouski to interview Lecavalier when he was seventeen, in his draft year, and that I was impressed by how serious he was about the game. In fact, I thought he might be *too* serious—all responsibility and no fun.

"He is serious, but I think in a good way," Esposito says. "I met Vincent when I was thirteen or fourteen, and for the past couple of summers I've worked out with him. He's taught me how to look at the game, and I think I'm like him—he takes the game seriously, and I do, too. I'm not a loud guy, and on game days I don't like to joke around. I don't think I'm wound up, just serious."

I ask him if he sees a common thread running through the players here.

"We're all looking to be something later on in life. This is a step to earning that spot. Everyone wants to be here to show our talents—what we want to do. It's part of the process of where we want to end up in the future."

We talk for more than an hour. I see Esposito eyeing the clock in the lobby. The team is checking out of the Hotel Satellit and will be busing over to Breclav shortly. Esposito's teammates are handing in their keys and lugging their suitcases through the lobby. I ask if he has to go, but he insists on answering all questions, as if it's just another of the captain's duties. Finally, his roommate comes down to the lobby with his luggage. "Espo, you better go," he shouts as he heads out the door. "The bus is going to leave in three minutes."

"Geez, I'm sorry, but I've got to pack," Esposito says.

August 12, 2006, Zimny Stadion, Breclav

IVAN HLINKA MEMORIAL, GOLD-MEDAL GAME
CANADA 3 U.S. 0

A few scouts went home yesterday. It might be hard for fans to imagine that scouts would cross the ocean to see a tournament but leave on the eve of the final. In fact, it's routine when there's a day off before the gold-medal game. Those who've bailed out assume that sticking around two days to see one game just wouldn't be worth the time and expense. And though Canada vs. the U.S. is a game of interest to them, they'll see the top Canadian and American players all winter long.

Almost everyone who stayed on is here in Breclav—few have gone to Piestany to see the Russians beat out Sweden in the bronze-medal game. The scouts' room is full to overflowing. As soon as the music goes up during the warmup, dozens of them file into the arena seats and take down the line combinations.

Only then do I cross paths with Don Boyd for the first time since the draft. He has the Blue Jackets crew along with him: Tichy, Larsson and Castron.

Small talk before the game starts.

"Kessel's agent was angry about us having a writer in the room at the combine . . . says his player's privacy was violated," Boyd says.

I tell Boyd I'm sorry if he took any heat.

"Anything surprise you about the combine and the interviews?"

I tell him that I thought that there'd be more gathering of infor-mation in advance of the interviews and more follow-up in the aftermath—like those lingering questions about Kessel: whether his family was financially comfortable enough to send him to Columbus for the sessions attended by Staal, Mueller and Brassard; whether he really had a 3.2 grade-point average at Minnesota, as he claimed; and whether he was even academically eligible to return for his sophomore year, as he said he intended.

I tell Boyd I think it's the stuff a reporter can cobble together with a few phone calls.

"Maybe," he says.

"Do you think there might be use for anything like that?" I ask. "Just a few calls, a bit of background checking. Maybe taking the top fifteen or twenty North American kids. Something that could just give you a bit of a head start in the interviews. I could do Esposito as a sample. I talked to him yesterday, got a few numbers and names I could follow up with."

"Let's talk about it. Let's stay in touch."

With that, the Canadian and American teenagers skate onto the ice for the opening face-off.

It's hard to pinpoint when the United States usurped Russia as Canada's chief international hockey rival. But feelings in international games run highest between teams from these two nations, and never higher than when junior-aged players are involved. A coach might have to try to rally his Canadian squad for a game against Switzerland, or his American kids for a matchup with the Finns, but motivation is never an issue when Canada plays the U.S. The challenge for the coaches is to keep the players grounded.

That's the case here in the gold-medal game. The coaches from the WHL do a better job of reading the situation and their players than does Ed Olczyk, Sr. who met his players—other than his son—for the first time in July. The Canadian players play with a level of discipline that has become a hallmark of its under-20 successes in recent years. The U.S. players, though, act out, the way you'd expect testosterone-charged teenage boys to.

The attendance will be announced as 879, the largest contingent being the parents of the American players. You can hear the players whooping and hollering all over the arena. And from the bench they're giving the Ric Flair "whoo-oo" not to slick passes and playmaking but to body slams. From the opening face-off the U.S. players, particularly Nick Petrecki, are bent on intimidating their opponents and they run at them recklessly at every chance.

The Americans draw only a few more penalties than the Canadians, but they're the difference in the game. Petrecki gets away with some stickwork and a charge or two early, but pushes his luck on a Canadian power play midway through the first period. Already down a man, Petrecki is sent to the box for a cross-check behind the U.S. net—a senseless penalty.

This sets up Angelo Esposito's best moment of the tournament. Not that it's worthy of a highlight reel. But with the two-man advantage, Esposito keeps it simple and takes what is given to him. Esposito controls the puck from the half-boards in the U.S. end for a good stretch and twice hits Brett Sonne with passes in the slot. On the first try, the surprise star of the Canadian team misfires. On the second, he one-times the puck into the back of the U.S. net.

It's the barest of leads, but even in the first period it feels large. The Canadian goaltender, Trevor Cann of the Peterborough Petes, has been sharp throughout the tournament.

During the intermission there's no surprise registered in the scouts' room. The consensus: Canadian teams in these tournaments usually play better with every game, while a significant asterisk is attached to this U.S., a reminder that it's not quite the best team that the Americans could have mustered.

When Kyle Turris takes a tripping penalty early in the second period, it seems that the Canadians are opening the door for the U.S. But just twelve seconds into the ensuing power play, Jonathan Blum gives the puck away at the point and takes a tripping penalty on the turnover. Sonne scores again, this time on a four-on-four, set up by Mark Katic.

Two goals would be a decent lead at any time, but it seemed all the more safe here because of the American teenagers' poor judgment. Two Americans take minors and misconducts for flagrant attempts to injure: Joe Diamond for a hit from behind, Nico Sacchetti for a head shot. Out of frustration, Petrecki runs around his own end like he's out for blood—he doesn't seem to know or care where the puck is.

Tyler Ennis, the buzzsaw from Medicine Hat, scores midway through the third period, but a third goal feels like insurance hardly needed. The game is far one-sided than the score suggests.

At the medal ceremony after the game, Angelo Esposito is called to centre ice for the presentation of the tournament trophy. He raises it over his head and turns to his teammates, looking less overjoyed than relieved. A sigh rather than a broad smile. It has been a victory for Canada—four wins in five days offshore—but for Esposito a less than compelling personal performance.

As the scouts head for the door, there's a low rumble of mixed reviews among the voices in the corridors.

"Esposito was only okay—not the best Canadian, not the best in the tournament."

"I would have liked to have seen Tavares here."

Before I close my notebook I file through my entries from the interview with Esposito. One quote jumps out. "I was fortunate going to Shattuck because *it took a lot of attention off me*. I think there would have been more attention playing closer to home." If he considers himself fortunate to escape attention at Shattuck, then he might consider himself unlucky to go into the season as the top-ranked prospect for the draft.

October 5, 2006, St. Michael's Arena, Toronto

OWEN SOUND 4 ST. MICHAEL'S 3

My junior hockey season on this side of the Atlantic begins with a game that is entertaining, but not meaningful for my research for Don Boyd. Neither team has an elite prospect eligible for the 2007 draft.

The Attack managed to land Trevor Lewis, that kid from Utah who passed unnoticed through the 2005 draft, only to be scooped up by the L.A. Kings in the first round last June. Lewis joins a roster of two other American-born first-rounders: forward Bobby Ryan, chosen second overall by Anaheim in 2005, and defenceman Bobby Sanguinetti, who was picked by the New York Rangers a few slots ahead of Lewis. It looks like the three will make for an electric power play this year—Lewis has great speed, Sanguinetti looks savvy on the point and Ryan has soft hands for a big forward. Ryan scores on a power play with three minutes left in regulation to tie it. Then the Attack's Anton Hedman scores the winner ten seconds later.

I track down Ryan at the team bus after the game. I wrote a story about him last season. He comes from unbelievably difficult circumstances: his family lived on the run and under assumed names because Bobby's father jumped bail after being charged with assaulting his mother. I was shaking when Bobby told me about the U.S. Marshals knocking down the door of the apartment his parents were living in and taking away his father. Somehow Ryan seems to have emerged from it remarkably positive, if not unscathed. Just a casual conversation and nothing more—except maybe a reminder that the toughest won't get dragged down.

October 8, 2006, St. Michael's Arena, Toronto

ST. MICHAEL'S 6 PETERBOROUGH 3

Even though the Petes made it to the Memorial Cup a few months ago, they'll likely be one of the league's weaker teams, especially with the Pittsburgh Penguins keeping Jordan Staal on their roster. The Majors are a lock to be dead last this season. Only 671 fans have made their way to the ancient high school arena at Bathurst and St. Clair.

It's not much of a game for casual fans and not for professional hockey watchers, either. The two teams have a few players who are eligible for the draft but are of little interest to the scouts. The best draft-eligible player on the visiting team is Trevor Cann, the goaltender from the Canadian under-18 team. Central Scouting has projected Cann to be a first- or second-round pick next June. The fall-off after Cann is dramatic. The Petes' next best prospect is

Branislav Rehus, a rookie right winger from Latvia. If Central Scouting has him pegged correctly, he won't be selected until the sixth round at the NHL entry draft—if he's selected at all. St. Michael's doesn't have a draft-eligible player rated as high as Rehus.

Even if the teams had a couple of decent prospects, some scouts in the Toronto area wouldn't bother coming out to St. Michael's. It has history, what with the dozens of photographs of alumni who went on to play in the NHL, a bunch of Stanley Cup winners and Hall of Famers among them. But, simply put, St. Michael's rink is not up to the standards of a major junior arena. Its ice sheet is twenty feet short of the standard 200 feet. This makes for big hitting and totals of shots on goal that read like basketball scores—which is to say that it makes for decent entertainment for fans, but way less than ideal conditions for viewing prospects (with the possible exception of goaltenders). So a lot of scouts avoid games at St. Michael's on principle.

A dearth of prospects and a bad venue. It sounds like an unpromising way to spend a couple of hours and yet it has its own fascination. Steve Downie is not a prospect for the draft. He has already been drafted—Philadelphia selected him in the first round in 2005. But if Downie is playing, you have to watch him. A threat to win a game, a danger to all—including himself. It seems unkind to say it of a teenage hockey player, especially one whose backstory reads like Downie's. He was eight years old when his father was killed in a car accident. In fact, Steve Downie was sitting in the front seat next to his father, who was driving him to a hockey practice. The crash left him without hearing in his right ear and severe loss in his left.

That part of the story has you rooting for him. And that straight inspirational story played out in his draft year. In the spring of 2005 he led the Windsor Spitfires to an improbable comeback victory over the Sault Ste. Marie Greyhounds. The Greyhounds, heavily favoured after finishing first in their division, won the first three games of the best-of-seven opening-round series. The Spitfires came back to win the last four games. Downie scored one winning goal in regulation, another in overtime. He also set up the two other goals that gave the Spitfires wins. But it wasn't just what Downie did on the scoresheet; it was the way he went about the task. Before all four of Windsor's wins, Downie didn't bother to skate with his teammates in the warmups; instead, he just stood at centre ice and stared down at the Soo's goaltender, his eyes looking like they'd been Photoshopped onto his face from Charles Manson's mugshot. It wasn't just theatre, either. Downie might not have lost a shift in those four games. One scout told me that Downie "practically willed them past the Soo . . . he just wouldn't accept them losing."

When Downie made headlines the following autumn, though, it was as a villain, not a hero. He was the captain of the Spitfires and he was involved in a hazing incident on the team bus. The Spitfires' top rookie, Akim Aliu, a sixteen-year-old from Toronto, balked when Downie and other Windsor players told him to pile into the tiny bathroom with other rookies. Downie carried the grudge over to practice the next day and cross-checked Aliu in the mouth, shattering a few of his front teeth. Aliu first went to the dressing room and then came back on the ice, where the two dropped the gloves for a no-holds-barred brawl, which was captured by the local television station's cameras, much to the CHL's embarrassment. Moe Mantha, the general manager, was suspended and then fired and Downie was suspended and then traded to Peterborough, while Aliu was later dealt to Sudbury.

Downie was a controversial selection when Hockey Canada named its team for the world junior tournament last December. In other years, Hockey Canada, an image-conscious outfit, might have passed over Downie.[5] But the pool of talent last year was considered a shallow one—particularly so with its forwards. So, Hockey Canada officials were willing to overlook Downie's transgressions—or, as they would characterize it, give him a second chance. Which is to

---

5. There are a few examples of this in recent years. For instance, Hockey Canada declined to invite Wojtek Wolski to its under-20 tryouts after he was involved in a fight at a party on the eve of the 2005 draft.

say that they found a rationalization rooted in principle to justify a pragmatic decision.

Downie did not disappoint them, scoring the key goals in the time of greatest need and unsettling opponents with a game and a mouth that grated on nerves. He even managed to beat the language barrier when it came to trash-talking—pointing at the scoreboard for the Russian goaltender's benefit when Canada led 4–0 in the final. Downie ended up leading the Canadian juniors to the gold medal, making the tournament all-star team and playing to slavish and forgiving reviews. Mark Spector wrote in the *National Post* that Downie had made "poor choices . . . stupid, ill-advised things that kids do sometimes" and that coach Brent Sutter saw Downie as "a kid who needed a second chance." Cam Cole in the *Vancouver Sun* called Downie "the embodiment of Team Canada's game." Cole pre-emptively dismissed any complaints about matters of character that would stem from the Windsor hazing incident, writing that "effete hockey purists and concerned moms . . . would say what a shame it was that we would celebrate the achievements of a crude, fearless, irritating, occasionally unsportsmanlike kid."

Downie went from reprobate to Canadian hero over the course of the tournament. It took less time for him to succumb to his demons when he made his way back to the Petes' lineup. In fact, it took just under sixty minutes. In his first game after the world juniors, Downie jumped Belleville Bulls captain Andrew Gibbons and pummelled him before he could get his gloves off to defend himself. The league suspended Downie for five games.

One junior coach—an effete hockey purist, by Cole's reckoning— told me that he wasn't surprised that the rehabilitation of Downie didn't take. "I get a sense he had to keep so much stuff bottled up during the tournament, you expected him to blow up the first chance he got. That's just part of the package."

It only takes a few shifts for Vince Malette to look as though he's suffering a migraine. Malette took the Petes' coaching job last summer after nine years as an assistant to Brian Kilrea with the

Ottawa 67's. When he took the job he assumed he'd have Steve Downie to work with. As it turns out, he has Downie to *cope* with.

Downie little resembles the dynamic player of last year's world junior tournament. He doesn't put out a lot of effort—except when it comes to making a show of putting out a lot of effort. That is, he slams his stick against the boards when the ref blows a whistle. He gives the ref a dirty look. He jaws at other players, even his teammates.

Rehus, for his part, plays a quietly effective game. He looks like a good skater with a decent skill set but lacking a big shot and flash. Barely a month into his initiation into the Canadian junior game, he looks like he's still trying to find his way around.

Peterborough leads 2–1 after twenty minutes, Downie setting up Daniel Ryder for the Petes' second goal on a power play. Ryder, the brother of the Montreal Canadiens' Michael Ryder, seems to be not just Downie's linemate but also a disciple. That is, when Downie acts out, Ryder jumps in and follows suit.

After a period I spot a scout, a former coach, in standing room. I ask him how Vince Malette could coach Downie. "He doesn't," the scout says. "That's no knock against Vince. Seems like everyone has a player who just kills you."

The way the scout tells it to me, Malette's greatest frustration is the fact that Downie kept it together with the Canadian under-20 team last winter.

"That's what kills you as a coach, the fact that Downie doesn't have to be disruptive—he chooses not to be a team guy. He wants to get out of Peterborough and he'll play his way out—not by playing well, just by playing like he doesn't want to be there."

Peterborough looks like a good bet to win this game, but it starts to come undone in the second period. On his second shift, Downie needlessly runs a Major into the boards and draws a minor for checking from behind—he didn't draw a major, but not for lack of trying. The Petes don't give up a power-play goal, but from then on Downie is on his own program, distracted.

The Majors score twice before the second intermission to take a one-goal lead. Early in the third, with the Petes still looking like a good bet to win this game, Downie takes a penalty for taking a shot at the Majors' goaltender, Jason Missiaen. Downie barks all the way to the box and slams the gate shut. Within less than a minute of play he's joined there by two other Petes who also draw minors. St. Michael's scores a power-play goal, and thereafter the outcome is never in doubt. All that seemed at issue is whether Downie would act out in a way that might result in a scene or a suspension. But he doesn't cross the line—he is doing his bit to *act* like he cares, but not appearing to back it up with his play or authentic emotion.

I catch up to Vince Malette after the game. Junior hockey has lots of high-pressure jobs and Peterborough is in the first rank. Coaches there are measured against those who've gone before him behind the Petes' bench: Stanley Cup winners in Scotty Bowman and Mike Keenan, a beloved Hall of Famer and coaching guru in Roger Neilson, a *wunderkind* winner of the Memorial Cup—at age twenty-six—in Gary Green.

Stress is written all over Malette's grille. He can't smile so much as wince. "We thought we'd have Jordan Staal back this season, but it looks like Pittsburgh is serious about keeping him up," Malette says. "We were expecting him to be one of the league's best players, maybe the best, this season. That's just a huge hole that we can't fill."

I fight the urge to add "an empty stall" and ask him instead about Rehus—a more agreeable subject than Steve Downie. Central Scouting seems to have Rehus tagged just about right: a marginal prospect probably. "A really good kid to work with, very coachable," Malette says. "He seems to be picking up everything fast, not just the game but the language and the lifestyle."

I hope that Rehus isn't depending too much on Steve Downie during this orientation. Tough enough that his introduction to the Canadian game, to juniors, comes on a losing team. Being around the maelstrom that is Steve Downie might give him the wrong ideas.

As far as I can tell, there are no handbooks for scouts—not for hockey scouts, not for scouts of any other sporting stripe. And as far as histories, biographies and other popular non-fiction treatments go, the publishing world seems not to have been much interested in the lives and work of scouts in pro sports. There's only one book that can be recommended: *Prophet of the Sandlots* by Mark Winegardner. Good luck finding it: it has been out of print for more than fifteen years now, and is considered a find in a used book store.

Hockey scouts have contributed to its scarcity. Many have read only a few books in their lives and some, may only have read one. Yet an unusually high percentage of scouts of a certain vintage— i.e., those who were around when the book was published back in 1989—have copies of it. One scout, Bob Tindall, who used to work for the Boston Bruins, told me he has four.

I re-read *Prophet of the Sandlots* before going into the Columbus war room, and took it with me to the summer under-18s. *Prophet of the Sandlots* is the story of Tony Lucadello, a phenomenally successful baseball scout.

Lucadello's story would never have been told had it not been for an unlikely sequence of events. It started when his most famous find, Mike Schmidt, hit his five hundredth homer. To celebrate the occasion, Schmidt and the Phillies invited Lucadello to Philadelphia. Though he had worked for the Phillies for a couple of decades and for the Cubs for a couple of decades before that, the scout had attended, by his reckoning, less than a dozen major league games over his career. He didn't do that type of scouting. He lived in the small town of Fostoria in western Ohio and knew every high school diamond in the Midwest, but he didn't know which gate to go through at the home ballpark of the team that signed his paycheques.

After Schmidt shook hands with Lucadello at a ceremony honouring the slugger, reporters on hand asked him, "Who's the little guy in the hat?" When Schmidt told them that this was the scout who signed him, the reporters pounced on what they thought was a good story. They soon realized it was a *great* story.

Here was a walking, talking slice of baseball history. How far back did he go? The first major leaguer Lucadello signed was his brother

Johnny—Tony got his signature on a contract for Rogers Hornsby, who was working for the St. Louis Browns. More? Tony Lucadello signed his first Hall of Famer, Ernie Banks, out of the Negro Leagues. In all, he had signed forty-nine major leaguers. No other major league scout was even close.

Lucadello gave more interviews in a few days than he had in the previous forty years. A *Washington Post* feature tweaked the interest of Winegardner, a young writer from Ohio who knew the region around Fostoria. Winegardner convinced Lucadello to let him accompany the scout on the road through the spring and summer of 1988—dozens of ball games at high school and college diamonds, weeks in budget hotels, thousands of miles in the passenger seat of an old Caprice.

To Winegardner and most of those who read *Prophet of the Sandlots,* this was a look into an aspect of pro sports that they knew nothing about. For hockey scouts, it was something else. Lucadello was a character they knew, a character they could identify with. They could identify with his desire to stay in the game even after the St. Louis Cardinals told him he had no future as ballplayer after one year of Class D ball. They could recognize the loneliness of the road and the repetitiveness of the games. Yeah, maybe Lucadello's scouting was a throwback to the old days of hockey scouting—when scouts had their regions and worked them exclusively, before they started to go to national and international events. This was close to home, maybe too close when it came down to the final chapters, in which the Phillies told Lucadello that they were letting him go, that he was too old to handle the demands of a job that breaks young men. In which Winegardner got a phone call from a friend of Lucadello's and was told that the scout had committed suicide by shooting himself beside Fostoria's diamond not long after filing his final scouting report for the Phillies.

I call up Mark Winegardner. These days he's a professor in the English department of a Florida university, but he's better known as the writer selected by the family of the late Mario Puzo to inherit the *Godfather* series of books. "It's funny that with the millions of copies of *Godfather* books out there I probably get as many questions about *Prophet of the Sandlots* as I do a best-seller. It touched a lot of people."

I tell Winegardner about the book's cult status among the NHL scouts, and he's not much surprised. When the book was published, he says, a lot of general managers in Major League Baseball read it and a few ball clubs placed orders for copies to hand out to their staffers. He also heard that a couple of executives with NFL teams were fans.

Winegardner says he hears rumblings every year or two about reprinting *Prophet of the Sandlots*. Maybe its time has passed. It seems quaint next to the best-selling sports book in recent years: *Moneyball*, Michael Lewis's book about the Oakland A's and their general manager, Billy Beane. Lewis lionizes Beane, an executive whose main philosophical tenet holds that traditional scouting like Tony Lucadello's is ineffective, outdated and obsolete. Lewis makes the case that Beane has managed to keep the A's competitive against richer teams by replacing scouting with statistical studies and scouts with computer analysts. What Lucadello saw as giftedness and craft and character, Beane would reduce to a spreadsheet of numbers and dollar figures; and just as Lucadello was the distillation of a bygone age, so is Beane the epitome of technology- and commerce-saturated times. *Moneyball* was as much a business and management book as it was a sports book, maybe more so. MBAs and CEOs ate it up. So did owners and executives with other major league teams who hired general managers to install copycat programs. I can't help but wonder whether Tom Golisano in Buffalo doesn't have a well-thumbed copy of *Moneyball* somewhere.

There's a striking difference between Lucadello's approach to scouting and the NHL scouts'. He travelled alone; they travel in packs. He'd watch a player in a workout and skip a game; their only interest is game action. Just that much I gleaned from the book and what I've learned over the years about the hockey scouts. I figured that I'd have to go an extra mile to get real insight into what made Tony Lucadello a great scout. In my fool's errand, the quixotic quest to learn to be any sort of scout at all, I could do worse than having Tony Lucadello as an inspiration, maybe even a role model. If I could learn just one thing about scouting, it would be worth making a side trip to the territory he used to work.

November 12, 2006, Wayne, Ohio

When I get out to Matt Stone's home on a road just outside of the town where he grew up, he's digging a trench in his backyard. The clay doesn't make for easy digging. The recent wet weather has worked against him, and the pain in his right shoulder doesn't help, either. No matter. He's been bent over a shovel since he got home from his shift in the custodial department at Bowling Green State University. He has to dig out a trench for the foundation of a cinder-block wall, five feet high, three feet wide. Standing all by itself, attached to nothing except memory.

Look around: corn fields on one side; wheat fields on another. Out here, there's not much use for fences, let alone a wall. Matt, his wife, Courtney, and their son, Tyler, have all the privacy they want.

"I remember when my father built me my wall in the back-yard," Stone says while he shovels. "He laid the block. It took him a few days and about eighty bucks in materials. This is gonna be just like it."

Matt Stone doesn't have a blueprint to work from. He knows what it's supposed to look like. After all, he spent thousands of hours across eight years, set in front of that wall. Every afternoon after school he was in his backyard, throwing baseballs against it, making his arm stronger, working on his fielding.

On the mantle of the Stones' home, there's a photograph of Matt Stone standing in front of the wall in his parents' backyard. A photo of Matt, age nine, in a Wayne Little League uniform, smiling. Behind him, with an arm around his shoulder, is an owlish old man.

That's Tony Lucadello. The lenses of his glasses are as big as base-ball cards and the brim of his houndstooth hat is pushed down.

A couple of years after that photograph was taken, Tony Lucadello told the reporters in Philadelphia that the best prospect in his terri-tory, from Pennsylvania to Indiana, from Kentucky right up into Canada, was an eighth-grader named Matt Stone. Out of all the high schools and colleges he scouted, the best prospect for the major leagues was the little boy who lived in a town of about 1,500, ten minutes from Fostoria. And when Lucadello conducted baseball clinics for American Legion and high school teams and coaches throughout the Midwest and even as far away as New York, it wasn't a former pro or an elite college player who demonstrated the drills. It was that same eighth-grader, Matt Stone.

Now in his early thirties, Stone stands behind the fence at Tom Thompson Field in his hometown. "I met Tony Lucadello right here," he tells me. "Our team was practising—I was eight years old— and I was waiting to take my five minutes of batting practice. I was so happy to get up to the plate, and at the end of my five minutes this man told my coach to keep letting me hit. It was Tony. I didn't under-stand who he was, but I knew he had to be important.

"My father spoke to him afterwards, and Tony told him about building a wall. He said that there were drills I could do to work on my arm and my glove [by] throwing against the wall. He told my father he was putting together a book with the drills. He was going to call it *The Lucadello Plan*. My father said he'd build a wall for me. Tony gave him the dimensions, but Tony said he had told lots of par-ents and nobody had ever built his son a wall."

That photo of young Matt with Tony Lucadello in the Stones' backyard freezes the moment when Lucadello saw a wall that Gene Stone had built for his son.

"Tony would stand out here behind the fence for a few innings," Matt Stone says. "He'd move around, go to the first-base side for a while, then the third-base side. He wanted to see the game from all angles, whether it was one of our games here or games other places. But he also came by our house just to watch me practise and to talk to me afterward. He wanted to talk not just about the technical things but about life in general. He would criticize me if he didn't think I was playing well or if I didn't behave right. I thought of him as my best friend. He was a good man. He didn't just want to find players and prospects. He wanted them to be good people. Character mattered—that was the lesson you could learn from his life."

Lucadello's doting on Stone reminds me of Bob Tindall, the scout who hoards copies of *Prophet of the Sandlot.* Back in 2001, Tindall took a particular interest in Seamus Kotyk, a goaltender with the Ottawa 67's. Tindall's club, the Boston Bruins, had selected Kotyk in the sixth round of the 1999 draft. It was easy to presume that Tindall's interest was purely professional—the Bruins had invested a draft pick and now had to decide whether to invest cold, hard cash in him or allow him to walk away as a free agent.[6] That spring I worked a lot of Ottawa 67's games as they made an improbable run to the Ontario league championship and a berth in the Memorial Cup. I had a sense that Tindall liked him, not just as a player but as a young man, and the fact was that anyone who met Kotyk came away liking him. He was a naturally funny and outgoing kid. It seemed as if Tindall was at every game, not just scouting for him but pulling for him, too. Other scouts would consider this a firing offence, or at least a breach of standard practice that would warrant Tindall's drumming out of the fraternity. As it turned out, although Kotyk was named the most valuable player of the Ontario league playoffs, Tindall couldn't convince the Bruins to sign Kotyk. Instead, he signed with the San Jose and even made it briefly to the Sharks as a backup before bouncing all over the minor leagues and Europe.

---

6. Kotyk had been eligible for the 1998 draft but had gone unselected. Thus, he would have been eligible for free agency rather than having to re-enter the draft.

On only a few occasions over the years have I seen an NHL scout seek out a prospect to talk to him the way Tindall did with Kotyk. Lots probably don't think it would be worth the bother. For others, though, it wouldn't be a lack of initiative but rather the abiding of protocol. A junior hockey coach demands a player's full attention, which would be tough enough if the teenager only had to filter what he hears from his parents, his friends and his agent. But the coach's message to the player might get drowned out completely if an NHL scout or two entered the picture. In the scouts' ideal world, a prospect would not know he was being watched. Handing him a business card and staying in contact with him—well, it's acceptable to a point if the scout's team has drafted the player, but only in that case, and only as long as it's a quick chat in the hallway outside the dressing room after a game.

I can't imagine any of the dozens of NHL scouts I know mentoring a player the way Tony Lucadello did with Matt Stone. Can't imagine they'd watch an eight-year-old, even a gifted one. Can't imagine they'd stop in a small town to see if there's a game going on. Can't imagine them sitting in anything but the corner seat of an arena. Can't imagine them watching a practice. Can't imagine them going out of their way to talk to a player.

There's Tony Lucadello's way of scouting, and then there's the NHL way.

NHL scouts pride themselves on being independent thinkers, yet they seem like slaves to convention. They too often seek comfort in consensus. Lots of times I've seen scouts sit around a restaurant or bar with their peers from other organizations and discuss prospects—who they like, who they hope will be there when their picks come up on draft day. For some scouts it's a form of amusement, a little shell game, even a disinformation campaign. But you'd never have found Tony Lucadello in a bar, or anywhere else, socializing with the competition. If he had been cornered by a bunch of scouts, he'd only give them his name, rank and serial number.

A kid in junior high as the best prospect among the hundreds, even thousands, he saw: it's tempting to presume that the scout saw something that wasn't there. Others, though, confirm that Matt Stone wasn't a figment of Lucadello's sentimental imagination. He may not have been a phenom comparable to Wayne Gretzky at age twelve, but he was something more than the best player in the Wayne Little League.

"Matt was a very talented kid," Mark Winegardner told me. "Everything he did was so fundamentally sound and looked so natural."

The most compelling evidence is A *Coaching Clinic*, an instructional video that Major League Baseball issued in 1988. Lucadello's drills are the foundation of the video. The scout takes the lead on the diamond, an odd figure in his houndstooth hat, cardigan and tie. And then the star of the video appears. Matt Stone doesn't show up in the credits, but there's no mistaking him—he'd walk out in his blue Wayne Little League uniform and perfectly execute every drill, from routine grounders to the toughest double plays, as if the kid in a coaching manual had come to life.

"I remember the day they shot that video," Gene Stone says. "Pretty well it was all done on the first take."

Was Matt Stone the best Little League player in America? There's no knowing, no telling. It's not quite like Sidney Crosby going out at fourteen and fifteen and dominating the Air Canada Cup and the Canada Winter Games. Still, Tony Lucadello believed Matt Stone would make the majors, and Matt Stone did, too. Lucadello probably believed it when he drew his last breath. Matt Stone did until he reached back for a fastball one night.

The phone rang at the Stones' home in the early evening seventeen years ago. Matt was already in bed. A good night's sleep was another of Tony Lucadello's lessons. A friend of the scout in Toldeo called with the news that Tony had driven out to the Fostoria diamond and shot himself. No red flags before. No suicide note after.

"We went in his bedroom and told him," Gene Stone says. "We could see the hurt. We told him that he didn't have to go to school the next day if he didn't want to. He said he was going to go . . . that it's what Tony would have wanted. When we turned off the lights, the last thing he said was, 'Now I'll never get drafted.'"

On the last page of *Prophet of the Sandlot*, Matt Stone is a high school freshman going through the first slump of his life—no less resolute, though. Winegardner has gone to Wayne to say goodbye to Tony Lucadello's favourite player. When Matt Stone shakes the author's hand it's with a firm grip—a tip from Tony Lucadello, a subtle way to impress scouts. Stone tells Winegardner, "Now I just want to prove to everybody that I can play pro ball. That Tony was right about me."

And there the book ends. As suddenly as Tony Lucadello's life.

Matt Stone leans against the fence at Tom Thompson Field in Fostoria. "I tried to make sense of Tony's death," Stone says. "I thought about things Tony said to me. He'd always say to me, 'Do you think I've still got it?' and 'Do you think I've got another year in me?' There were other red flags, too—ones I realized after. He'd tell the same stories over and over again—he didn't realize that he had told them to me and my parents before."

Life was different for Matt Stone after Tony Lucadello's death. He became a loner, on the team but not part of the team. "Other players drank and did drugs and even did steroids," Stone says. "Tony warned me about those things. He had told me that I had to stay away from that stuff if I wanted to be a major leaguer."

Matt's parents thought he lost his enthusiasm, his joy, for the game. But he didn't quit the game. He starred through three years of high school. He threw against the wall and took grounders, sticking with the Lucadello Plan, even though he was confused and even angry about the scout's suicide.

In late summer before his senior year, Matt Stone was pitching an American Legion game. He had two out and a two-strike count to a batter when the catcher called for a fastball. "It felt like my arm went with the ball to the plate," Stone says. "I got out of the inning—I got the batter with junk—but my fastball went from mid-eighties to mid-sixties. I got in to see a specialist a couple of days later and he told me that my rotator cuff was torn, practically the whole way through."

Matt Stone didn't have surgery. His hopes of making the majors dangled by a slender thread. He played the whole season for Elmwood, didn't miss a game or a start. But he lost something off his fastball and he knew that it could be over with just one pitch.

"I tried to hide the injury from scouts," Stone says. "Tony always told me not to let scouts know if I had something like that—it would hurt me in the draft."

It didn't matter. He had been a prospect as an underclassman, but major league scouts had short memories. Or the word got out about the tear. Maybe the scouts just looked at the readouts on their radar guns and put it together. Matt Stone wasn't drafted. By that point, he didn't expect to be.

College recruiters had longer memories. He got a scholarship from a junior college in Illinois. He went to a day's worth of classes and to a team workout in the afternoon. The coaches looked at him as if he was imposter. "I had nothing," he says.

He was back home in Ohio a day later. He didn't pick up a ball and a glove for more than ten years.

"It's hard to get past the personal disappointment, but if I consider myself unlucky with my injury, I consider myself lucky to have known Tony Lucadello," Stone says. "I can appreciate what Tony did for me. And I can see a wisdom and a decency in what he did. Maybe the best thing you can say is that he cared. He cared about his job and he cared about other people, maybe even more than he cared for himself."

Out here on the field behind the church in Wayne, Matt Stone's story has me thinking about the scouts I know who've read *Prophet of the Sandlots*. If they had read it as a handbook, a guide to scouting, then they'd probably go about their business in a much more idiosyncratic way. Maybe they've read it as the life and times of a saint, the patron saint of their trade. Maybe they've also read it as a cautionary tale, one where there's a high price for being too emotionally invested in your work.

I can probably afford a little personal involvement in my sideline, my bird-dogging for the Blue Jackets. It's a season-long project, not my living, not my life.

And professionally the considerations are different for me than the real working scouts. No coach will be offended if I talk to a player or two, and I couldn't turn a prospect's head if I tried. I'm up front. I tell the coaches and the players that I'm working on a story. I make no secret of my friendship with NHL scouts or the project I'm working on.

As far as remaining emotionally detached, well, that's part of any writer's day-to-day reality. I figure most come by it easier than I do.

November 14, 2006, Interstate 90, west of Cleveland

I was planning to drop in on Don Boyd in Columbus on the drive home from Fostoria. Those plans were put on hold a couple of days ago. Nobody in the Blue Jackets' executive offices feels much like entertaining visitors. The team has already fallen four games below .500, on course for yet another season out of the playoffs. Feeling the heat from ownership, Doug MacLean fired Gerald Gallant and the team is shopping for a new coach. I was going to call Boyd from the road to ask him how he's doing, to see if the situation has settled down at all. There's no need to when I hear a report on a local radio sportscast.

"In Columbus, the Blue Jackets have hired Ken Hitchcock to replace Gerald Gallant behind the bench . . ."

Even though Hitchcock might be the best-qualified coach available, I know that he's not MacLean's first choice. In fact, he might be one of his last ones. The general manager didn't make this hire. It was likely made over his objections. It was the owner's call, a vote of non-confidence.

There's no need to make the call. I'll drive right past the turnoff for Columbus.

November 19, 2006, Hershey Centre, Mississauga, Ontario

MISSISSAUGA 6 OTTAWA 1

Every draft seems to have its hard-luck prospects. Early in the season, it's already clear that Logan Couture is the player who is skating
under a bad star this year. Getting knocked out of the summer
under-18s with the cut on his leg on the last shift of the tryout was a
bad break, but not a critical one. Once Ottawa's season started,
Couture was a little sluggish. Eager to make up for that lost showcase at the under-18s, he tried to skate right through the bad patch.
It turned out he didn't have the flu, but rather mono. Word was he'd
be out until December. In fact, he missed five weeks, just ten games.

Like any other kid in his position, Couture would never admit
to being wrapped up in draft-watching. Common sense would tell
you that's a non-starter. In Couture's case, so would history. Back
when he was playing Junior B for the St. Thomas Stars in the
spring of 2005, Couture was rated as the top player eligible for the
Ontario league's midget draft. The Oshawa Generals, owners of
the first-overall pick, made a handshake deal with the player and
his parents, and Logan was destined to play for Oshawa. But then
the Generals proved the minimal value of pressed flesh. Even
though they had committed to Couture, the team petitioned the
Ontario Hockey League to make an exception for John Tavares
and grant him draft eligibility a year ahead of time. Once the
Generals pulled off that gambit, they got out the Handi-Wipes and
shook hands once more, this time with Tavares and his family.
Couture was ready to bail out on junior hockey entirely and consider the U.S. college system instead. That seemed to be an
extreme overreaction—if going to Oshawa at No. 1 was such a
dream scenario, what difference could it make to be taken by
someone else in the Ontario league early in the first round?
Clearly, Couture and family saw prestige in being the first-overall
pick and wanted to be in a position of control. By the time draft
day came around, Couture had thrown a scare into enough

Ontario league teams that he wasn't selected until Ottawa's pick rolled around, the twelfth in the first round.

Eighteen months ago, Couture was Ontario's top-ranked player among those with 1989 birthdates.[7] Whether it's a teenage hockey player who's the subject of involved negotiations, a prodigy who's tapped as a future valedictorian or just a high school grad proclaimed "the most likely to . . ." in his yearbook, it's hard to imagine a head not turning. It's hard to imagine a kid whose thoughts wouldn't become a swirling vortex of expectations. It's easy to imagine a kid who declared himself to be fit just out of hope. That's the case with Couture this late Sunday afternoon in Mississauga.

In his first game back last week, Couture racked up three points in a shootout loss to Kitchener, making it seem that perhaps he *hadn't* been rushed into the lineup. Today, though, playing in his third game in three days, Couture just has nothing to give. That said, he's no different than the rest of the 67's. It's not that Couture is dragging them down, just that even at his best he couldn't pull them up. In less than nineteen minutes the 67's are trailing 5–0, and at the end of the first period they're outshot 18–6.

Dozens of NHL scouts make it out to Sunday afternoons in Mississauga — it's a good opportunity to squeeze two or three games in a day. A doctor would require blood work and a physical exam before making a diagnosis, but the scouts see all they need to from the corner seats. There's not a good word about Couture that they can attach to their scouting reports today.

I figure that Ottawa's coach Brian Kilrea will shut down Couture in a game that's a lost cause. Couture has rushed back, and there seems little sense in draining his battery. Worse, his reactions are dangerously slow. He's used to moving faster and eluding hits, but fatigue is making him a stationary target. Kilrea, though, keeps

---

7. And though five dollars and the clipping will buy you a latte, the International Scouting Service proclaimed Couture its pre-season top-ranked prospect in all of hockeydom among those eligible for the 2007 NHL entry draft.

rolling Couture over the boards. In the third period, I leave the corner seats and take a place behind the Ottawa bench, just to get a closer look at Couture. Referees have stopped a lot of title fights and saved fighters who look better than Couture does in his last few shifts of the game. He looks disoriented. Even if Couture wanted to keep playing, he should have been sent to the dressing room.

After the game, I track down Brian Kilrea in the hallways of the arena. "Couture came back too soon," he tells me. "That's what he wanted."

It also might be what Kilrea wanted—he does fill out the lineup, and he was still sending Couture out in the last two minutes of the game.

The glazed look in Couture's eyes during the game remind me of Alyn McCauley, another 67's player who had his own issues with injuries in his draft year and throughout his junior career. The 67's had selected McCauley with the third-overall pick, but in his draft year he suffered a knee injury and tried to play through it. The New Jersey Devils chose him in the fourth round of the NHL entry draft and he went on to a great junior career, eventually being named the CHL player of the year. But even after his selection by the Devils, McCauley tried to tough it out through injury, dressing when he had no business being on the ice. I recall seeing him in Belleville when Ottawa was locked in a tough opening-round playoff series with the Bulls. McCauley had been sidelined with a concussion for a few weeks but felt the psychic pull of showing up when his team's season was on the line. Ottawa won the game, and McCauley was good if not great in the game, but nothing he did in the sixty minutes stuck with me as much as talking to him later in the dressing room. "Everything is a blur out there," McCauley said almost drunkenly. He told me the concussion wasn't the first of his young life and that he wasn't sure how many times he'd had his bell rung. With McCauley that night, and Couture this evening about a decade later, I figure it's a scout's dilemma: Do you give them points for bravery, or subtract a few for recklessness?

—

I doubt Couture knows the story of Adrian Foster, one of the most unlikely first-round draft picks in recent years. Foster is a testament to the staying power of a good, if brief, impression.

If you look up Adrian Foster's career statistics, you'll see that he played in only twelve games in two years leading up to the 2001 draft. What you won't see is the cause of all that time lost: a severe injury to abdominal muscles. With the knowledge of that injury and all of one goal scored in the Dub over those two seasons, the New Jersey Devils selected Foster in the first round, twenty-eighth overall. It looked like the ultimate reach, but was less so on further review. David Conte, the New Jersey Devils' top amateur scout, explained it was a strategic gamble based on three markers. One: Foster had been one of the best three or four players in western Canada as a bantam. Two: The Devils viewed the other players available at No. 28 without any enthusiasm. Three: If Foster didn't recover from his injuries and the Devils weren't inclined to sign him, the club would receive a compensation pick two years down the line.[8]

As it turned out, the biggest day of Adrian Foster's career was that draft day. New Jersey ended up signing him after his junior career, but he never made it to the big club. He's still property of the Devils, but his career has been stalled by injuries—some tied to that original abdominal wound, others just the result of the run-of-the-mill knocks in the game. If New Jersey's scouts remembered Foster, others would overlook a few games that Logan Couture lost to bed rest in November. If there's urgency here, it's not in the eye of the beholders, but rather the beheld.

---

8. In fact, it was easier to rationalize spending a first-rounder on Foster, than a second-rounder—or even a third- or fourth-rounder. If a team chose not to sign a first-round pick, it would receive a compensation pick between the first and second rounds. Later picks that went unsigned were not subject to compensation. "We figured the compensation pick that we might be looking at two years later would likely be better than the players who were available at No. 28," David Conte told me.

November 26, 2006, General Motors Centre, Oshawa

SARNIA 7 OSHAWA 3

Several players who'll figure prominently in the coming NHL entry draft are out here tonight: Oshawa forwards Brett MacLean and Dale Mitchell and Sarnia's Mark Katic, that swift-skating but undersized defenceman from the summer under-18s. For scouts in attendance these players are the priority, the main course. But if this is a dinner for the scouts, they'll skip everything and go directly to dessert: Sarnia's Steven Stamkos and Oshawa's John Tavares, players who are projected to be the first-overall picks in the 2008 and 2009 entry drafts.

When the Ontario league granted Tavares "exceptional" status and allowed him to enter the 2005 Ontario league draft, that opened up the top slot in this year's OHL draft for Stamkos. Not that it cheapened it at all, mind you. In almost any other year, Stamkos would have been the top pick. A five-foot-eleven centre who draws comparisons to the era's exemplar of all-around play, Steve Yzerman, Stamkos heads up what figures to be one of the great draft classes in recent years. The next two picks in that OHL draft were two defencemen, Alex Pietrangelo of the Mississauga Ice Dogs and Michael Del Zotto, Tavares's teammate with the Generals, and are almost as highly regarded as Stamkos. They're bound to be fixtures in the Canadian under-18 and under-20 programs and projected to be in the top five picks in the 2008 entry draft. Remarkably, not only did Stamkos, Pietrangelo and Del Zotto come up through the ranks and become friends, but their families became close and their parents have travelled together to tournaments.[9]

It's fascinating to see the contrasts in style between Tavares and Stamkos—they're desserts for entirely different tastes. Tavares's skills with the puck are obvious every time he touches it but he doesn't

---

9. The three are also represented by Newport Sports, the Mississauga-based agency founded by Don Meehan.

impress you with his skating. No matter; when he gets the puck within ten feet of the net—anywhere around it, even behind it—the two teams can save time and skate directly to centre. Tavares inevitably finds a way to pot any ball that's around the pocket. To pile on another metaphor, he is a closer.

In personality as well— as much as two sixteen-year-old hockey players from the greater Toronto area could—they stand in significant contrast. Tavares is a very sober, serious-minded kid who measures each and every word, grounded in the understanding that one day he'll be the focus of the hockey world's attentions. Stamkos, meanwhile, seems to be the kid who's just happy to be here. That might owe much to the fact that his future stardom has been less of a sure thing. Though he was named the top player in the Quebec pee-wee tournament, he was so tiny that there was doubt he'd ever be big enough to become a pro, especially in the heights (or depths) of the NHL's clutch-and-grab era.[10] He grew, and the NHL game can be said to have done the same.

On this night Parker VanBuskirk, the Sting's goaltender, turns aside 37 of 40 shots, including a couple of Tavares breakaways. I'm tempted to say that he could be thankful that the Generals are whistled for thirteen penalties, leading to four Sarnia power-play goals.

If it seems as though Stamkos plays the point as much as centre, well, that's par for the course when you play nearly a full period with the man advantage. Few forwards are trusted with the keys to the power play, fewer still at age sixteen. Yet back on the point, Stamkos's playmaking and vision are on display as Sarnia runs out to a 7–1 lead after two periods. He has just two points on the PP, and he's a zero in the plus-minus column, but the numbers don't call his skills into dispute.

---

10. In the interest of full disclosure, I attended high school with Steven Stamkos's father, Chris, and Steven's godfather has been a close friend of, sigh, more than forty years.

Katic is almost as compelling to watch. Here he's jumping into the rush, not quite with reckless abandon nor reflex. Fact is, he seems to pick his spots well, seems to read plays as quickly as he skates. It doesn't translate into points, but that's not the first step.

Still, if the scouts had their druthers they'd skip dinner and go to dessert.

November 27, 2006 General Motors Centre, Oshawa

ONTARIO HOCKEY LEAGUE ALL-STARS 4 RUSSIA 3

An ill-tempered game and a less-than-impressive show by both teams, but a result that sends the fans home with the desired result. A win over a team in Russian sweaters offers them some satisfaction, but CHL officials are disappointed that something less than the Russians' best have been sent—this loss is their fourth in a row on this tour.[11] The game doesn't want for notable performances. The best among them comes from Steve Mason, the goaltender scooped up by Columbus in the third round in June. Mason makes twenty-nine saves and is arguably the OHL team's best player.

The game descends into chaos in the last minute. On the Ontario team, Chris Stewart of the Kingston Frontenacs takes two majors, one for spearing and one for slashing, and Steve Downie is hit with a major for high-sticking. Meanwhile, the Russians are on the end of a major for cross-checking and two match penalties—at one point, a linesman grabs a Russian player and body slams him in a way that would have made Hulk Hogan proud.

Whenever I talk to a scout or coach, one theme always enters the conversation: "Players are different now than back in my day." That

---

11. The Russian Selects will wind up their tour winless, dropping both of their games to the Western Hockey League all-star teams.

"day" depends on the scout or coach. If it's Brian Kilrea in Ottawa, his day was back when *Hockey Night in Canada* was on radio. But even the hockey men who are fresh out of the playing ranks say the same thing.

In the old days, the Steve Downies of the game, the square pegs, were rare, and they were quickly hammered into round holes or discarded. These days they're no longer rare and, because of the multitude of teams and scarcity of talent, they're not so easily put into their places. More of them have short attention spans—or none at all. More are likely to act out. More come from dysfunctional families. More are trying to filter out distracting voices— of family, friends, agents and assorted other meddlers who get them off the team message.

I feel like I have to get my bearings, to get some sense of a baseline: the new normal with players. Sitting in on interviews at the combine doesn't help on that count. There's nothing average or normal about the hundred teenagers who come out to the combine— they are the elite of the sport. There's nothing average or normal about the circumstances at the combine—they face inquisitions with the team execs in the conference rooms. I want to see average junior players in their native state, their comfort zone. And just as I won't get that at the combine, I won't get it at world juniors or the under-18s—again, elite players in something significantly different than a conventional team set-up.

I wish I could claim that I scientifically selected the Swift Current Broncos as the targets for my test. Such, though, is not the case. I had to be in Regina for other work when the first hard gusts of winter blew across the Prairies. Only then did I start looking for teams in that region that would suit my purposes. Swift Current is dead square in the middle of the standings. And then there's the roster: no stars, nobody who has been a selection in the first four rounds of the NHL entry draft.

Granted, Swift Current is hardly average in some ways. Swift Current, population 16,000, is the smallest community in Canada with a major junior team. Downtown you're as likely to bump into a family in traditional Hutterite garb as a ranch hand in a cowboy hat—not everyday occurences for players on the St. John's Fog Devils, Oshawa Generals or Vancouver Giants.

The franchise has an infamous history. Across the country, hockey fans still identify Swift Current with Graham James, a former coach who was convicted of sexually abusing two Broncos players. A lot of people in junior hockey still find it hard to believe that James abused players for years without people around town—or around the team—at least having suspicions about him.

Still, I'm hoping I can see the players' lives there in something close to a vacuum, a long way from the distractions of the big cities, a long way from the big business of the NHL.

I phone Dean Chynoweth, the coach and general manager of the Broncos, and at first he's leery about letting me behind the scenes with his team. The problem is a spate of bad press that the Canadian Hockey League has recently received.

"What do you think of Ken Campbell?" he asked me. "What did you think of *The Hockey News*'s story about the CHL?"

These are fully loaded questions.

I know Ken Campbell from the hockey beat in Toronto. I've spoken to him only days before. And I know about the *Hockey News* story that Chynoweth is referring to.

Campbell wrote a piece about how one former junior had been run around and short-changed when he went to collect on the education clause that's part of the standard CHL contract all players sign. The player was like any other who signs on with a junior club—he went in with the expectation that the team was going to honour the contract and pick up university or college expenses if he fulfilled his playing commitment.[12]

Campbell took this story and others and developed them into a screed that portrayed team owners—increasing numbers of them former NHLers—heartlessly exploiting innocent young junior players.

---

12. A player voids the education clause if he signs a professional contract.

Campbell's criticisms of junior hockey were pointed, well-researched and well-reasoned, but they were not quite original. A while ago I came across a story written by Don Townson. His position was captured in the title: "Hockey's Child-Stealers." The story detailed how players leave home at fourteen or fifteen to get a head start in better bantam and midget leagues in other provinces. It documented how precious few succeed in making it to the NHL. How junior hockey "more often leaves ordinary players with little but faded clippings from small-town newspapers, old scars and nothing to fall back on when they reach the top age limit of 20 and are replaced by other youngsters." Townson also described how "beardless youths," believing that they were only a season or two away from the pros, from NHL money, let their marks slide, killing their chances at higher education.

Townson's story appeared in the *Star Weekly* in 1962. The piece quoted the *Toronto Star*'s veteran columnist Milt Dunnell as a "longtime critic" of junior hockey, which suggests that in a dusty archive you might come across a piece upbraiding the Montreal Canadiens for looking after young Howie Morenz but not legions of others.[13]

Back in 1962, every significant junior team in Canada was affiliated with and controlled by the six NHL franchises. The contracts of those times—"C-forms," they were called—effectively tied a player to an NHL team from adolescence to death. Nowadays, teams are owned by private interests or, in a few cases, community ownership. Today's standard junior contract ties up a player only to age twenty, but it still puts a player at the mercy of others. A player can be traded to a team hundreds of miles away at the drop of a hat. If a player lands in a coach's doghouse, he may never dress for a game—a team isn't obliged to give a player a chance to make a fresh start elsewhere. The critics would say that little is changed—that what was once a cruel and inhuman system is nowadays only cruel.

---

13. Dunnell celebrated his 100th birthday in 2006. It's not clear whether he has changed his opinions about the injustices of junior hockey.

This is, of course, not what Chynoweth want to hear. Then again, it's not a viewpoint I entirely endorse, either.

"There are probably good and bad teams, just like there are good and bad players," I tell Chynoweth. "I don't think that the players are right every time, and I don't think that the teams are, either. I think some kids do very well by junior hockey, and I think some would struggle in any set-up."

I can say this with a clear conscience. I believe it to be true. It's enough to get me onside. Chynoweth gives me my pass. He lets me blend in with the scenery with the Broncos for a working week. I don't know if Tony Lucadello ever rode a bus to get to know a prospect, but I'd bet he never did it just to know about players as a demographic. Still, I doubt he'd find fault in the exercise.

December 1, 2006, Swift Current, Saskatchewan

Sometime in the early afternoon, Dean Chynoweth calls me in my room at the Best Western. "The bus is going to leave a half hour early," Chynoweth tells me. "The weather is supposed to take a turn for the worst."

Anywhere in Canadian junior hockey this would just sound like the sensible thing to do. But a bus leaving early in Swift Current because of a bad turn in the weather is more ominous than anywhere else. It evokes a tragic day in the history of the junior game: December 30, 1986.

The weather that day was supposed to be mild by southwest Saskatchewan's standards: just around freezing, clear, dry. But by midday temperatures had dropped and a freezing rain started to fall. After lunch that day the Broncos' team bus left town for a road game in Regina and only made it as far as the overpass on the eastern edge of town. Just a few minutes out of the parking lot at the Centennial Civic Centre, the bus, an old Western Flyer, skidded off the Trans-Canada Highway, went into a ditch at full speed, hit an embankment and went airborne, landing on its side.

The crash killed four players. Brent Ruff was perhaps the most talented sixteen-year-old in western Canada, and the little brother of Lindy Ruff, who was playing for the Buffalo Sabres. Chris Mantyka was the Broncos' designated tough guy. Trent Kresse was a nineteen-year-old with a fiancée and an eye on going to college if hockey didn't work out. And Scott Kruger was the feisty, undersized Swift Current native and fan favourite.

At the memorial service a few days later more than four thousand crowded into the arena, which was designed to hold about three thousand. Called "The Solidarity of Sorrow," the ceremony attracted players from across the Western Hockey League, all wearing their team sweaters. Among them was the present-day coach who has just told me that the bus is leaving early. Twenty years back, Dean Chynoweth was a star with the Medicine Hat Tigers. His father, Ed, was the WHL's commissioner and spoke at the memorial.

"That memorial service was something that stays with you all your life," Chynoweth says. "I catch myself thinking about it some days at the arena."

Chynoweth and the other teenagers in their sweaters shared a common experience with the four lost Broncos: the life of a junior hockey player. They knew that for all the cheering it's a lot less glamorous than it looks.

It's much colder today than it was on December 30, 1986. It's going to drop down to minus-27. When the bus pulls out of the parking lot, the windshield is coated with a sheet of ice that, if horizontal, would make for a serviceable backyard rink. The driver has cleared an open patch, no bigger than a dartboard, to peer through.

If anything symbolizes the junior hockey life, it's not a game or a sweater—it's the bus. Whoever first called it the "Iron Lung" missed his calling as a poet. The bus is a constant in the game, the ride the players have to take to make it to the NHL. Chynoweth has spent hundreds, even thousands, of hours on buses, playing four seasons in the Western Hockey League and coaching the Seattle Thunderbirds for two before coming over to Swift Current two years ago. Even before he took the job in Swift, Chynoweth had ridden past the site of the Broncos' bus crash dozens of times—it's on the Trans-Canada Highway, just a couple of minutes outside of town, en route to Moose Jaw, Regina and points east.

Most scouts have spent more time on team buses than I have. Most rode them when they played junior or college hockey. A lot of them rode in buses when they played in the minors. Some of them rode up front in the seats reserved for the coach of the team. Don Boyd had the front seat in Newmarket, London and the Soo in the Ontario league and Regina in the Dub. Even if a scout only rode a bus for a season, he'd know the junior hockey life more intimately than I ever will. I've only ridden on a team bus as part of the media covering a team, which meant that I sat where I'm sitting today: in the idiot seats, the ones behind the coaches and in front of the players, who prize the rows closest to the back. Like other aspects of the game, the bus ride is wound up in a weird series of rituals that no one can explain. Everyone sits in the same seats on every trip—veterans beside veterans, rookies with fellow initiates. And the rookies are expected to do the heavy lifting, loading the skate sharpener and other hardware into the hold.

Dean Chynoweth is up front and the players load and board and take their places. Just a couple of minutes out of the parking lot, the bus rolls onto the Trans-Canada Highway, and just a couple of minutes after that Chynoweth points ahead to the spot on the road where the Broncos' bus crashed twenty years ago. There's nothing to mark the spot, no wreath off the soft shoulder.

I ask a couple of players sitting behind me if they know the site of the Broncos' bus crash. They shake their heads. They say they know a bit of the story behind the patch that Broncos teams have worn on their sweaters the last twenty years, but no, they don't know where the crash happened. Just as we roll past it.

I ask the team captain, a twenty-year-old from Winnipeg, Myles Rumsey, if some of the bus rides in the dead of winter worry him.

"You don't think about it," Rumsey says. "I mean, we've gone off the road before. Happens all over hockey, probably. I don't remember too much about it. Middle of the night. I was asleep."

I look behind Rumsey. Less than five minutes out of Swift Current and he's one of the few Broncos still awake. It's not just that many don't know where that bus went off the road twenty years ago; I'd bet some of them haven't ever been awake to see it.

Moose Jaw Civic Centre, Moose Jaw

MOOSE JAW 6 SWIFT CURRENT 2

For years I've heard about the Moose Jaw Civic Centre. Nobody had ever called it the Civic Centre, mind you. No, it's always "the Crushed Can." When the bus first pulls up I think that might be a little unkind. Yes, the roof does collapse in the middle. Not your usual arena architechture but not so unusual that it needs knocking. Only when I get inside does it hit home: the arena really does look like the inside of a crushed can, and one that's been dug out of a garbage dump after fifty years. With its rolling metal roof, it looks like Frank Gehry might have been conceived here. It's cold—as cold inside as it is out. It's cramped. There's no in-arena restaurant, just hallways redolent of fries and popcorn. It doesn't have interactive displays or fan zones, just photos on the walls—old black-and-whites of Fred Sasakamoose, the Cree from the Sandy Lake Reserve who was a goal-a-game legend for the Moose Jaw Canucks before becoming the first Native to play in the NHL in the early '50s.

The game between the Broncos and the Warriors won't match the atmosphere. It's a down year for the home team. Moose Jaw's best player is a centre named Riley Holzapfel, a second-round pick of the Atlanta Thrashers in June. This season the Warriors don't have much in the way of draft-worthy prospects. Their top-ranked '89 birthday is defenceman Travis Ehrhardt, who's projected to be a late-round pick on Central Scouting's players-to-watch list.

The Broncos are ahead of the Warriors in the standings, but their spot in the playoffs is no sure thing. Joe Sakic was the rising star on that Swift Current team in 1986, but there's no one like him in

Swift Current now and hasn't been for a long time. Broncos coach Dean Chynoweth tries to make a virtue of necessity. "We don't have stars, so we have to have a great work ethic," he says. "No one can afford to take a shift off. The team can't afford to have anyone take a shift off."

The Broncos' top draft prospect is Paul Postma, a defenceman from Red Deer. In NHL Central Scouting's early-season rankings, Postma is slotted just outside the top ten in the Western league. If he holds onto that slot, Postma is probably looking at being selected in the second or third round. That seems a little high for a kid who is six foot three but a pencil-thin 160 pounds.

I strike up a brief conversation with Postma. His best friend and teammate growing up in Red Deer was Brandon Sutter. Postma tells me that he and Brandon had always talked about playing together in major junior, but they realized in the season leading up to the WHL draft that it was a longshot. Everyone in the league knew that Brent Sutter was going to take his son with the sixth over-all pick, and the best guess was that Postma would be long gone by the time Red Deer's pick in the second round came up. The Broncos selected Postma just six slots after Brandon. "We're still best friends and we still work out together in the off-season," Postma says. "That's not going to change. It would have been great to have played together and to play at home. But things turned out that way for a reason, and I'm just making the best of it."

I ask Postma for the skinny on his physique—he looks as if he could get pushed around at the starting line of the Boston Marathon, never mind in the corners of an NHL rink. "I've tried to put on weight and Brandon has, too," Postma says. "My father's a decent size. I just have to work out and be patient. I know that it would prob-ably help me with [the draft] to have that extra weight. Scouts would look at me differently."

When I see Postma step on the ice during the warm-up, one name comes to my mind: Jane Russell. Postma's ability to pass for a pro prospect probably owes as much to modern equipment design as much as anything else—he is padded enough and draped in a large enough sweater that his ectomorphic frame is thoroughly disguised. There hasn't been such a form-flattering outfit since Howard Hughes came up with the underdress that cantilevered Russell to spectacular effect in the 1943 film *The Outlaw*.

The Broncos' work ethic is apparent early on. Through the first five or six shifts it looks as though they'll run the Warriors out of the rink. Swift Current's energy starts to dissipate when the Warriors' goaltender, Joey Perricone, keeps turning aside what look like sure goals. And when Riley Holzapfel scores midway through the first period, the Broncos flat-line. They're never really in the game after that.

With Swift Current down 3–1 through the second period, a Broncos forward named Brady Leavold drops the gloves with Moose Jaw's Brennen Wray. Leavold is no heavyweight, not even really a middleweight. In fact, the Broncos don't have a tough guy, no one resembling a Chris Mantyka. There's no clear winner in the fight, which is as good as a loss for Leavold, who went looking to start something, and for the Broncos, who needed a lift.

At the end of the night, Holzapfel and Travis Ehrhardt look like sure NHLers. Holzapfel has three goals, and Travis Ehrhardt racks up five assists from the blueline.[14]

Dean Chynoweth has his critics in Swift Current. Some of Chynoweth's knockers will never get over the fact that he's not from Swift Current. It's not good enough that he was willing to come to Swift to coach major junior; no, some fans think that the team should be coached by one of their own.

Others say he's not emotional enough behind the bench. I overheard that at a diner in Swift Current this morning. I've seen it on

---

14. He'll end up with only 24 more points, all assists, in 68 more games this season.

WHL fan websites. Accusing a coach of being a cold fish would pass for libel in the business—a coach without passion is nothing.

You'd never convince the Broncos that Chynoweth is cool or detached tonight. Chynoweth loses it on the team when he spots a couple of players smiling on the bench late in the game. He wouldn't have accepted that sort of indifference to defeat when he was a player—Chynoweth was a captain of a Medicine Hat team that won the Memorial Cup back in '88—and he won't accept it as a coach.

Chynoweth is not yet forty. His playing career was done by his thirtieth birthday, because he had to play hard to play at all. The idea that players would laugh when losing offends him. At a time like this, Chynoweth must wish he were still a player—then someone would get pinned to a wall. He's almost trembling with anger by the time he walks out the back door of the arena to the idling bus and takes his seat without a word. The players load their equipment into the lower hold in silence. As each player boards he has to walk past Chynoweth, who greets him with a withering glare.

The rest of the night will be as silent inside the bus as the great, snowy Prairie void outside it. Almost a monastic silence. Solidarity of sorrow of a different sort, I suppose. Eventually, that will give way to the solidarity of sleep.

Just before we pull into the arena parking lot in Swift Current, just before midnight, I ask Chynoweth about the kid who was in the fight tonight. Brady Leavold. The coach tells me Leavold left the team last winter and went home to British Columbia. Last summer he asked Chynoweth if he could come back to the team, and the coach makes it sound as though he even surprised himself by agreeing to give Leavold another shot—although on a very short leash. "When I was playing, if a player did that, it would be over for him," Chynoweth tells me. "I let him come back this season. It's not that I was making an exception for a top player in the league. Brady was just having some trouble, like a lot of kids who play junior and a lot who don't. A second chance here was going to be good for him."

It's hard to reconcile the coach who laid into the team with the one who'd opened the door for Leavold to return. But I'm more interested in the player than the coach. Leavold didn't just choose to play junior—he chose it twice. Maybe there's something to glean from a player who had enough misgivings to walk away, yet enough desire to endure the humbling of coming back to play again.

December 2, 2006, Swift Current

I meet up with Brady Leavold for breakfast at the Smitty's Restaurant out on the North Service Road running parallel to the Trans-Canada Highway.

Like most of the Broncos and most in major junior, Leavold wasn't drafted when he was first eligible back in 2005, and not last June, either. The consensus among thirty NHL teams has twice been that he's no prospect. If he makes a dollar in the game someday he'll have beaten massive odds. Those are just the cold realities that most kids in junior hockey have to face: even on the very best teams, fewer than half the players are drafted.

The way Leavold describes it, a team is divided along the lines of those who are drafted and those who aren't and aren't likely to be. The players at the top of this caste system are those who are back in junior after having signed NHL contracts. Those players are the ones with chronic cases of entitlement.

"Ian White was the big player when I came here," he says. "He'd been drafted by the Leafs and he had gone to the world juniors. He was just going to do things his way. In training camp we were supposed to show up for fitness testing in the weight room at the rink, and we were all there in our gym stuff. He shows up in jeans and a cowboy hat. He didn't even take it off when he had to do the bench [press]. He did one rep and put the bar back on the rack and said, 'That's all I feel like today.' He coulda done dozens of reps. And he gave it to the rookies, too. I was scared shitless. On the bus, I was afraid to even look around my first season. I sat near the front—all the veterans were in the back—and one time when I turned around White saw me and said, 'What the f— are you lookin' at?' After that I didn't look back the rest of the season. I'm a veteran now, I don't want to be like White was to the younger players. It doesn't mean anything to me."

White has since made it into the Toronto Maple Leafs' lineup but also into the headlines recently, first for a drunken-driving charge, then for driving with his licence under suspension. The people least surprised by that news were the Broncos. White had asked Chynoweth if he could skate with team before the Leafs' training camp, then proceeded to carouse around a town where news of that sort would get back to the Broncos' dressing room before he would. His farewell from the Broncos wasn't marked by a pre-game tribute but by Chynoweth tossing his equipment out the back door of the arena when White didn't show up for a practice and breached the coach's rules. The equipment lay unclaimed for several hours.

Players on other junior teams might be hometown heroes, but not the Broncos, not the way Leavold tells it. The players, who come from all across western Canada, get a lot of cold shoulders and cold stares at the local high school. "Walking through the halls, we'll hear them cracking about us," Leavold says. "Kids I don't know, never talked to, will say, 'Nice jacket, Bronco.' The guys will try to pick fights with us, because they have nothing to lose and they know that we're finished here if we try to stick up for ourselves."

When Leavold says this, I can sense the frustration: what is supposed to be a charmed life turns out to be cursed a lot of the time. Being with the team turns out to be not a licence, but baggage. It's not just the likes of Ian White, the little princes of the game who laid rubber on Main Street in sports cars bought with NHL money. No, every team has its share of troubled kids and troublemakers. But police in Swift Current investigated a claim that players sexually assaulted a teenage girl a few years back. Ultimately, no charges were filed, but the team's reputation was tarnished.

Every year it seems a story like this plays out in junior hockey. When I started writing about junior hockey, charges of sexual assault were filed against three Windsor Spitfires. A few years later, when I was covering the Ottawa 67's, police charged a player with the same beef. In both cases the charges were dropped. This season, several Saginaw Spirit players are being investigated by the local police.[15]

Deals tend to be struck with the complainants and cases tend to go away—or at least not make it to court. But that doesn't mean that everyone forgives and forgets.

"Whatever happened years back, we pay the price," Leavold says. "I feel comfortable with the guys on the team, but I don't know if I'll ever feel comfortable with Swift Current. We're here to play for the people, but truth is they want nothing to do with us."

The Broncos' dressing room has the low hum of the early afternoon before a game night. Players are prepping sticks. The trainer is sharpening skates. Other equipment is getting blown dry. Hunchak, the assistant coach, will put a couple of players rehabbing injuries through a non-contact skate.

Dean Chynoweth is exasperated as he leaves the arena. Instead of spending Saturday afternoon at home with his family, he has to meet with Darrell Moir, the father of the Broncos' goaltender, Kyle Moir. Darrell Moir knows how a team should operate. He played in the Canadian Football League for seven seasons and was, until recently, a vice-president of the Calgary Stampeders. He probably never had to deal with a father pushing for his son to be traded, but that's why he has asked to meet with Chynoweth. Moir wants his son to have a chance to play for a winner, and he's convinced that the top teams in the Dub would have Kyle.

Chynoweth will have to take it all in, politely. He might even hold back the fact that his phone hasn't been ringing off the hook from coaches asking about Kyle's availability, even though the Nashville Predators called out his name in the late rounds of the

---

15. Charges of simple assault would be filed against four players.

draft a couple of years ago. Maybe Chynoweth will let Darrell get an early start on the drive back to Calgary, telling him that he's giving the start against Brandon to Kyle's backup, Travis Yonkman.

Centennial Civic Centre, Swift Current

SWIFT CURRENT 6 BRANDON 4

Less than 1,800 make it out to the arena. That's a small crowd for a Saturday night, even by the standards of the smallest town in junior hockey. Part of it is the cold, around minus-30 at game time. Part of it, though, is dissatisfaction with the Broncos. The people in Swift Current are used to competitive teams. The Broncos have made the playoffs every year for a generation, but this year's Broncos don't get anybody excited.

Dean Chynoweth gets a better effort out of his team at home. Levi Nelson, the Broncos' only forward who has been drafted (Boston, No. 158 in 2006), scores twice in the first period to stake Swift Current to a lead. The Wheat Kings score three consecutive goals in the second period to take the lead. After that, though, Yonkman stops the bleeding, and by the end of the game he has saved 39 of 43 shots. Brady Leavold scores on a penalty kill in the second period to tie the game at three. Then Jeremy Schenderling, an overager from British Columbia, a kid who's kicked around the league since the 2001–02 season, gets a hat trick's worth of power-play goals to clinch a much-needed two points. Two points much needed by the embattled coach and general manager, who sees the empty seats. Two points much needed by the players to avoid more silent meditation on their failings.

The other players have showered, dressed and are clearing out of the Broncos' dressing room. They'll be lighting out for Boston Pizza and other bright lights of the Swift Current social milieu. Only their captain, Myles Rumsey, is left behind in the dressing room. He sits at his stall, barefoot, draped in a towel. His head hangs down. He's crying.

I knock on the door of the coaches' office and ask Chynoweth what's wrong with Rumsey.

"He found out after the game that a friend of his had died back in Winnipeg. Todd Davison, a kid who played for the Pats," Chynoweth says. "Cancer. An aggressive cancer. It had gone into remission, and he even came back to play, but there was no stopping it."

As it turns out, Rumsey had played with and against Davison from atom right up to the Dub. They were '86s. Rumsey was a second-round pick, Davison was picked later. Rumsey was drafted by the Calgary Flames. By the time Davison was in his draft year, he was undergoing chemo.

There's no going back to Rumsey to talk about Davison tonight. No going back to talk about anything at all.

When I get to my hotel room I look up Davison's stats on a hockey website. He had played 48 games for Regina as a sixteen-year-old centre back in the 2002–03 regular season. No goals, two assists. He played two playoff games that year and didn't get a point, but ended up with seventeen minutes in penalties. That was the end of his career in the Dub. He didn't even come away with a puck to mount as his first goal. He didn't come away with much to show for his short time in the league except a small place on a site that a fan started, a site that lists every fight in the WHL and every player's record in those fights, like they're professional boxers. Even there, Davison's shorted: two fights, no decisions. The Pats listed Davison as only five foot eight and 162 pounds, so playing much beyond junior was a longshot. Still, he had been a pretty promising player and was even invited with Rumsey to try out for the Manitoba team that went to the Canada Winter Games but he never made it back to the Pats. He played parts of a couple of seasons with the Lloydminster Blazers in the Alberta Junior Hockey League, Tier II. And back in the fall, after rounds of chemo and surgeries that stalled but didn't stop the spread of his cancer, Davison helped out behind the bench of the Winnipeg Thrashers AAA midget club.

The other players left Rumsey alone to grieve. He didn't want a shoulder to cry on. He didn't knock on the coach's door. As captain he's supposed to be the brave face. He's supposed to look out for himself and for others.

December 3 2006, Centennial Civic Centre, Swift Current

SWIFT CURRENT 3 REGINA 2

Maybe the silent bus ride still resonates with the Broncos. They come out with a second consecutive competitive game. It's not a spectacular win, but it's not as if Swift Current has stuff that comes close to spectacular. It's a methodical win. The Broncos take the lead midway through the first period, Brady Leavold and Kyle Bortis setting up Zack Smith, and never trail. Midway through the third period Swift leads 3–0. Down 3–1, the Pats pull their goalie with two minutes left, and manage to score once, but mount no pressure after that. The Pats outshoot Swift Current 32–17, but again the Broncos' backup, Travis Yonkman, stars while the goal-tender who was looking to get traded to a contender, Kyle Moir, has to watch.

The Pats have one player projected by Central Scouting to be selected late in the first round or early in the second round of the 2007 draft: Nick Ross, a defenceman who played on the summer under-18 team. I set up a heading in my notebook with his name and number but write nothing under it over the course of sixty minutes. That's not to say that he's bad or indifferent, and he probably does have something to do with the Broncos' getting only seventeen shots, but he doesn't jump out.

December 4, 2006, Smitty's, Swift Current

Before I head out of town I meet up with Myles Rumsey for breakfast. Rumsey was drafted, though he's no lock to get a contract offer from Calgary, who selected him in the seventh and final round, 221st overall—220 picks after Sidney Crosby—in 2005. If he had been a priority item for the Flames at their training camp last fall, they might have assigned him to their American Hockey League affiliate in Omaha.

"If I made it to Omaha next year, that would be great," he says. "Just a chance to show what I can do—to find a role and learn to fill it. That's what I want."

In his voice, there's a resignation. It's not just that it's a longshot to get to Omaha; to get past Omaha is one longshot parlayed after another.

It's easy to see why the Broncos would want Rumsey as an overage player and as their captain. He's soft-spoken, not gregarious; but there doesn't seem to be anything the least bit impulsive about him at all—in contrast to Leavold, who's almost manic in his energy. It's not simple maturity. He might not seem mature by the standards of twenty-year-old university students or twenty-year-olds who've had to go to work on the farms outside of Swift Current. No, Rumsey seems *old* for a junior hockey player. He has been around. He has accepted his lot. He's fallen into line. He has soldiered on.

The old saw is that players make the best scouts, that there's nothing you can observe as a scout that players don't already know about those they play with and against.

I ask Rumsey who the best player in the Dub is this season, and he doesn't hesitate. "Peter Mueller, hands down," he says. "He's just so good with the puck. Everett is the toughest team right now and he's the one who makes them go."

I ask Rumsey about Postma. He says Postma's "a good kid," but he says so without enthusiasm. Rumsey also says that he likes the other defenceman, Derek Claffey, more than Postma. I'm suspicious of false witness. It sounds like Claffey is tighter with Rumsey off the ice. It also sounds as though Postma's draft pedigree—a first-rounder—and his connection with the Sutter family might rub the honest workman/plugger in Rumsey the wrong way. Maybe he sees himself in Claffey.

I ask Rumsey about Geordie Wudrick, a sixteen-year-old rookie from British Columbia. Wudrick isn't a prospect for the 2007 draft — born in 1990, he's not eligible until 2008. I'm just interested in the tall poppy syndrome — how players look at a young teammate who comes in hyped and heralded. Wudrick became the highest draft pick in Broncos franchise history when the team selected him No. 2 in the Dub's bantam draft in 2005. Wudrick also became, as far as anyone can remember, the first out-of-town player to arrive in Swift with his mother — the first who didn't move in with a billet.

Rumsey has only good things to say about Wudrick. "A big kid who can be a power forward when he fills out . . . a smart kid for sure." But Rumsey expressed some concern about what might be lost — by Wudrick and by the team, by the precedent that was set. Other play-ers say that the Wudricks can afford an arrangement that other players' families can't — not that it has escalated into class warfare or resent-ment, just that it might separate Geordie from the team. "We all try to get along and we all try to fit in. That's what I've done, and I think that's what everyone on this team has done. Yeah, it's tougher for sixteen-year-olds, but others have done it. Will Geordie move in with a billet family next year? Maybe that would be for the best."

Finally, I ask Rumsey about Todd Davison. A sigh. A nod. He cowboys up. "He really did love the game, and his teammates liked him. When he couldn't play, even though he knew he probably didn't have a lot of time left, he wanted to help coach the team back in Winnipeg. Life's unfair sometimes. If you had twenty guys with his attitude and some talent, you'd win a lot of games."

You could probably say the same about Myles Rumsey.

December 27, 2006, FM Matsson Arena, Mora, Sweden

CANADA 6 U.S.A 3

A Boxing Day departure from Toronto gets me to the arena, a couple of hours from Stockholm, just in time for the best matchup of the opening round: Canada vs. the U.S. I've missed the opening games—Canada vs. Sweden and the U.S. vs. Germany—but no matter.

Canada and the U.S. met for the gold medal at the 2004 under-20s in Helsinki, and the Americans rallied from a two-goal deficit in the third period to win their first-ever world junior title. It looked like a turning point in tournament history. Much had been expected of the U.S. under-20 teams over the years, yet they had little to show for it— a silver in '97, a couple of bronzes. Given their resources and deep talent pool, the Americans should have been up there with Canada and the Russians. Many, including those scouts in the corner seats of arenas, thought that the Americans' victory in Helsinki was the dawn of a new era—from then on the U.S. would have to rank as one of the favourites every season.

American hegemony has yet to materialize.

The Americans first had a chance to defend their title at home. The IIHF awarded the 2005 tournament to USA Hockey, which opted to stage it at the University of North Dakota. The tournament was a box-office success—tickets sold out—but the U.S. team didn't enjoy much of a home-ice advantage because most tickets were snapped up by fans driving down from Winnipeg. Then again, it wouldn't have helped the American team if the organizers had shipped in 15,000 fans from Madison Square Garden. I made it to that tournament after Canada's first two games and asked one friend in the scouting biz for an update. "The other guys are beaten before they step on the ice," he said. The 2005 Canadian team, an outfit that featured Sidney Crosby in a *supporting* role, was the most dominant squad in tournament history. They knew it, and so did the other guys. The Canadians steamrolled the Russians 6–1 in the final. The U.S. was spared an undressing, losing to the Russians in the semis and then falling down to the Czech Republic in the bronze-medal game.

Many pundits picked the U.S. as the favourites before the 2006 under-20 tournament in Vancouver, but the Americans again under-achieved. Phil Kessel was supposed to be the best player at the event, yet he failed to impress, scoring only one goal in seven games. Switzerland scored a goal late in their opening-round game against the U.S. to come away with a 2–2 tie. Nor were the Canadians anything like the powerhouse team of the previous under-20 tournament. They looked small and unskilled up front. They struggled to score. Their goaltender, Justin Pogge, was so lightly considered that he wasn't even invited to the Canadian team's summer evaluation camp. Yet they managed to edge the Americans in the opening round and then smoked the Russians in the final, 5–0.

So, feeling a bit beaten up by a day in transit, the lessons of recent history are still fresh in my mind. The American team is supposed to be a threat to the two-time defending champions. Many U.S. players are bound for long careers in the NHL. So I do a double take when I look at the results from Boxing Day. Canada 2 Sweden 0—okay, that I can see. But the other game has me wondering if jet lag has blurred my vision: USA 3 Germany *four* in overtime.

Many fans presume that NHL prospects are found at this tournament. This is almost never the case. Any player worth scouting has shown up on the radar years before—even by the time they appear in the under-18s this is true. The vast majority of NHL prospects at this tournament are already drafted. This year's tournament is an instructive example. The 2007 draft consists of the class of 1989 birthdays. When you factor in late birthdays, that means players born from September 16, 1988, through September 15, 1989, are eligible for the NHL draft for the first time. Eligibility for this world junior tournament extends as far back as January 1, 1987—in other words, the oldest players at this tournament were eligible for the 2005 draft, a.k.a. the Sidney Crosby draft.

Scouts go to the world juniors mostly to keep tabs on players already drafted—especially players that their own teams have already drafted. The key players for Canada at this tournament were snapped up in 2005 (goaltender Carey Price, who was selected fifth overall by the Montreal Canadiens, and defenceman Marc Staal, who was selected by the New York Rangers) or 2006 (centre Jonathan Toews, who was selected by Chicago third overall). Likewise, the U.S. team is made up almost entirely of draftees from 2005 (defenceman Jack Johnson, selected third overall by the Carolina Hurricanes) and 2006 (winger Kyle Okposo, chosen seventh overall by the Islanders, and centre Peter Mueller, who was selected with the next pick by Phoenix).

That's how it runs through most teams at the under-20s. The Slovaks, Swiss or Germans might have a bunch of players here who were eligible for the 2005 and 2006 drafts and went unselected, but that doesn't mean that they were missed or that they'll be "found" here. No, the fact is that they were seen at other tournaments, they were "viewed" dozens of times by scouts in every organization, and their names are logged in databases beside the notation "No prospect."

Still, Canada and the U.S. do have a couple of players apiece who are eligible for the upcoming draft, and all are priorities for the scouts here: forwards Patrick Kane and James van Riemsdyk of the U.S. and forward Sam Gagner and defenceman Karl Alzner of Canada.

The player who figures to play the most is Patrick Kane of the London Knights. Kane, a late '88 birthday, is in his rookie season in the O, but he's been among the league's leading scorers since the start of the season and has won a place on the wing of the Americans' top line.

Sam Gagner's case is a curious one. The son of former NHL journeyman Dave Gagner and a teammate of Kane in London, he was unexpectedly invited to the world junior tryouts earlier in the month—unexpectedly, because he was invited to the under-18 tryouts last summer *and was cut*. From that under-18 team, only Angelo Esposito was invited to the under-20 tryouts, and he was quickly dropped. So was John Tavares. Maybe Gagner had a poor camp in the summer, and maybe he raised his game over the fall, but it's still hard to figure out how he came from so far back and passed so many players to make the Canadian team.

Alzner and van Riemsdyk aren't likely to play that much. Alzner, a late '88 birthday, is just a depth player on the Canadian blueline— the top defencemen from the championship team of last winter

(Marc Staal, Luc Bourdon, Ryan Parent, Kristopher Letang and Kris Russell) are back. Van Riemsdyk starred at the under-17s, but the U.S. is just looking at his trip here as an enrichment exercise—he's expected to deliver at the 2008 and 2009 world juniors.

No player has more to prove at this year's tournament than Jonathan Toews. His season has been poor so far. The scouts are saying it, and he admits it. His team at the University of North Dakota has struggled mightily, and he has all of four goals for the Fighting Sioux. Chicago's selection of Toews at No. 3 looked like great value in June, less so now, given that Phil Kessel has scored more goals for the Boston Bruins than Toews has against college players.

In Vancouver, Toews had a limited role, much like Sam Gagner's assignment here: defence and energy first. Here he's supposed to centre the first line, man the power play and kill penalties. Even with Steve Downie, Canadian Anti-Hero™, on hand, even with all the returning defencemen, the defending champions are likely only going as far as Toews can take them.

Canadian coach Craig Hartsburg matches him against Peter Mueller on every shift, and Toews owns him. Mueller may be the best player in the Western league in Myles Rumsey's estimation, but he's the second-best centre every time he steps on the ice here.

Downie opens the scoring in the first period, scoring with a wrist shot on a two-on-one. I don't get the number of the Canadian player who's skating up the ice with Downie—and evidently Downie doesn't, either, because he never even glances at him. From centre ice until he hits the top of the face-off circle, Downie's focused on U.S. goaltender Jeffrey Zatkoff. He never has any intention of passing the puck, which is fine if you score.

The Canadians go ahead 2–0 later in the period on a goal by Tom Pyatt and seem in control of the game at the intermission. It looks as if a rout is in the making when Toews scores on a power play early in the second period, skating through some heavy traffic and bouncing off U.S. defenders, flashing a sleight-of-hand deke that he must have kept under wraps at the last world juniors.

The Americans rally late in the period. Goals by Erik Johnson, the first pick in the 2006 draft, and Mike Carmen, another University of Minnesota player, make it 3–2 going into the third and pump oxygen and energy into an American team that looked ready to roll over.

All this sets the stage for Toews. With about ten minutes to go in regulation, he slips behind the Johnsons, Erik and Jack, and has a clean breakaway. Erik Johnson slings his stick thirty feet like a javelin in an attempt to try to knock the puck off Toews's stick—an impetuous act you'll see every now and then in a peewee game, but not with near-pros. The ref awards Toews a penalty shot, which he coolly finishes off, snapping the puck into the top corner on Zatkoff's glove side. In their war room the Blue Jackets scouts expressed doubt about Toews being a "game-breaker", but the finish on the penalty shot might be cause for reconsidering that.

Capping a bravura performance, Toews is sent out late in the game when the U.S. has a five-on-three power play and forces a face-off in the Canadian end. Toews wins the draw cleanly and clears the zone, snuffing out the last U.S. threat.

Toews isn't the happiest person in the rink. Top honours would go to Dale Tallon, the Chicago Blackhawks' general manager. Tallon won't admit to having been concerned about Toews's play at UND, but the Hawks needed some validation of their selection in the last draft. This game gives them that and more. Tallon says Toews's last turn, the penalty kill, says as much about him as the clinical finishes on his two goals. "He's very conscientious defensively and has great instincts for the game," Tallon tells me. "He's not chasing the puck but going where the puck is heading."

While the Canadian players are getting on the bus to head back to their hotel, USA Hockey is giving its players time to spend with their families and their agents (or, in the case of the collegians, their family advisors who are certified NHL agents). They wait for the arena to clear and then mingle around the foyer. I've seen Canadian teams in defeat many times in these tournaments, and in all those gloomy wakes I have never seen as many clear eyes or as much self-satisfaction as I do at this gathering of the extended U.S. team in Mora. I look for Patrick Kane to see how he's handling it, but he's on his own. His parents didn't make the trip.

December 28, 2006, Ejendals Arena, Leksand, Sweden

RUSSIA 6 SWITZERLAND 0

This year's Russian junior team isn't as highly touted as the last two sent to the under-20s, though likely only because it does not feature players already highly drafted by NHL teams. Last January in Vancouver the focus was on Evgeni Malkin, drafted second overall by the Pittsburgh Penguins in 2004 and regarded as the best player not in the NHL. Two years ago in North Dakota, Malkin was understudy to Alexander Ovechkin, the first-overall pick of the Washington Capitals in 2004. The most prominent names on this year's team would be recognized by scouts, but not by casual fans: Semen Varlamov, the phlegmatic goaltender drafted by Washington in the first round, and Artem Anisimov, the skilled forward selected by the Rangers. Prospects of interest to scouts, but a long way from making the cover of *The Hockey News*.

Though this is a team of '87 birthdays, the priority of the scouts at this game is an '89, Alexei Cherepanov, last seen at the summer under-18s. At that tournament, and in Russian elite league games since then, he has emerged as the top-ranked draft-eligible talent in Europe. In fact, he's putting up more impressive statistics against seasoned professionals in the Russian league than Ovechkin, Malkin and Ilya Kovalchuk did at the same stage. (Rumour has it that Cherepanov is making as much as $1.5 million. That might be his most impressive statistic, though a lot less so to a NHL team that drafts him and has to convince him to take a pay cut.)

The Russians rout the ever-game Swiss team, and the one-sided score looks like it might reach double digits but for a near-heroic performance by Reto Berra, Switzerland's live-wire goaltender and aspiring banker. Berra keeps his team within a goal through a relentless onslaught that lasts the first thirty-five minutes.

Meanwhile, Varlamov's end of the rink barely needs flooding. The Russians are too good to hold at bay, scoring four in the third period and racking up forty-four shots for the game. Cherepanov ends up with a goal and an assist, looking supremely skilled if, well, a little sleepy. Ovechkin and Malkin seemed determined to put their imprint on a game, while Cherepanov is a little more subtle, as if waiting for it to come to him. That said, it's not as if this game was ever in doubt.

Getting a line on Russian teams—or, more precisely, the *players* on Russian teams—is no easy exercise. It might seem clear-cut with Cherepanov—a player who has success as a teenager against the best Russian pros is a safe bet to be a real NHL prospect—but with others it's far more of a crapshoot than you might think. The cautionary tale is that of the Russian team that won the 2003 world junior tournament.

The Russians have sent many good—and several great—teams to the under-20s. Back in the 1970s, the USSR went undefeated and untied through the first four world junior tournaments. The 2003 Russian team that won the world under-20s in Halifax would be regarded as the best of the post-Soviet troupes, featured Ovechkin and Nikolai Zherdev as underage players. They were, in fact, just members of a talented ensemble, the Russian '83s, that defeated Canada 3–2 in the gold-medal game. The score was close, the play a lot less so.

It's hard to imagine a one-goal victory as the bottom line on an imperious performance, but it never seemed like Canada was going to come back to tie the game. The Russians looked bigger, faster, more accomplished in every facet of the game. No one knew this better than the players at both ends of the ice. In fact, the Russians taunted the Canadians throughout the game without fear of retribution. Though Ovechkin has since carved out a reputation as a fun-loving kid, that night he trash-talked his way through the game and was firing f-bombs at the Canadians right through the medal presentations.

Those who watched that Russian team had good reason to presume that players on its roster would boost the level of talent in the NHL for a generation—that they would form the core of a Russian squad that would take the measure of Canada's best for years to come.

But to the amazement of those who watched that team, most of the players on the Russian '83s just faded into the background. Ovechkin has gone on to stardom, and Zherdev to infamy, but most of the rest are still in Russia. Some NHL scouts today might claim that it's no surprise to them, but that's only wisdom acquired after the fact.

Just going down the roster of that team:

Those in the NHL

- Alexander Ovechkin beat out Sidney Crosby for the Calder Trophy and will be a fixture on future NHL All-Star teams.
- Defenceman Fedor Tyutin is in his second full season on the New York Rangers' blue line and looks like he'll have a decent NHL career, though he's unlikely to emerge as an All-Star.
- Nikolai Zherdev, as noted before, is a talented enigma and a potential serial coach-killer.
- Right winger Alexander Perezhogin was Montreal's first-rounder, twenty-fifth overall, in 2001. He's in his second full season with the Canadiens, and while he doesn't seem like he'll ever develop into a big scorer, it looks as though he can carve out a decent NHL journeyman's career.

Works in Progress

- Alexei Kaigorodov, a centre with Magnitogorsk; Ottawa's second-rounder, forty-seventh overall, in 2002;

has yet to play in the NHL, but the Senators are trying to get him across the Atlantic.[16]

- Andrei Taratukhin, centre, Omsk, Calgary second-rounder, forty-first overall, is playing his first season in North America with the Flames' affiliate in Omaha.[17]

BACK IN THE MOTHERLAND

- Evgeny Artyukhin, a forward who was brought over to play with Moncton in the Quebec league after Tampa Bay drafted him in the third round, ninety-fourth over-all, put in two full years in the minor pros before making it to the NHL in the fall of 2005. He lasted a year with the Lightning, scoring four goals in 72 games, before heading back to Russia this fall to play for Yaroslavl.
- Maxim Kondratiev, a defenceman with Tolyatti Lada, was Toronto's sixth-rounder, 168th overall, in 2001. He played in North America for three seasons, making it into 36 NHL games with Toronto and the New York Rangers, before heading back to Russia to play with Tolyatti Lada.
- Timofei Shishkanov, a left winger, was already playing for the Quebec Remparts when the Russians won the world-under-20s. In the 2002–03 season he put up numbers not quite up there with Alexander Radulov's, but impressive nonetheless: 36 goals and 46 assists in 51 games. It looked as if Nashville had chosen wisely when

---

16. Kaigorodov will end up playing six games for the Senators before the season is out and then be traded to Phoenix.

17. Taratukhin will end up with 17 goals and 43 assists in 80 games with Omaha.

the Predators selected him in the second round, thirty-third overall, in the 2001 draft. But, four seasons into his pro career, Shishkanov played just two games with Nashville before being shipped to St. Louis. He played in just twenty more games with the Blues before heading back to Russia last summer. These days, he's with Chekhov Vityaz and looks like a washout.

- Kiril Koltsov, a defenceman with Omsk, was selected by the Vancouver Canucks in the second round, forty-ninth overall, in the 2002 draft. He played one season with the Manitoba Moose and part of the next before rejoining Omsk Avangard, where he has spent the last two seasons.

- Denis Grebeshkov, a defenceman with Yaroslavl, was Los Angeles's first-rounder, eighteenth overall, in 2002 (a late '83 birthday). After a brief American Hockey League apprenticeship, he played thirty-three games with the Kings and Islanders in a couple of seasons, but went back to Russia last fall and looks like he's there to stay with Yaroslavl.

NEVER LEFT RUSSIA

- Mikhail Lyubushin, a big defenceman with Krylia, was Los Angeles's seventh-rounder, 215th overall, in 2002 but has never left Russia and is playing with Omsk Avangard.

- Igor Grigorenko, a short, squat right winger, was Detroit's second-rounder, sixty-second overall, in 2001 and has put up some decent numbers with lesser Russian league teams but has not yet come to North America.

- Alexander Polushin, a forward with Moscow Red Army and later Cherepovets, was Tampa's second-rounder, forty-seventh overall, in 2001, but has yet to play outside of Russia.

- Konstantin Barulin, the backup goaltender on Russia's world junior championship team, was a third-rounder of St. Louis, eighty-fourth overall, in 2003. He has bounced around the Russian leagues ever since.
- Yuri Trubachev, a centre with St. Petersburg and Cherepovets, was Calgary's fifth-rounder, 164th overall, but has never left Cherepovets.
- Dmitri Pestunov, a centre with Magnitogorsk, was Phoenix's third-rounder, eightieth overall, in 2003 (an '85 birthday). He has never left Russia and is still playing with Magnitogorsk.

FALLEN OFF THE FACE OF THE EARTH

- Konstantin Korneev, a defenceman with Krylia, was not drafted by a NHL club. Whereabouts unknown.
- Denis Ezhov, a defenceman with Lada, was not drafted by an NHL club. Whereabouts unknown.
- Andrei Medvedev, a rotund goaltender who played for Russia's under-20 championship team in 2002, was Calgary's second-rounder, fifty-sixth overall, in 2001. He has never played professionally in North America and hasn't played in a couple of seasons.
- Dmitry Fakhrutdinov, a defenceman with Yaroslavl Lokomotiv, was not drafted by a NHL club. Whereabouts unknown.

Those who have returned to Russia and those who never left include a first-rounder, five second-rounders and three third-round picks. If a scouting staff had that many clear-cut wasted picks, they'd be roasted by their bosses and ridiculed by peers. There are bound to be complicating issues, a variety of backstories. And I'm sure some of them play out like the Blue Jackets' frustrations with Plekhanov—that promises were frequently made and, at the last minute, broken, that third parties emerged to bog down negotiations. Still, it's a sorry record after the expectations raised at the world juniors in 2003.

The professional underachievement of the Russian '83s becomes even more mystifying when held up against the careers of their Canadian counterparts. This was far from the best Canadian under-20 team in the eyes of the scouts. Yet somehow the players on its roster far exceeded the low expectations that were set. Pity poor Alexandre Rouleau, a defenceman who was playing for the Wheeling Nailers of the East Coast league before being shipped over to the San Antonio Rampage this winter. A third-rounder of Pittsburgh in 2001, Rouleau is the only alumnus of the Canadian under-20 team in Halifax who won't play in the NHL this season.

NHL scouts will admit that the hard feelings between the NHL and the Russian hockey federation have had a chilling effect on the stock of Russian players in recent drafts. I suspect that the disappointing '83s have scared NHL scouts off subsequent Russian classes. The roster of the Russian team here has only one player selected in the first round of an NHL draft—and only one more who is likely to be, Cherepanov.[18]

December 28, 2006, Hotel Dalecarlia, Leksand

The only player with as much to prove as Jonathan Toews is another collegian, Jack Johnson of the U.S. team. Johnson's not struggling at the University of Michigan the way Toews has been at North Dakota. No, for Johnson it's a matter of getting past image and innuendo.

There's one image of Johnson that comes to Canadian hockey fans' minds when his name is mentioned. In the waning seconds

---

18. Evgeni Malkin, a 1988 birthday and a rookie star with the Pittsburgh Penguins, would be eligible to play for Russia.

of Canada's victory over the U.S. at last year's world juniors, Johnson almost decapitated Steve Downie with a stealthy elbow out of the view of the officials. If Downie's performance was to be believed, Johnson landed a blow that qualified as criminal assault. If Johnson's who-me expression was to be trusted, no harm was intended.

The scouts aren't worried about Johnson's penchant for rough stuff. Fact is, they like the edge he plays with. No, the scouts question his decision-making—not decisions on the ice as much as career choices.

The Carolina Hurricanes were eager to sign Johnson last season, but they gave him a pass when he enrolled at Michigan. Johnson could have signed with the club at the end of the Wolverines' season and joined them on their run to the Stanley Cup. Johnson told the Hurricanes that he was heading back to Ann Arbor for his sophomore year. Nobody in hockey thinks he needs another season of college hockey; he's spinning his wheels at Michigan. The Hurricanes heard the rumbles that he was planning to stay in school beyond his sophomore season, even through to his senior year. Not that he was a particularly dedicated student, just that he loved being Joe College.

Carolina decided it had had enough and traded his rights at the start of the NHL season—seemingly at a discount—to the Los Angeles Kings. Having suffered a small plague of injuries, the Hurricanes needed immediate help, and Johnson was their best asset.

I'm prone to jet lag on trips to Europe. Tonight, after several hours of staring at the ceiling and overhearing the contented snoring of scouts in neighbouring rooms, I head down to the lobby, just to have a better view of the sun rising and to beat the rush to the breakfast buffet. There I see Jack Johnson—not the player, but the father of the player. For the sake of clarity, I'll just refer to him as Mr. Johnson.

I've never felt like I had a line on Mr. Johnson's son—Sidney Crosby's best friend when the two were at Shattuck–St. Mary's. Two teenagers couldn't seem farther apart in personality, Johnson as brash and outgoing as Crosby was cautious and respectful. Yet at their draft a couple of years ago in Ottawa, Johnson and Crosby seemed inseparable—having breakfast together, heading to the gym. It was the nearest thing in hockey to, say, the enduring friendship of Don Rickles and Bob Newhart. And I couldn't figure out why Johnson would stay in college if he had a chance at a Stanley Cup. At that point I'd think that "The Victors," the Michigan fight song, would sound sort of tinny. Anyone who has covered the NHL would presume that it's a bit of gamesmanship, players and agents using college to leverage out a better deal from NHL clubs.[19] And media types would also presume that meddlesome parents had signed off on the squeezing of the NHL.

The late-night session with Mr. Johnson puts it all in perspective. I've seen him around the hotel my first two days here—he has been in the company of the missus and their grade-school-aged son Kenny. The Johnsons have mostly kept to themselves—it seems other American parents have a bit of history together, and so the Johnsons are off on their own.

Mr. Johnson introduces himself. I've heard that he's as much a wild card as his son. What's more, I've seen his video on YouTube: footage of Mr. Johnson dancing around in the stands at a Michigan game. On campus, Mr. Johnson is almost as well known as his son. During stoppages in games, students will chant, "Hey, Mr. Johnson!" and after a time he'll stand up and shake and rhythmlessly shimmy. Just think of Dancing Homer brought to life, albeit with a hip replacement.

Over a couple of beers, with dawn not so far off, Mr. Johnson gives me the rundown: he was a player himself, a member of an NCAA championship team at the University of Wisconsin, coached

---

19. *Cough.* The NCAA prohibits scholarship athletes from having agents, so players who attend U.S. colleges have—*cough*—"family advisors" who, to a one, are certified as agents by the NHL Players' Association.

by Hall of Famer Badger Bob Johnson. After the championship season he transferred to Michigan State because he wanted to play
hockey and football. "I didn't try out for the NHL after my college
career," he says. "I went out for the Dallas Cowboys and got cut."
The way he talks—and *talks*—about his days on campus makes it
sound as if playing in the NHL or the NFL would have been a
comedown from the college life.

These days, Mr. Johnson works in promotions and marketing for
car-racing outfits, which affords him the comfort of a home in a tony
Detroit suburb. He's able to indulge a fantasy that must be harboured
by many forty- and fifty-somethings: reliving his glory days through
his son. That Mr. Johnson attended Michigan's fiercest rival doesn't
diminish the warm, fuzzy feeling he gets when he hears "The
Victors" and sees Jack. After all, Mrs. Johnson attended Michigan, as
did her father, a two-sport man in days of yore. Any sort of attachment
Mr. Johnson might have had to Wisconsin or East Lansing was severed long before Jack went to Ann Arbor. "Jack was seven years old
when he used to get autographs from players coming off the ice at
Michigan games," Mr. Johnson says. "People ask when did he decide
to go to Michigan . . . Jack was so young, I don't know if he can actually remember the first time he said he was going there."

Mr. Johnson may be a fierce defender of his son (repeating time
and again that Jack is "just a great kid") and fantasist (believing that
one day his son and Sidney Crosby will be reunited as teammates
with the Montreal Canadiens). But while it's a favourite pastime of
parents of American players to bash the families of opponents and
teammates alike, Mr. Johnson doesn't have a bad word to say about
anyone.

By dawn I have my read on Mr. Johnson—he seems more like
Jack's older brother than his father, his friend more than a mentor,
his teammate more than a coach. I have to believe that there are no
complications in the Johnsons' story, no ulterior motive, no plot to
leverage a deal. Money seems like the last thing the Johnsons have
on their mind. Jack has years to make money, but just one chance to
wear the Maize and Blue.

December 29, 2006, Ejendals Arena, Leksand

CANADA 3 GERMANY 1

Everyone has a favourite flavour, and I presume that scouts are the same. The best example is a friend, a goaltending scout. A high draft pick back in his day, he fell short of a lasting NHL career, though not for lack of talent. No, ultimately he was undone by bad timing, bad injuries and a bad attitude that was a byproduct of his bad timing and bad injuries. In his scouting career he has shown a preference for physically unimpressive goaltenders who are more upbeat than he ever was. Another scout summed up his friend's underdog fixation neatly: "He was a good athlete with a bad attitude. When it comes to goaltenders, he looks for what he wasn't—an average athlete with a good attitude."[20]

I have a soft spot for swift and skilled defencemen who might be a tad small, blueliners who will take off with the puck or join the rush as a third man. I'm not quite old enough to feel a nostalgic pull for the rover position. It's just a matter of action. Stay-at-home players are valuable to a winning club, but did anyone go to games to see Ken Daneyko rather than Scott Niedermayer? Of course, I'd be a sucker for Mark Katic of the Sarnia Sting, the speedy but undersized blueliner from the summer under-18s. A defenceman on the Canadian team, Kris Russell of the Medicine Hat Tigers, falls into

---

20. This scout's interest in goaltenders whose profiles contrast with his own evokes Billy Beane, the Oakland Athletics' general manager and the central character in Michael Lewis's *Moneyball*. As a high school ballplayer, Beane was a physical specimen and immensely gifted. Scouts liked him even when his play tailed off in his draft year, just because he *looked* like a future great. That he was an indifferent professional he put down to his lack of instincts and desire. As a scout and a general manager, he didn't care about what a player looked like. All he cared about was performance, which meant he sometimes placed his chips on not-in-the-mould players who did the little things well.

the category as well. He's listed as five foot ten and 175 pounds, but that seems at least an inch and ten pounds too generous. I'd be following him with interest even if he hadn't been drafted by Columbus in the third round of the 2005 draft.

Canada's win over Germany clinches a spot in the semifinal for the defending champions and also offers a nice showcase for Russell. He opens the scoring seven minutes into the game in a situation made to measure for him: a four-on-four on an Olympic ice surface. Russell is the trailer on a rush up the ice—it almost seems like he has to hit the brakes to avoid overtaking the puck carrier, Andrew Cogliano, a slick and speedy centre who plays at the University of Michigan. Cogliano finds Russell with a drop pass and beats German goaltender Timo Pielmeier with a one-timer. It's a one-sided game, Canada outshooting the Germans 16–3 in the second period. By the time Russell scores his second goal in the third period, the outcome isn't in any doubt.

Russell's farther along than Katic—Russell's a couple of years older, and this is his second turn with the under-20 team. I don't know what Russell's game looked like at age seventeen and how it would compare to Katic's. One measure would be their respective draft positions coming into junior. The Medicine Hat Tigers selected Russell in the eighth round of the WHL's bantam draft. In his draft year, Katic was high up on OHL teams' lists, and the Sting selected him in the first round, second overall. The edge here would seem to go to Katic, but there's a problem with the math—the fact that the WHL drafts its players as fifteen-year-olds and the OHL as sixteen-year-olds. Russell must have looked like a runaway from a Cub Scout troop when he was fifteen. By eighteen, he had started to look like a prospect, but not an elite pro prospect—he was still there when Columbus's pick came up in the third round, sixty-seventh overall.

Russell took home a world junior gold medal and was named to the WHL's second all-star team last season, but he's still typecast. Canadian coach, Craig Hartsburg, has leaned on his top four defencemen: Marc Staal paired with Ryan Parent, Luc Bourdon with Kristopher Letang, all returnees from last year's team, all pro prospects in the conventional mode. Hartsburg has given Russell spot duty and made him a power-play specialist, as if he were too small to succeed in a greater role at this level.

Russell's an intriguing player: less than a sure thing, but one with big risk and reward. What's more, he has a colourful story—his father worked in the rodeo but pushed his sons away from the cowboy life because "you can't buy anything with belt buckles." Blue Jackets scout John Williams told me he made an unforgettable first impression. The first time Williams viewed Russell, Medicine Hat was in against the Kootenay Ice, the team that drafted Kris's twin brother, Ryan, the first time the brothers had ever played against each other. *And* the first time they fought in a game. "They came out to centre ice and took off their helmets and went at it," Williams said. "Their teammates and the crowd went crazy."

Many scouts wouldn't have given a second glance to a defenceman a couple of inches under six feet in the old NHL. But the league's rule changes have put a premium on mobility and skill rather than just size—the scouts need only look at the successes of players like Buffalo's Brian Campbell. Russell won't skate into the NHL next season. He might not make it the season after that. Or at all. But wherever he lands, he'll be fun to watch, and the Blue Jackets, as heavily criticized as they have been for their draft record, seem to have done all right with a third-rounder in 2005. To a one, scouts in other organizations give fair credit to Columbus for the selection of Russell. Plucking a third-rounder who'll land on two Canadian teams at the world juniors and win all-star berths in the WHL is no small feat.

December 31, 2006, Ejendals Arena, Leksand

USA 3 Sweden 2 (overtime)

It's a game that the Americans need desperately and that the host Swedes can afford to lose, so maybe the result shouldn't come as a surprise. How it comes about, though, could hardly be more dramatic.

Midway through the second period, the U.S. trails 1–0 and looks to be reeling. The Swedes try to physically take the game to the Americans, which is like David running Goliath, given that the U.S. players are at least ten pounds heavier on average. For a time, it works, but then, against the tide of play, the Americans pick up goals from Patrick Kane and Ryan Stoa barely ninety seconds apart. That silences the crowd, and the energy of the Swedes drops a notch thereafter.

The precocious Kane is a revelation. He had an impact in previous games, but here he's playing with surpassing confidence. Not that he's playing alone—on the opening goal, Kyle Okposo creates a turnover and a scoring chance for Kane with a crushing forecheck on defenceman Niklas Hjalmarsson behind the Swedish goal. Kane finishes his chance with sure hands, then goes into an exaggerated dip and pose after the goal—something that might fit right in on a stage with bodybuilders during a posedown, but sort of laughable here, considering how scrawny he is.

Through the third period, it looks as though the Americans will make the lead hold up. The big names from last year's draft struggle. Erik Johnson picks up a couple of minors and a misconduct, while Nicklas Backstrom is on the periphery of the play, at least for fifty-nine and a half minutes. With fourteen seconds to go, with the Swedish goaltender pulled in favour of a sixth attacker, Backstrom sets up Fredrik Pettersson for the tying goal and sends the game into overtime. It would be tough enough for the American teens to keep their composure in any situation, but this is absolute crisis—they need a win in overtime. Given the tournament's scoring system, a win in a shootout would not be enough to advance to the medal round.

Regulation time is Kane's showcase, overtime Jack Johnson's. Swedish defenceman Jonas Ahnelov takes a chintzy cross-checking penalty a minute into sudden death. Ahnelov's stickwork wouldn't crush a grape, but no matter. The Swedes look to have killed off the penalty, Ahnelov standing at the gate, when Jack Johnson walks in from the point and unleashes a howitzer. A highlight-reel goal that ranks alongside his father's dancing on YouTube. And as his father might, Jack Johnson slamdances with teammates and the plexiglass in celebration.

I'm already down at ice level when the Americans skate off the ice. The crowd—mostly Swedes in blue and gold, though flecked with face-painted blood-red Canadians—gives a polite round of applause to the winners as they walk through the Zamboni gate en route to their dressing room. "Yeah, they booed us and now they love us," Jack Johnson yells as the U.S. team leaves the ice.

Well, maybe not.

The U.S. dressing room is so awash in teenage testosterone that I wish I'd worn Wellington boots to the rink. In contrast with Canadian players, who seem to go through the tournament with an exaggerated stoicism, the Americans fall somewhere between the kids who line the ring at a WWE show and the wrestlers inside the ropes. The contrast between the teams and programs couldn't be starker.

Patrick Kane fits in beyond all expectations on the ice, but off the ice seemingly less so. That's not to say that he lacks confidence, just that he doesn't feel the need to shout out. Though he's making his debut with the U.S. under-20 team, Kane acts as if he's been here before. He may look callow, standing on the periphery of the scene, taking everything in with a deadpan, wide-eyed expression. On looks, he could pass for a waif in a velvet painting. But as soon as he talks, it's clear that has grown up fast. It seems like he's already a pro.

I ask him what it's like to be one of the younger players on the team, but he's quick to point out that he's not the youngest—van Riemsdyk being the lone '89 birthday—and that he knew a lot of the players going into the tournament.

"It's different being here instead of London," Kane says. "My parents aren't here, but they've made it out to practically all my games with the Knights. My father had a business selling cars, but he sold that. It's not just that my parents are back home. It's different here in a lot of ways—not just the bigger ice surface. The team is different. It's maybe a bit more businesslike with the Knights."

When I ask him which he prefers, the rah-rah of the American team or the Knights' pro ethic, Kane won't commit. You might presume that there's not such a big difference, but I'd counter that the hockey cultures of the two countries are as far apart as Jeremy Roenick and the most circumspect Sutter brother. I suspect that, in time, Kane may end up closer to the Canadian model. As a fourteen-year-old looking for better competition than he could find in Buffalo's youth leagues, he headed off to Detroit, where he moved into the home of Pat Verbeek,[21] who settled there when his NHL career wound down. Kane ended up richer for the experience, though perhaps not the way he and his family imagined. Verbeek gave him an introduction to NHL family values. Many suspected he'd go the college route, like most of the others on this U.S. under-20 team, but he had to figure that what was good for a billet with a Stanley Cup ring would be good for him.[22] Kane's had more of the same NHL grounding in London with Dale Hunter as the head coach, Dave Gagner as the assistant coach and Mark Hunter as the general manager. Just seeing Kane up close with his teammates here, he looks more like a bemused spectator than a participant. Save van Riemsdyk, he's the youngest among them, but Kane still seems older than them all, probably older than some of the parents.

January 2, 2007, FM Matsson Arena, Mora

U.S.A. 6 FINLAND 3

The American juniors looked vulnerable against the Swedes, but against the Finns their confidence is abundant, even toxic. The

---

21. Has there ever been a less celebrated 500-goal scorer in the NHL? Verbeek was fairly openly derided by his own teammates when he neared the milestone. "Pat getting 500," Brendan Shanahan said. "That's a lot of rebounds."

22. A native of Sarnia, Verbeek played with the Sudbury Wolves.

Finns stay in the chase against a bigger, more talented U.S. team—the score is tied two-all after two periods, three-all midway through the third. But four consecutive minors with about ten minutes to go, successive five-on-three penalty kills, hand the game to the U.S. and put the spotlight once more on Patrick Kane. Kane, who picked up a goal in the second period, sets up the winning goal by Peter Mueller and the insurance goal by Trevor Lewis on the next shift. Though Mueller is supposed to be running the power play from the point, Kane takes the lead in this quarter-final.

The Finns' frustration mounts and they're whistled for four minors and a game misconduct with less than three minutes to play—not that they're running the U.S. players, they're getting nabbed for slashing and hooking and beefing to the ref about the unfairness of it all. With a two-goal lead and yet another two-man advantage with less than a minute to go, the decent thing would have been to call off the dogs and just keep the puck away from the Finns. Instead, the Americans run their five-on-three power play as if they need a goal for victory. And when Jack Johnson scores with twenty seconds to go, he celebrates as if he has scored in overtime of the seventh game of the Stanley Cup final—skating to centre ice, away from his teammates, as though he doesn't need to be congratulated by them when he can congratulate himself. Again, it's stuff you'd see at a pro wrestling show.

I have questions for Johnson, Kane and the rest, but U.S. team officials say that there will be no media access to the players after the game, citing the demands of games on back-to-back nights. Not that the American kids were too drained to run their power play needlessly in the last minute. Later on, the U.S. players mingle on the arena concourse with their parents. That's the USA Hockey program in a nutshell: the players aren't held accountable by anyone, while the program is hostage to the parents.

January 3, 2007, Ejendals Arena, Leksand

CANADA 2 U.S.A. 1 (SHOOTOUT)

Other games between Canada and the U.S. have featured better players—just think of the Hall of Famers on the ice in the 1996 World Cup or the 2002 Olympic final. But it's hard to think of a more dramatic contest between the two nations than this game.

A lot of games fade from memory five minutes after watching them—it's true of reporters, true of scouts. Not this one, though.

The IIHF's rules are so arcane that you'd swear they're making them up as they go along. The Canadian team comes up against an example in this game. Even though the Canadians are undefeated and finished atop their group, the Americans are designated the home team in this semifinal game and own the last line change. It's in the fine print in the IIHF rulebook—a stipulation that teams meeting for the second time in a tournament must alternate the home-ice advantage. Canada had the last change in the opening round, so the U.S. gets it in the medal round.

The Americans have saved their best for this game. They also get the benefit of a lucky bounce. After a scoreless first period a pass attempt by the U.S. captain, Taylor Chorney, banks off Canada's defenceman Marc Staal and past goaltender Carey Price. Through the rest of the second period and deep into the third it looks like that single goal might hold up. Canada's forwards struggle to generate any chances against the Americans' Johnsons on the blueline.

As he did last year, Steve Downie seizes the moment, and does so in character. Downie has been goading the Americans all game long with profane threats of bodily harm, though to no effect. It's unclear what he does to set off Mike Carmen, but it provokes the American forward to draw an elbowing penalty. On the penalty kill, Blake Geoffrion, great-grandson of Howie Morenz, is whistled for interference. Canada generates chances in a flurry, and defenceman Luc Bourdon wires a shot past U.S. goaltender Jeff Frazee.

The sixty minutes of regulation are tense, but the ten minutes of overtime are excruciating. The Canadian captain, Kristopher Letang, takes a high-sticking penalty four minutes in, and on the ensuing four-on-three power play the Americans buzz the net for the full two minutes without a whistle, without a loss of possession. Mueller and Kane own the puck, and it seems like they're enjoying having the Canadians sweat it out. The sequence that will stay with me after this tournament is the play of Ryan Parent during the penalty kill. Parent, a first-round pick of Nashville in 2005, is the right defenceman, on the far side of the ice from the Canadian bench, so he's stranded out there—too far away to get over for a line change. The Americans have several glorious chances to score but can't close the deal, thanks to the work of Parent, Jonathan Toews, Marc Staal and, especially, goaltender Carey Price. At the buzzer, Price has turned aside twelve shots in the overtime, while Frazee saw the puck only twice.

The game goes to a shootout, and again the rules of the IIHF are at variance with those North American fans are familiar with. The teams alternate shooters in a round of five attempts—but a team can send a player out for more than one attempt, just not consecutive ones. If the teams are still tied after five attempts, then it's sudden-death on the shootout—the first make-and-miss determining the victor.[23] Toews and Price are again the stars for Canada—Toews scores on all three of his attempts, including the winner on Canada's seventh shot, while Price shuts down a deke by Mueller on the Americans' last chance.

Mueller looks wounded while the Canadians celebrate. On the U.S.'s first attempt of the shootout, after Downie had missed,

---

23. The IIHF rules are so arcane that even its own officials mess up on the shootout. Canada has the first shot in the shootout's round of five, but when the shootout goes to the sudden-death tiebreak, the first shot should have gone to the U.S. The IIHF on-ice officials miss this, and it will lead to a halfhearted protest by the U.S. after the game.

Mueller beat Price with a wrist shot to the glove side, then skated by the Canadian bench with palms turned up, a shrug and a big smile, as if to say that it couldn't have been easier. Lost in youthful hubris, Mueller didn't know from tempting fate, though he might have learned about it by the time he skates off the ice. Mueller scored later in the shootout—another wrist shot, this one just under the crossbar, a pure goal scorer's goal, but his smug theatrics make the Canadians' victory sweeter and his role in the American defeat that much tougher to accept. There's no dancing in the end zone for running the ball down to the one-yard line.

RUSSIA 4 SWEDEN 2

The second semifinal doesn't match the drama of the afternoon session. The Swedes run out to a lead in the first period on a goal by Jonas Junland, but thereafter the Russians take over, scoring four times without a reply, without the Swedes registering a memorable chance. In the second period, Semen Varlamov only sees the puck twice, neither shot a real tester.

Alexei Cherepanov picks up his fifth goal of the tournament, doing nothing to betray the fact that he's the youngest forward in the Russian lineup. Watching him, I think he'd be the perfect complement to Patrick Kane—Kane has a way of controlling the puck on the cycle and finding teammates in traffic, while Cherepanov seems to do a lot of his best work without the puck, getting himself in position to score.

I sit with Don Boyd during the second semifinal. He seems weary, though I wouldn't bank on it being jet lag. I'd put it down to another disappointing season in Columbus.

I show Boyd a sample background profile of a player. I want to keep it simple—400 words if possible, no more than a page. And I don't want the profiles to reflect my opinions about talent—I can't pretend to be qualified to make judgments about players. I just want to talk to a few trustworthy sources who've worked with or played with a prospect. I want to be able to provide a quote sheet that Boyd and other scouts can refer to quickly prior to an interview with a prospect, something that can give them a running start in their twenty-minute sessions at the combine. I chose to do a player that his staff is familiar with.

Junior coach: "Hard on himself—harder than we are on him a lot of the time. Very up and down emotionally. He's a hyper kid a lot of the time. He's had a couple of setbacks and he doesn't get over them quickly. They stay with him longer than they would most other kids."

A teammate: "He's in the gym all the time. He wants to watch video [of games] all the time. He thinks the more time that he spends on the game, the better he'll be."

A former billet: "We had him his first year away from home [when he left to play midget AAA]. He went home after a month or so. He said he was homesick and I think he was. I also think that his father wasn't real happy with [the son's] playing situation. Anyway, he came back after a time. He wasn't a bad kid—there weren't issues with the rules of the house—but he wasn't the most socially adept player we've put up, and we've put up kids from very small towns."

A coach who worked with him in a tournament: "It was a bad situation for him. We just had other players and I knew them. I didn't know him that well. I knew he had physical talent, some great skill, but I wondered about his game judgment sometimes. Of course, he was younger, but still, compared to other players his own age, I don't think he was reading the game as well as he should have been—trying to do too much sometimes. I think that's a question that's still hanging out there."

Another source: "His father seems to be an issue."

The backgrounder has six sources in all—I talked to a few more people, all telling the same story. I whittled them down to six, taking a representative sample. Boyd pores over it without expression.

Finally, he looks up. "I knew the father could be an issue," he says. "Yeah, something like this could be useful."

Boyd asks me how many of these I would put together. I suggest as many as twenty—using the Columbus scouts' designations, that would be their Top Tens, the next best, and a few other players of interest—this season's Tom Sestitos. Because of language and geography, I'd stick to those on North American teams.

I tell him that I've started a work-up on Esposito and a few others who are high up in NHL Central Scouting's rankings. He says he'd be interested in seeing what I come up with about Esposito and anyone else.

"I don't know that any of it can help, but it can't hurt," he says.

With that, I don't feel as though the bar has been raised too high. And of course he'll get the material at the Al Ritchie discount—I'll do it for nothing.

January 5, 2007, Ejendals Arena, Leksand

CANADA 4 RUSSIA 2

Canada and Russia meet in the final for the third consecutive time. And for the third time in a row, the Canadians come away with gold medals. Unlike the previous two finals, however, the Russians lose by fewer than five goals. The outcome remains in doubt into the waning minutes. In the previous two under-20 finals, the Canadians dominated. This time, they look physically and emotionally spent midway through the second period.

Then again, their victory over the U.S. must have felt like the perfect denouement rather than the penultimate game—even a victory lap would be a letdown, never mind a whole other game.

The Canada–U.S. semifinal was emotionally tortuous—too many swings in fortune to count. The final, though, is one ebb, one flow. The Canadians storm out of the gate and take a 3–0 lead on three furious shifts late in the first period. Jonathan Toews again is the defining player—drawing a penalty setting up Brad Marchand for the second goal, then roofing a shot from the slot that beats Semen Varlamov and would have beaten most NHL goaltenders.

The Russians score twice late in the second period to make a game of it, but the Canadians tighten their defensive game in the third, peeling back, clogging up the neutral zone and shutting down any passing lanes inside the perimeter in their own end of the rink. They suck the oxygen out of the rink and run out the clock.

The IIHF officials name Cherepanov the tournament's top forward, and the fact that he's even in the mix for the award is no small accomplishment for a draft-eligible player. Still, Toews was the best player in the moment of greatest need for the champions. It would be hard to explain the decision to bypass him—maybe the officials want to spread the wealth around after giving Canada's Marc Staal and Carey Price the tournament awards for best defenceman and best goaltender, respectively.

Price is an interesting case. When the Montreal Canadiens drafted him with the fifth-overall pick in the 2005 draft, the critics instantly ridiculed the decision. On the TSN broadcast of the event, Pierre Maguire described it as "off the reservation." It was probably an attempt to rework the idea of a choice coming "out of left field," but it was in dubious taste, given that Price is a Native Canadian and that his mother serves as a band leader.

Last year at this time, the Canadiens' choice of Price seemed to come out of left field because he was cut from the under-20 team after a brief tryout. Price's play here has been above reproach and yet, after the game, while his teammates celebrate, he's subdued. He looks satisfied, but nothing more than that, almost like he's outside the circle.

"There are always going to be doubters," he says. I ask him to expand on the theme, but he will go nowhere with it.

It's a tacit admission that the wound from Maguire's "off the reservation" line hasn't healed. It's also a fair indication of how young players track the media about the draft.

Eight a.m., January 6, 2007, Hotel Dalecarlia, Leksand

Most scouts moved on to Stockholm after the game and are flying out of Arlandia this morning. Only a few have stayed on at the hotel. One sits down at the table next to mine in the dining room.

"Did you hear the news about L.A.?" he asks me. "They whacked a bunch of their scouts yesterday."

On New Year's Day I was talking to Dave Taylor. Just a couple of days ago I was having breakfast with Grant Sonier, told him that I'd give him a call when I made it home.

The scout doesn't have all the details. The list of casualties will come out later. It's hard to figure out why a team would dump its staff midway through a season—especially a team that will miss the playoffs, a team that owns its own draft picks and will likely acquire others through trades at the deadline. It's harder still to figure out why a general manager would dump scouts he signed to two-year contracts last summer.

"Stuff always happens when scouts are in Europe," the scout says. "In this business you feel like you're out of the loop. You should never feel confident. Maybe they do shit like this just so we don't get a false sense of security."

Two p.m., January 6, 2007, Hovet Arena, Stockholm

DJURGARDENS 3 FROLUNDA 2 (OVERTIME)

With a couple of days before my flight home I catch a ride to a Swedish league game with Joe MacDonnell and Hakan Andersson, the Wings' European scout. Maybe some clubs would claim to have pulled as many players out of Europe in recent years as Detroit has, but none could claim to have as many late-round finds as the Red Wings. Their two franchise forwards, Pavel Datsyuk and Henrik Zetterberg, were selected 171st in 1998 and 210th overall in 2000. Going back, they selected Tomas Holmstrom 257th in 1994. Looking ahead, a player they selected with the last pick of the 2002 draft, Jonathan Ericsson, is in his first year with the Wings' AHL affiliate in Grand Rapids. When Andersson first saw Ericsson he was an ungainly centre, and he has since been converted into a defenceman. He might have a shot at the NHL in a season or two.

I'd hoped that I would see the Wings' magic at work at this Swedish league game, but if there's magic here I'm missing it. The game is deadly dull. I would nod off, but my ticket has put me beside a bunch of Frolunda fans who have driven in from Gothenburg. I suspect they might have been shirtless and fully body-painted when they started the drive. The Frolunda fans stand all game long, chant and sing nonstop, and the drummer banging the bass drum four seats to my left takes only one washroom break.

Frolunda has built its team around a bunch of older pros, many of whom have had a taste of the NHL. The best known would be Tommy Salo, the goaltender who had some playoff glory with the Edmonton Oilers and some lasting infamy for letting in an 80-foot floater that allowed Belarus to knock Sweden out of the 2002 Olympics. The Red Wings aren't interested in Salo or the others who have come home, almost certainly to stay. No, MacDonnell and Andersson are looking at prospects drafted by Detroit over the last few years. They're fringe players at this point. Christofer Lofberg is an example. The eightieth pick in the 2005 draft, Lofberg is a twenty-year-old centre who's still working his way into the Djurgardens lineup from the club's junior team. There are four players in all who could play, but only Anton Axelsson, a Frolunda forward and a Detroit seventh-round pick in 2004, sees any ice time. By the third period, the Red Wings' scouts are looking to bail out.

I'm reminded of my limits as a wannabe scout. When I watched Finland at the world juniors back in 1997, I was impressed by Tomi Kallio, a winger and the captain for the Finnish team. He seemed to have a great read of the game. I saw that Colorado had selected him eighty-first overall in 1995—a prescient pick, I thought. Kallio did come over—not as quickly as I thought—and did play a bit, but with less impact than I expected.[24] I'd ask Kallio, now with Frolunda, what happened, but there's no point—time that you waste investigating lost causes is time that could be spent on the looking for the next Zetterberg or Datsyuk.

January 16, 2007, Le Colisée, Quebec City

CANADIAN HOCKEY LEAGUE TOP PROSPECTS GAME
TEAM RED 5 TEAM WHITE 3

The summer under-18s are a frantic exercise for scouts—a scout would need the compound eyes of a housefly to track twelve draft-eligibles every shift—but it's easy to see that it would be a worthwhile one. On the other hand, I've reported from the Top Prospects Games over the years, and I have no idea why it's a significant fixture for NHL scouts. Yes, it gathers up most of the top prospects from the three major-junior leagues—not just those with Canadian birth certificates, but also players from the U.S. and Europe who've landed in the CHL. But it doesn't put the players in a position to play particularly well. They're divided up into two teams almost randomly—linemates learn each other's names one day and are expected to impress pro scouts the next. Rather than put teammates together, they're split up—tonight Patrick Kane is in white and Sam Gagner in red. It looks like a tournament game or a league playoff game, but it's a lot less. Thankfully, it's not like the NHL All-Star Game—if the players aren't positioned to play well, at least they're motivated to. They know that the scouts come out in force.[25]

---

24. Over parts of three seasons with the Atlanta Thrashers, Columbus and Philadelphia, Kallio appeared in 140 games, scoring 24 goals and adding 31 assists.

25. Unlike the NHL All-Star Game, there are not only checks thrown in this game, but even punches. My favourite dates back to the regional format. Back in

Those who have to sell the game—the broadcasters trying to attract viewers, the CHL trying to generate ticket sales—bring in celebrity coaches. This year it's Scotty Bowman, Pat Burns, Jacques Demers and Michel Bergeron. This presumes that fans will pay to see grown men stand behind the bench and occasionally pull their hands out of their pockets or whisper in the kids' ears. The real, built-in storyline should be more compelling: they're pitching this year's game as a showcase for Angelo Esposito, the star of the home-town Remparts and Central Scouting's top-ranked North American player at the mid-term. It seems like his top ranking is based on career accomplishment and not on his play this season. Every scout I've talked to who has made a trip out to the Quebec league has come away underwhelmed by Esposito. And if the lack of familiarity with teammates should hurt every prospect, Esposito, a member of Team White, and his Remparts teammate, forward Ruslan Bashkirov, would seem to have home-ice advantage. Some players here have flown in from the Pacific time zone or spent the better part of a day on the road and in the air to make it to Quebec.

But just days ago it seemed that Esposito might not play. He has had a case of the flu and dropped a few pounds. He's in the lineup, but he has told reporters he's far from 100 percent. Even if true, it's not what the scouts want to hear. They'd prefer that he not even mention the flu and just play through it—they think he's lowering the bar for himself, that he's copping a plea in advance just in case he needs it.

Esposito doesn't have a bad game, but he fails to score and comes out on the losing side with the White team. I think he has a couple of good moments. The best of them—and the most unlikely—is an

---

1995, when the game was in Kitchener, there was a classic dust-up between the Detroit Jr. Red Wings' Bryan Berard, the top-ranked draft-eligible player, and Terry Ryan, a Newfoundlander who played for the Tri-City Americans in the Dub. Just for added flavour, the fathers of the two players happened to be sitting on either side of their sons' agent, Mike Barnett. Awkward.

open-ice bodycheck that drops Sam Gagner for an eight count in the first period. Esposito also has a couple of good moves in the open ice, but really he can't win. Flu or no flu, there's no lowering of expectations. No matter how the fans urge him on, he's not Sidney Crosby or anything remotely close. He knows the reviews will be harsh.[26]

Others steal Esposito's thunder. Gagner and Kane have the puck on a string. For the Red team, Gagner's is a vertical game in straight lines, going through traffic, ducking and dodging checks on a couple of end-to-end rushes. For White, Kane's is a horizontal game in a constant weave, rolling off checks on the cycle and, when defenders least expect it, hitting his linemates with passes through tangles of sticks, skates and bodies.

It's not just these names featured near the top of Central Scouting's midterm list who are eclipsing Esposito. More come from way down the page.

Keven Veilleux, a forward with Victoriaville, ranked No. 16 according to Central, is listed at six-foot-five and 205 pounds but plays bigger. His crushing checks have players on the Red team looking over their shoulders when gathering the puck in their own end of the rink. Jakub Voracek, the Czech forward who landed with the Halifax Mooseheads, is almost knocked into the Atlantic time zone when Veilleux drills him on a forecheck that sets up the game's opening goal for Oscar Moller. Veilleux picks up a goal of his own later on and makes a strong case to be named the White team's best player. Instead, the honour goes to Moller, a Swede who plays a face-first game (with missing teeth to show for it). No. 35 on Central's midterm list, the franchise player with the expansion Chilliwack team, Moller is the rare Euro you couldn't pick out of a Dub game without a program.

---

26. The Canadian Press story filed by Bill Beacon began: "It was Ruslan Bashkirov and not Angelo Esposito who made the Quebec Remparts fans stand and cheer."

On the winning Red side, there are all kinds of candidates for the player of the game. On the blue line, Nick Ross, the Regina defenceman who blended into the scenery in the Pats' loss in Swift Current, delivers a slew of old-school open-ice hip checks. Stefan Legein, the industrious little forward with Mississauga, No. 33 on Central's list, wasn't even originally invited to the game — he was brought to Quebec as a last-minute addition when a few other players were scratched due to injury. Legein hacks and whacks all night long, bringing a little menace to the game and outplaying a lot of more heralded names. And bringing both menace and some outrageous skill to the game in a far larger package is Akim Aliu, who won the one-lap race in the prospects' skills competition by a comfortable margin last night. At the end of the game, Pat Burns cites Aliu as the player who impresses him the most.

Five slots below Legein on Central's midterms, Aliu picks up a couple of assists, but he has a shot at a hat trick in a five-minute stretch of the third period. Three times he bursts in on goal — the first time hitting a crossbar in traffic, the second time chasing down a puck on a penalty for a partial breakaway and finally fighting through a check, barrelling into goaltender Tyson Sexsmith of the Vancouver Giants. Just in case scouts might not have noticed him, Aliu gives Angelo Esposito a facewash with a couple of minutes to go and tries to goad him into a fight. The officials have to separate them, though Aliu won't go quietly. Maybe he doesn't like the fact that Esposito hammered Gagner, Aliu's friend and teammate from the Toronto Marlies minor midget team a couple of years ago. Aliu jaws at Esposito all the way to the penalty box — and the top-ranked draft-eligible player looks utterly defeated.

January 28, 2007, St. Michael's Arena, Toronto

PLYMOUTH 6 ST. MICHAEL'S 3

About seven months have passed since I heard Tom Sestito's name mentioned in the Columbus war room. He wasn't on

Central Scouting's radar. I saw his team, the Plymouth Whalers, last season and I had no recollection of him. A player who's landed at No. 31 on Columbus's list should have made some impression. Not until Plymouth comes to St. Michael's do I get to see what all the fuss is about.

Sestito is a load. James Neal—a teammate and the best measure to set against Sestito—was the muscle up front for the Canadian team at the world under-20s in Sweden, the biggest forward, easily the biggest hitter. Neal, a Dallas second-rounder in 2005, is the best player on the ice against the Majors, with a goal, two assists and three punishing right hands in a unanimous decision over St. Michael's tough guy Rob Kwiet. He has pro size, at six foot three and 210 pounds, and looks like he could step right into the Stars' lineup. Yet when Sestito scores the insurance goal in the third period against St. Michael's, Neal comes over to pat him on the back—and has to reach up. Neal looks a helmet shorter than Sestito.

Altitude is a significant part of Sestito's upside, but not the only part. He scored ten goals last season but he's on pace for more than forty this year. He's still learning to use his size—he's not a great skater, more upright than the textbook power forward. But that's stuff he can work on. His read of play isn't a strength, either. Still, he plays hard. The fact that he was the Whalers' first choice to be on the ice for a five-on-three penalty kill says something about the coach's confidence in him.

The doors of the NHL are now supposed to be open to the little man, thanks to the rule changes. But NHL guys love size—always have, always will. The Flyers are famously the most size-obsessed franchise. A Flyer exec once told me that his definition of a prospect was "a guy who can stand flat-footed and shit in a pickup truck." And when you look at the breakthrough of a guy like Dustin Penner in Anaheim, you have to presume that size is never going to be held against you. Fact is, with giants like Penner and Sestito, size buys them time. A team will be more patient with the big player, presuming it takes him more time to get his act together.

Funny thing, but in bygone days you didn't see the likes of Zdeno

Chara, Hal Gill, Penner and other contemporary giants of the game. I remember when Bob Dailey was a giant with the Marlies. At six foot four, maybe six-five, Dailey would be a big guy today, but no giant, not out of the box. I'm sure that in days of yore guys like Sestito and these others would have been considered too big to play the game—some sort of bunkum about bad backs, like the old NFL teams that thought weight-lifting made players muscle-bound.

February 2, 2007, Credit Union Arena, Saskatoon

RED DEER 4 SASKATOON 1

The Blades are the weakest team in the Dub. Red Deer is better, but not one of the league's powerhouses. It's a chance, though, to see two players from last summer's Canadian under-18 team: Colton Gillies with the Blades and Brandon Sutter with the Rebels. Both are, barring injury, guaranteed a place in the first round of the NHL draft. Gillies is the nephew of Clark Gillies, the hard-rock winger who was a cornerstone of the Islanders' Stanley Cup–winning teams. Sutter is the son of Red Deer coach Brent Sutter, who was also on a couple of the Islanders' championship teams. Brandon also has five uncles who had long, distinguished NHL careers. His cousin, Brett Sutter, Darryl's son, is captain of the Rebels.

It seems easy to project Gillies into a pro role—it won't be much different than the one he plays here. He's a big winger whose strongest assets are his skating and his willingness to throw his weight around. His puck skills are basic. He crashes and bangs against the Rebels and he'll crash and bang when he gets to the NHL—the defencemen he'll be running into the end boards will be bigger, but by that time so will he.

Sutter is a more intriguing player—a better player than Gillies, but one more difficult to project. I track him through every shift. He's not gifted—or at least, not gifted with something obvious. His game isn't beautiful to watch. His skating mechanics are awkward, coltish. Back in the summer I mentioned to one scout that Brandon Sutter was a runner, not a skater, and his rejoinder was swift. "Did you ever watch the other Sutters skate?" True enough. Brandon Sutter's uncles played thousands of games in the NHL on the strength of everything but their skating. It's not just that he's a smart player, but rather that he makes the right decision on every play.

I hear a couple of rumbles around the Rebels. One: that Brandon Sutter has to take more crap on the ice than any other player in the Dub. The name on the back of his sweater makes him a target of every tough guy and miscreant around the league. "They keep pushing him and pushing him and he never backs down," one league regular told me. Two: that Brent Sutter won't let Brandon use creatine, a legal though somewhat controversial supplement as commonplace as chewing gum in many hockey dressing rooms. Players and other athletes have told me about creatine being nasty stuff, about some gawdawful side effects. There had to be at least a few creatine users on the Canadian teams Brent Sutter coached to world junior titles. The same holds true of his Red Deer dressing rooms over the years—not that he, the team or even the CHL or Hockey Canada signed off on it. At one level it has to be a hockey judgment of a coach—that Brandon's development as a player wouldn't be helped by creatine and might even be hurt by it. It also has to be the judgment of a father who wouldn't put his son in harm's way.

February 23, 2007, Hershey Centre

OTTAWA 5 MISSISSAUGA 2

"Courage" is a word thrown around sports pages so freely that it's about as devalued as the Mexican peso. So I won't use "courage" or any derivative to describe the performance of Logan Couture in this game. "Guts"? Fine. "Courage," though, is a little much. And if it's a little much for sportswriters—those who write about "teams of destiny" and the like—it would only get a laugh out of scouts.

Logan Couture's bad-luck streak must be approaching a Canadian junior hockey record. First the cut on his leg at the under-18 tryouts, then mono, now both knees. He hasn't played in a couple of weeks and hasn't even made it through a hard skate in that time. Over that stretch, the 67's have plunged in the standings. And over that stretch, he must be scaring off scouts and teams.

I've come away with one impression from the times I've talked to Couture: He's a little young for his age. He's admittedly "quiet." He says he had never been away from home for more than a few days before going off to Ottawa to play for the 67's. He's an honour student, product of a middle-class background (father a firefighter, mother a gym teacher). If a criticism could be levelled against him as a player, it would be "shy" in a hockey sense, or the pejorative "soft." Couture and "guts" aren't a couple of words I'd throw together. Coming back from the cut leg wouldn't cut it. Rushing back into the lineup after mono wouldn't do it, either. Those would get him marks for attendance not transcendence.

Couture shouldn't be any good at all against Mississauga. Ottawa coach Brian Kilrea tells me before the game that he's going to try to spot Couture early in the game to see if he can contribute. He's as good as his word. He gives Couture a shift here and a shift there—he might be on course for a total of ten minutes of ice time. By the third period, though, Kilrea is double-shifting him and Couture winds up with closer to twenty-five minutes of ice time and the first-star honours.

It's a game of power plays: Ottawa has eleven, the Ice Dogs seven. It's a game of oddities: Both Mississauga goals are short-handed, Stefan Legein's coming on a three-on-five, and one of Ottawa's three powerplay goals comes on a *six*-on-three situation (two Ice Dogs in the box and Ottawa's goaltender pulled on a delayed penalty). But most of all it's Couture's shining moment. His numbers (two goals, an assist, plus-one) don't tell the story. He's his best at the time of greatest need.

Late in the first period, Couture's bad luck seems to carry over to the team. Ottawa out-shoots the Ice Dogs 26–11 but is trailing 1–0 on Legein's goal. Couture, who struggles in his first shifts back from injury, beats Mississauga goaltender Andrew Loverock late in the period to tie the game at one. Thereafter he finds his timing and confidence. On every shift, he dictates play. He scores the winning goal late in the second—the only even-strength goal until the empty-netter at game's end. It's no classic: Couture lets loose a long floating slapshot and Loverock channels Tommy Salo vs. Belarus. The pucks hits his shoulder, bounces twenty feet in the air and then trickles into the net.

It's not the goals, not the plays he makes for teammates, not anything at all on the ice that impresses most. What sticks with me is the scene in the trainer's room after the game. When Couture gets off the trainer's table after being iced down, he can barely walk. It looks like he won't play another game this season he's so banged up. I don't know if rushing back from mono was brave or reckless. This game, though, leaves no doubt about his guts. I'd mention that to Kilrea but I'd get a profanity in a cloud of cigar smoke for my trouble.

I checked Adrian Foster's season stats before the game—he's been out since mid-December with a knee injury and it doesn't look like he's coming back soon.

No one accuses Stefan Legein of being shy. On the three-on-five goal he scored, Legein could have dumped the puck into Ottawa's end and peeled back. Ninety-nine percent of players would have done just that. But Legein took on two 67's without any help and drove to the net without any support except for the fans' cheering. After the game I catch up to one coach who had worked with Legein in an all-star game and tell him about the double-shorthanded goal. The coach gives me a profile that seems a perfect fit: "He'll be a pest in the league. The question is whether he's Darcy Tucker, who has more offensive skill, or Sean Avery, who's just annoying but effective. I think he's more like Tucker offensively but personality-wise he's Avery. He's the most confident kid in a room full of better players. Sean Avery dates starlets that star players in Los Angeles wouldn't have the nerve to go up and talk to. That's Stefan Legein. Three-on-five, no problem. One-on-two at centre ice, go for it. He's a WTF [what the f—]player. You need those guys just for energy but if there's any skill that goes with it, you've got a player."

February 24, 2007, Hershey Centre, Mississauga

SUDBURY 5 MISSISSAUGA 4 (SHOOTOUT)

A weird and at times not so wonderful game.

Weird: Sudbury looks to be in control when Akim Aliu finishes off a set-up from Kevin Baker to give the Wolves a 3–1 lead late in the first period. The Ice Dogs look like they're done when they give up another goal in the second period. They're listless and they're playing without their offensive catalyst, Stefan Legein, who's under suspension for a game misconduct at the end of the 67's game. Other regulars are also out of the home team's line-up.

Not so wonderful for the Wolves coach Mike Foligno: He puts Aliu out on a penalty kill in the second period and the big winger runs a Mississauga forward into the boards, setting off a minor melee. Aliu gets a minor (and it could have easily been a double minor), the Ice Dogs get a new life and the game turns on one shift.

Mississauga comes all the way back and gains a point when it looks like none is to be had. The shootout is an exercise in futility— the first fourteen shooters can't find the net, a credit to the goaltenders, Sebastien Dahm for Sudbury and Andrew Loverock for the home team. Patrick Lusnak finally beats Loverock in the eighth round and everyone can go home.

I put my ear to the ground—okay, to the door at the arena—and I hear rumblings about Aliu from those around the team. I hear more negative stuff than I've heard about any other player this season. Supposedly Aliu has had trouble with billets, issues with teammates and trouble with coaches. On the last count, the operative phrase is "maintenance every day"—suggesting that the coaches have to either light a fire under him or put out one that he started with alarming regularity. Coaches seek the self-sufficient, get-along, no-maintenance types. So do NHL teams.

It's a matter for further investigation. Even discounting the buzz, Aliu's an enigma. The goal he scores here is his twentieth of the season, but he seems capable of a lot more. He looked better in that jumble of high-level draft-eligibles at the CHL Prospects Game than he does here against a Mississauga team that should easily present less of a challenge. Mike Foligno would seem to be just the right coach to get the most out of Aliu. He should be able to command his respect both as a player who dominated this league back in his day (140 points in one season with the Wolves back in the '70s) and a long-time NHLer with a 41-goal season on his resumé. Yet Foligno hasn't managed to tap into the full reserve of Aliu's potential. Twenty goals is still a pretty decent number for a draft-eligible player but Aliu must leave the Sudbury coach wanting more.

The boys at Hockey Canada have no interest in Aliu for their spring under-18 team—whether the buzz has reached their ears or they're just not that impressed with what they see on the ice doesn't matter. It's telling that a player ranked as high as Aliu is on NHL Central Scouting's mid-term list wouldn't be of interest to them.

I leave the arena thinking about the boarding penalty Aliu took—not an awful play, but awfully timed, coming when the Ice Dogs still had a life. A three-goal lead with five minutes to go in the game—that would have been the appropriate time for Aliu to settle a score and get some payback. It's like he didn't know the score or, if he did, didn't care about it. Either offence would be enough to drive a coach to distraction and to put a scout or a team off the offender.

March 9, 2007, Sudbury

I called up Akim Aliu and asked if we could meet up for lunch when he has some free time. He suggested one of the Fridays that were teacher-development days at his high school.

Aliu's bearing isn't what I expected. He's soft-spoken. He doesn't make eye contact easily. He's a little socially awkward. When we go to a restaurant downtown, he doesn't want to order anything. When he finally does, he sees a garden salad on the menu and asks the waitress if "that's the one with tomatoes.."

Aliu seems like a complicated case on the ice and from what's common knowledge about his personal history—the hazing incident and fight with Downie in Windsor, his suspensions, his performance at the Top Prospects Game. His backstory, though, is stuff you couldn't write as fiction.

Aliu's father Tai is Nigerian. I assumed as much when I saw that Akim was born in Okene, Nigeria. What I didn't know was that Akim's mother is Ukrainian and that he grew up in Kiev.[27] Tai Aliu was a geology student and a sprinter at the University of Kiev when he met Larissa, a native of the Ukraine. They married and lived in Nigeria until moving back to Kiev shortly after Akim was born. "My family didn't come to Canada until I was twelve," he says. "I didn't speak any English. We spoke Russian at home."

I ask Akim if he considers himself Canadian, Russian, Ukrainian, Nigerian, or some mix. He leans to the Ukrainian-Russian side. He says he has good memories of Kiev. "I like the Russian way of doing things in school," he says. "There are lots of things they do better."

He sounds disappointed about his family leaving Kiev—at least until he talks about his father. "The police would harass him," Akim says. "They'd pick him up on the street and take him in just because he was black. That's why my parents wanted to leave. They didn't want that for my older brother and me."

I've presumed that his skating and the speed that placed him first among the prospects at the Top Prospects Game were products of

---

27. That would explain one entry on biography of Aliu, which listed his favourite food as perogies.

Russian training. Not even close. Aliu tells me he never even put on skates until his family came to Canada, never even tried sports until he was in seventh grade. By age 12, the other players in that Top Prospects Game had been skating for eight, nine, even ten years. They already had played hundreds of games and worked on their skills at summer hockey schools. Some of those prospects, like Brandon Sutter and Sam Gagner, had learned the game from fathers who played in the NHL.

Until he came to Canada, Akim Aliu hadn't even watched hockey. The first skates he tried on were borrowed. "We were too poor to buy equipment when we first came to Canada," he says. "The four of us lived on welfare in a one-bedroom in a Portugese neighbourhood [of Toronto]. I wanted to play but I had to wear other people's stuff. I couldn't pay the fees to play in leagues or go to hockey schools. I didn't have any way of getting to games. I had to count on other people helping me."

Aliu says that some helped but some didn't. "When we first came here from Kiev I had a fight every day," he says. "I didn't understand what people were saying, so I thought they were saying something about me."

A few years back, a friend in minor-hockey told me about Aliu when he was with the Toronto Marlies minor midget team along with John Tavares and Sam Gagner. That Marlies team lost only two games all season. Tavares was regarded as the Next Big Thing, but in retrospect, Aliu might qualify as the real prodigy. For a kid to go from never having skated to skating along with the top minor-midget players in Ontario is akin to sitting a twelve-year-old behind a piano for the first time and coming back to hear him banging out songs like Jerry Lee Lewis two or three years later. (I choose Lewis out of the academy of great pianists not just out of personal preference but also because he can't read music. That seems apropos—the idea that Aliu might excel at playing hockey without being ground in the culture of the game.)

When I put it to Aliu that he's still learning the game, he doesn't object. "In junior, everyone is learning," he says. "I got a late start. I have to learn more [and] faster than everybody else."

Aliu knows that I'm going to ask him about the incident in Windsor, just as the NHL teams will at the combine. Still, what comes out is not a reading from a text prepared by his agent or some sort of clichéd dodge. It has an honest and unaffected ring.

"Nobody wanted to hear my side of it," he says. "When they told me I had to go in [the hotbox on the bus] I wouldn't do it. I wouldn't do that to anybody else, they shouldn't do it to me—that's just how I see it. It's not part of the game or the team. We're here to play hockey.

"At the practice Downie cross-checked me in the mouth. I went to the dressing room and saw that three of my teeth were chipped and broken. That's when I lost it. I came back out on the ice and I went after him.

"I feel sorry for Moe Mantha—it shouldn't have cost him his job. And I don't have a problem with Downie. We've spoken about it since then. It's in the past. When we've played against each other since then, people tried to make a big deal of it but it's over. It's like a lot of things—there's a lot of talk about me but nobody's talked to me."

Aliu only picks at his salad. He starts to ask me about the draft, if I've heard anything about which teams like one prospect or another. When I mention a couple of names, he tells me where they stand on NHL Central Scouting's mid-term. When I tell him about my experience in the Columbus war room last June, he asks me what type of questions they hit prospects with.

"They'll ask 'What kind of player are you?'"

He sits up straight and goes into performance mode. "I work out with Rick Nash in Toronto. I'm like Rick but I want to be like Rick and Todd Bertuzzi—skilled but tougher."

Gulp. I don't think he'd be well advised to compare himself to Bertuzzi, whose star crashed after his assault on Steve Moore in 2004. I move on without comment.

"They'll ask you questions about other players in the league, because they're not just doing research on you but on other players. They'll ask you, 'Who's the best defenceman in the league?'"

"The way I'd answer that," he says, "I'd tell them, 'I think every time I get the puck I should beat the defenceman I'm going against. I don't take any pride in beating a sixteen-year-old defenceman. That's someone I should beat every time.'"

I tell Aliu that maybe a straighter answer and a name might go over a little better, but I can't help thinking that his interviews at the combine might be more entertaining than most.

After almost two hours I ask the waitress for the bill. Aliu reaches for it. "I'll pay for it," he says.

"It's okay," I say, taking it.

"Please," he says. "It's okay."

Just at that moment he seems anxious, almost desperate, to repair an image that has taken a battering, but it's forgivable. He's not like other prospects. I don't know how a team could get to know him in just twenty minutes at the combine.

March 11, St. Michael's Arena

ST. MICHAEL'S 4 SUDBURY 1

I've followed the Wolves from Sudbury Friday night (where they lost to Brampton), to Belleville (where they lost to the Bulls) and on to St. Michael's (where they're looking to salvage a lost weekend by picking up the two easiest points in the Ontario league).

I can tell that the relationship between Akim Aliu and Mike Foligno is strained. The other night up in Sudbury, after the loss to Brampton, I went to Foligno's fan forum, attended by a hundred or so fans in Wolves sweaters, at a Don Cherry's restaurant. Foligno promised to answer any questions submitted in writing. I submitted a couple of questions about Aliu—I can't imagine that I was the only one who wanted to know about him. My questions never came up. In fact, Aliu's name was never even mentioned. And at the end of the night, the broadcaster who hosted the show claimed that the coach had taken every question from the floor.

Trying to go in through the front door with Foligno hasn't been

working for me either. For several days I've been asking for a few minutes to talk about Aliu and Foligno, and he's always put me off. Now he
says that he'll give me some time after the game at St. Michael's, before
the team boards the bus back to Sudbury. Still, he's hardly enthusiastic
about it—and I've never had a problem talking to him before.

I meet up with Akim Aliu's father Tai before the game in the lobby
of the arena. Tai still has the muscularity of a sprinter. He hands me
his business card—he wasn't able to put his geology degrees to use
here but he has his realtor's licence. He hasn't been able to show any
houses this weekend. Like me he'll have logged about 1,200 kilometres going to the Wolves' games. Even in the worst weather, he won't
miss a game. His wife makes it out to games closer to home and to
some in Sudbury but she gave this weekend's road trip a pass.

"Very hard weekend for the team," he says, in an accent that owes
more to Lagos than Kiev. "Very important game today. I still get
nervous, like it's Akim's first game."

I want to get some sort of read of Tai's and Larissa's involvement
in their son's career. If Tai is driving all those thousands of kilometres then Akim might not quite be up there with Ottawa 67's coach
Brian Kilrea's best players—"orphans". Still, just showing up at
games, coming out to support their son, hardly constitutes excess
parental interference.

A few general managers around the league have told me they've
done their own work-ups on Aliu. One told me that he decided not
to trade for him because of concerns about Tai becoming meddlesome, a distraction both for his son and the team.

I ask Tai point blank about it. He says he's surprised to hear that.
"Maybe someone thinks that after what happened to Akim in
Windsor," he says. "That was very disturbing for my wife and me.
This wasn't something that we knew anything about. Larissa just
wanted him to come home and not play hockey after hearing what
they were doing. But we trust Akim to know what's best for him in
hockey. He has an agent who advises him. We just support him as
our son."

I take Tai at his word, but it's a something to follow up. I tell him that I'll stay in touch and see him at playoff games, even though, the way the Wolves are playing, I suspect they won't get out of the first round.

I watch the game up in standing room with Daniel Doré, the Bruins' scout based in Gatineau, Quebec. Doré, says he has seen Aliu a few times this season—he won't tip his hand about his list, but he does say that "someone will take a chance on a kid that big and that fast," even if he's lugging some baggage.

At the start of the game it looks like Aliu is intent on making the scouts forget about any baggage. Aliu is skating on the first line, on the wing of Nick Foligno, the coach's son and the Ottawa Senators' first-round draft pick last June. It seems like a nice complement. Nick Foligno, a heady, hyper-competitive player, figures out ways to get Aliu the puck. In turn, Aliu's a menace on the forecheck—it seems like Aliu can go from centre ice to the net in three strides with a head of steam. He creates turn-overs for Foligno to pounce on.

Aliu's best moment has nothing to do with his speed or his hands. With St. Michael's on the powerplay in the first period, Aliu skates out to the point and dives in front of a slapshot. Not a safety-first slide, shin pads out in front, face turned away. Almost a swan dive, arms and face first. The puck could have rattled off his helmet or hit him in the throat. Instead, it hits him square in the chest. If the scouts (and his coach) have questions about Aliu's commitment, plays like that should put them to rest.

Aliu has a good moment on the first shift after the second inter-mission. He sets up Nick Foligno for a goal that ties the game at one. The Wolves have been dominating play, outshooting the home team 34–20 through two periods, but the Majors' goaltender Chris Carrozzi has been stoning Sudbury. Foligno's goal gives his team hope that they'll come away with a point, maybe two.

But all the good done comes undone. Late in the game, with St. Michael's back out in front by a goal, the ref whistles Sudbury for-ward Andrew Self for slashing, a weak call. When Aliu complains, the ref tags *him* with a minor for unsportsmanlike conduct. St. Michael's scores with the two-man advantage and the game is effectively over. Aliu's troubles, however, are not. He comes out of the box to complain after the goal, but the ref lets him know that it's Self who's back in the game, and that Aliu could get tagged with another minor or misconduct. When Aliu serves out his two minutes, he skates back to the Sudbury bench. Mike Foligno benches him the rest of the way.

After the game I go down to the Sudbury dressing room. There are loud shouts, a few profanities. When Foligno emerges he tells me there's going to be no interview. "I'm disappointed in Akim Aliu as a player and person, and that's all I have to say," he says, stalking away. Aliu comes out a few minutes later, looking dazed. He doesn't want to talk. He carries his equipment bag and sticks to his father's car and throws them in the trunk.

I call Tai Aliu later that night for an update. He doesn't pick up. I find out that he had been rushed to hospital with chest pains.

March 12, 2007, London

It's not scouting of a conventional sort, I'll admit, but maybe Tony Lucadello would sign off on it. I was planning on catching Sam Gagner and Patrick Kane at a London Knights practice. I've seen Gagner and Kane, Nos. 3 and 4 respectively according to Central Scouting's mid-term rankings of North American skaters, in a few games since the world juniors and they've been lighting it up as the playoffs near. I figure I'll get more time to talk to them after a practice than I would after a game. The added value: The day I book to come out to London is the day after Aliu has been suspended by Sudbury, and Sam Gagner knows him from their time with the Toronto Marlies midget club. One trip, three bases covered.

As it turns out, London coach Dale Hunter decides at the last minute to make the practice optional and gives Gagner and Kane the day off—more or less. They don't have to go to the rink but they do have to go to a mall for an autograph session. I figure I'll be able to interview them while they sign for a small cluster of kids, something that shouldn't take more than a half hour. That notion goes out the window when I pull into the mall's parking lot and have to steer around a line-up that snakes through the mall and out into the street.

Gagner and Kane sit together in their green Knights sweaters at a table in a vacant store given to the club for the day. Without their pads on, the pair's sweaters hang down loosely to their thighs, making them look even more boyish and indistinguishable from the autograph hunters. The doors won't open for another fifteen minutes. Kane is slumped in his chair, tapping a felt marker on the tabletop. Gagner is leaning forward, looking out at the crowd. They neither seem impressed nor inconvenienced by the signing. In fact, they seem blasé, which would be exactly a NHLer's attitude in the same circumstances.

"I heard the last time, this took four hours," Kane says, shrugging.

The Knights seem closer to an NHL outfit in scale and attitude than to many junior franchises—with crowds of more than 8,000 they're closer to, say, the Edmonton Oilers than the Swift Current Broncos. So it stands to reason that London's best players could pass for veteran pros—but for the beardlessness.

The doors open and the fans start to file in. They have programs, photographs, hockey cards and autograph books in hand.

"What's your name, buddy?" Sam Gagner asks an eight-year-old who wordlessly passes him a crumpled-up piece of paper.

I sit behind the two and try to keep a dialogue going over their shoulders while they keep on signing.

If the Knights are a quasi-professional team, then the same might have been said of the minor midget Marlies team Gagner played for along with John Tavares, Akim Aliu and Justin Vaive, son of former Leafs captain Rick Vaive. I ask him about the complaints you'd expect with from players and parents with a team so crowded with talent—the bitching and moaning about ice time. Gagner says it was never an issue. "The players understood that being around other talented players is a challenge," he says. "My father was a coach on the team but that was never a problem for anybody. It was just great preparation for the next level."

For Gagner, the next level was the Sioux City Musketeers of the USHL—he and his father were keeping their options open about NCAA hockey. (Gagner made an oral commitment to the University of Wisconsin before opting to play for the Knights.) When London landed his rights and offered his father an assistant coaching job in the bargain, it promised a perfect situation for the son and a home-coming for the ex-NHLer. The Knights were a few minutes east along Highway 401 from the farm where Dave Gagner grew up.

There's a difference of attitude between the Glimmer Twins—it seems like Kane is more purposeful. Circumstances influenced that. Gagner has been able to be with his family but for Kane hockey meant moving away. "I learned a lot from Pat Verbeek when I went to Detroit," says Kane. "I was homesick the first day, when I got dropped off but it was what I had to do for hockey."

Again, the team that he played for, Detroit Honeybaked, is closer to a Canadian major junior franchise in spirit than any minor-hockey program Kane might have played for had he stayed on with his family in Buffalo. Honeybaked, major dough.

Kane says he has had to make "sacrifices" to play hockey: being away from family friends, giving up his second favorite sport, basket-ball. "I'm sort of a 20-point 10-assist point guard," he says in all mod-esty. Coming to London has meant seeing more of his parents than he did while he was playing for Honeybaked or in the U.S. under-18 development program in Ann Arbor last season.

"It's been a great experience," Kane says. "My father sold his business—he had a car dealership—and he and my mother have made it out to all our games."

The word around the league is that the Knights had to shell out significant coin, around $150,000 to $200,000, to convince Kane to come to London rather than accept a scholarship to a U.S. school—Mr Kane's showroom negotiating skills would have come in handy. Given the revenue the Knights generate in their 9,000-seat arena, the money spent on Kane is a shrewd investment.

One scout (not in the Columbus organization) expressed a concern about Kane. "Everything seems to be a big production with him," the scout says. "He took so long to make a decision about going to London. There's all this foot-dragging. Why not just commit? Now it's the agent deal . . . everyone else has one but you."

Another scout (again, not with the Blue Jackets) didn't seem bothered by Kane not having committed to an agent. "Supposedly the father thinks he can do it and maybe he can," he said. "How much does an agent have to do to get a No. 1 pick signed to a salary-cap contract? He can just take Sidney Crosby's first contract and change the name on it. Hire a lawyer and pay him by the hour rather than a percentage."

When Kane is on the ice, he dictates the pace of the game. Off the ice, the same seems to hold true.

March 16, 2007, Le Colisée, Rimouski

RIMOUSKI 5 SHAWINIGAN 0

L'Océanic de Rimouski is best known for three alumni: Brad Richards, Vincent Lecavalier and Sidney Crosby. Richards and Lecavalier, teammates for a season in Rimouski, lifted the Stanley Cup with the Tampa Bay Lightning two NHL seasons and a lockout ago. Just about that time Crosby became the biggest name in hockey while still a teenage player in this town of 25,000 on the south shore of the St Lawrence a couple of hours east of Quebec City. When the Q granted a franchise to Rimouski in the mid-90s it seemed like it would be a challenge to get top prospects to go to there. Now Rimouski's a preferred destination—for players and scouts alike.

It's the last weekend of the season for l'Océanic. The team will miss the playoffs by more than twenty points. That makes it sound like it wouldn't be a priority for scouts but in fact Rimouski is a must-see team. L'Océanic was the only team to place four players in the

CHL Top Prospects Game[28] and the only team other than the U.S. under-18 team in Ann Arbor to place four players in the top 50 North American skaters in NHL Central Scouting Service's mid-terms. All four are forwards: David Skokan is ranked 14th, Maxime Tanguay 29th, Maxim Gratchev 41st and Olivier Fortier 45th. What's more, Rimouski might have that many players who'll be that high up on Central Scouting's list for the 2008 draft.

It's one of scouting's workaday ironies: many weak teams are priorities because their lineups are like Rimouski's this season—they're heavily populated by seventeen- and eighteen-year-olds who are bound to struggle against nineteen-year-olds. Rimouski acquired Tanguay from Chicoutimi, Gratchev from Quebec and Fortier from Drummondville, all clubs loading up for the playoffs. Acquiring these players and a couple of promising sixteen-year-olds, Rimouski's management has built a team that will be competitive next year and likely a contender for the Memorial Cup in 2009. General manager André Jolicoeur will be hiring a new coach to take over for Doris Labonté, who took the team to a national championship with Brad Richards and to the title game with Crosby. They'll also be expanding the fifty-year-old arena in hopes of being named the host of the Memorial Cup two years down the road. The CHL has been inflating the Mem Cup for several seasons now, putting the games in the biggest arenas and the biggest cities in a push for bigger gate revenues and a more prominent place in the Canadian media. Now the event seems out of reach of many towns with great programs. If Rimouski wins the right to host the event, l'Océanic would be striking a blow for junior hockey's little guys (who actually outnumber the big guys but wield much less influence).

I've been to Rimouski a half dozen times over the years and it always seems to be an adventure. On my first trip I was nabbed for

---

28. As it turned out, Olivier Fortier and Maxime Tanguay missed the Top Prospects Game with injuries.

speeding, about 25 kilometres over the limit (100 km/h), even though I had just been passed by four vehicles, one of them bearing the provincial government's logo. The next time I decided to take the train, and it deposited me there at two a.m. on a bitterly cold night with the town's taxi not in sight, no change in my pocket for the pay phone and a two-mile walk on icy sidewalks to my hotel. You get the idea. It's a beautiful town with great restaurants, a wonderful place to watch a hockey game—and the spot where my good luck goes to die.

On the drive out to Rimouski this time around my luck seems to be changing for the better—no speed traps; clear, dry roads, not a flake of snow in sight; just a peaceful, uneventful drive along the south shore.

You wouldn't imagine a big crowd making it out to le Colisée for the last home date of the season. Nothing rides on the outcome of the game, and Sidney Crosby and the Pittsburgh Penguins are taking on the Canadiens in Montreal in a game broadcast on RDS tonight. Still, the announced attendance, just under 4,400, seems to be an honest count.

Up in standing room I bump into three scouts from an NHL club that not long ago flogged some draft picks on the deadline—a source of frustration to the scouts. They're out here to see the four Rimouski players—they have to be: Shawinigan doesn't have any ranked draft-eligibles, and if les Cataractes did, these scouts could see them closer to home during the playoffs. No, this is a last chance for scouts to have a look at three of the four Rimouski prospects.[29]

"What the hell are you doin' all the way out here?" one asks me.

"Everyone has to be somewhere," I say. "At least there's a good French restaurant here."

---

29. Olivier Fortier has already been invited to the world under-18s in Finland in April. His three draft-eligible teammates are all late '88 birthdays and aren't eligible for the '89 tournament.

FUTURE GREATS AND HEARTBREAKS   223

They flew into Quebec City and will drive back after tonight's game, looking to catch a game with Angelo Esposito and the Remparts Saturday. I tell them I'm planning to staying on in Rimouski for a day to talk to the draft-eligible kids.

"You know it's supposed to storm tonight," the one scout tells me. "That's why were not staying over."

The travel and the prospect of a long night makes the scouts testy. The game hasn't even started and they have the acid out. When "O Canada" is played, a good portion of the crowd doesn't stand, a sight you'll see around the Q. One of those who stays seated is an old man sitting in the last row of seats directly in front of us. One scout bumps the oldtimer's seat with his foot but looks straight ahead, like it's an accident. "I guess that means you won't be cashing your Canada pension cheque," the scout says.

After only two or three shifts it seems hard to imagine that Rimouski isn't in the playoffs and Shawinigan is. The home team dominates play.

The biggest and brightest talent for the home team is already drafted: Michael Frolik, the Florida Panthers' first-rounder, tenth over-all last June, is lighting it up on every shift. He scores two goals, the second of them the result of the undressing of a Shawinigan defenceman and an explosive descent on the net—the best goal I've seen all season. Frolik has breathtaking jump once the puck hits his stick.

The four draft-eligibles all have their moments. Fortier and Gratchev pick up goals. Skokan does decent work on Frolik's line. Tanguay is a little less conspicuous than the others. But at 2–0 after one period and 3–zip after two, Shawinigan just mails it in for the last twenty minutes—it's something less than a crucible that will sep-arate prospects from pretenders. I leave the game convinced that Central Scouting's mid-term rankings of Rimouski's quartet of draft-eligibles would be more accurate if it were turned upside down. I think that Fortier would be out in front of the other three by a fair bit and that Tanguay would edge out Gratchev and Skokan. Tim Bernhardt, the longtime Dallas scout, warned me about reading too much into one game. "You can't judge a kid when you see him once," Bernhardt said. "You might be seeing his best game, or maybe his worst." It's my second look at Gratchev and Skokan—they played in the Top Prospects Game and they both had moments there, Gratchev scoring a goal, Skokan playing beside Akim Aliu on the winning Red team's most effective line. I only have a foggy memory of Fortier from the summer under-18s—he was a third- or fourth-liner and a penalty killer. And this is my first look at Tanguay. Still, I can't see Fortier being the fourth-best player in this group.

I'd tell this to the scouts up in standing room at the end of the game, but with about seven minutes to go, garbage time, they're beating a retreat to Quebec, mindful of the weather report.

March 17, 2007, Le Colisée, Rimouski

L'Océanic practice

The next morning in my hotel room I pull the curtains to look out at the St Lawrence. I do a double take. It's Rimouski that's frosted over. More than two feet of snow has fallen overnight, and the snow is giving way to sheets of freezing rain. The weather channel is advising that the highway westbound out of Rimouski is closed. Things in town are no better. There's no point digging my car out. So, underdressed and drenched to the bone, I trudge uphill to the arena, a walk of maybe a mile. Usually I'd use this time to mull over questions to ask the coaches and the players, but instead I'm dwelling on two dark thoughts. One: *If anyone ever tells me they love hockey, I'd love to put him to this test.* Two: *My luck in Rimouski has hit a new low.*

By the time I get to le Colisée, a figure-skating program for tots is just winding down and l'Océanic's players are lacing them up. It's Doris Labonté's last practice with the club, the last bit of business he'll do here in his hometown. There's a game in Victoriaville tomorrow, but that's it. He had been a gym teacher in Rimouski and worked his way up to the highest reaches of junior hockey. It might have turned out to be a sentimental affair, maybe even an event—a fair number of fans turn out every day for l'Océanic's practices. But the weather has cut into it.

I came to know Labonte fairly well when I was writing a book about Sidney Crosby a few years ago. Most coaches are more protective of their opinions than poker champion Doyle Brunson is of his hole cards, but Labonte fears saying nothing as long as it's true. He's a little man, maybe five-six, with a rough, growling voice that would better suit a lumberjack a foot taller.

One scouting axiom holds that players make the best scouts—that those who play with or against a prospect know his strengths and weaknesses better than anyone else. If the players know what a prospect can do, the coach knows what a player will do. If you go by a coach's decisions inside the game—how much ice time he gives a player, what situations he uses him in, when he holds the player back—rather than what he'll tell you, you can filter out the personal stuff, the flattery of a less-talented kid he likes, the criticism of a solid player who might have crossed him.

I'd bet that Lebonté's opinion about Fortier is about the same as mine. Against Shawinigan, Fortier was the one all-purpose player among Labonte's group of forwards—first line, first power-play unit, first penalty kill. The departing coach smirks when he describes Skokan as "a typical European . . . one shift hard, one shift not so hard." He likes Gratchev as "a skilled player, a scorer." And he twists the knife with Maxime Tanguay, saying that his brother Alex, a first-rounder, was "more competitive, more aggressive player than the little brother." But when he talks about his players, he talks first about Fortier.

"Fortier is the perfect player," Doris Labonté says. "On the ice, there's no doubt about effort, no doubt about understanding. Tell him once, show him once, it's done. Off the ice, the same thing. A good player gets to the rink on time. A perfect player gets others to the rink on time. I put Fortier with Tanguay [off the ice] and he'll help him in every way, whether it's with hockey or school."

Others I talk to in Rimouski give me the same work-up on Fortier. The CBC reporter who covers the team says he always goes to

Fortier after games because he gives "not just a good quote but one with some insight . . . very smart, very analytical." The reporter tells me that Fortier had been in a program for gifted students in Quebec City before being drafted into the Q, that he's a lock for the award the team gives to its top student.

Fortier lives up to the advance billing when I catch up to him after practice. He wears a t-shirt saying "TV is my friend," but it seems like he has spent far more time on the ice or over an open book than in front of a television. He takes time with every question I ask. When I ask him about leaving the gifted-student program to play in Drummondville, he gives the question about as much thought as an essay question on an exam.

"I'm proud to be a good student. I wanted to do math and science, but I knew going away for hockey to Drummondville that [an enriched course] wasn't available. It's a hard decision but I thought that junior hockey was an opportunity I had to take. I talked it over with my family. I want to do [university] for maths someday and I hope hockey can put me in a position to do that. Maybe there were times last season in Drummondville when I didn't know that it was right thing, [but] when we [the Quebec team with Angelo Esposito] won the under-17s in Regina I knew that it was a good decision."

Fortier is impressively clear-eyed about his decision—nothing emotional nor impulsive about it. He seems to have mastered the calculus of junior hockey. He determined the value he could derive from the game and weighed it against staying in school. That approach carries over when he talks about the summer under-18s. Fortier was limited to a role as a checker and penalty killer. He saw a lot less ice than Angelo Esposito and the other front-line players.

"I think I could do more than they asked me to, but it's better to be there in that [role] than to stay at home and think I should be on the first line," Fortier says. "When Derick [Brassard] went with the summer 18s they had him do the same thing. He showed them that he can do that if he's asked, and in the Q he showed them that he's a first-liner. It's an opportunity and you take it and do your best. Once you are in the program, Hockey Canada knows you."

Fortier fills in the gaps in his story. His father was a good player, he says. His little brother Jon-Michel will likely be drafted into the Q. His best friend on the Drummondville team was Derick Brassard. If the Blue Jackets have an interest in Fortier, they can ask their top pick last year about him, just like they can ask Rick Nash about Akim Aliu.

I talk to the other prospects for about a half hour each in the team's recreation room. That's the upside to the lousy weather—nobody is in a rush to go outside.

Tanguay has the best bloodlines—in his draft year, his brother Alex was invited to the Canadian under-20 team's tryouts because others were injured and he turned out to be one of its best players. He was expected to be the key player on the under-20s in '99 but suffered a concussion that put him on the sidelines. That's been the story with the older Tanguay brother: the perception that he should have been more. It's hard to say a player is a tease with his talent when he has scored a goal that clinched a Stanley Cup in Game 7 of a final, like Alex Tanguay did with Colorado. Still, many have thought that Alex Tanguay should have become an automatic choice for Team Canada. That hasn't happened. That Maxime Tanguay trains with Alex in the off-season, that he has competed against his older brother since he was a tyke, would be viewed by teams as positives. But Maxime still suffers by comparison to Alex, who himself suffers when measured up to others' expectations. "It's more of a good thing than a bad thing to have a brother in the league," Maxime Tanguay tells me, but not too convincingly.

Gratchev has the best story—he was born in Russia and his family moved to Boston when he was five years old. Thus he has a Boston accent but has played internationally for Russia and says he's "more Russian than American." He makes it clear that he's driven to be a player, that he trained at his father's hockey school since he was first-grader, that he came to the Quebec league rather than attending a U.S. college because it would best prepare him for the NHL. "Maybe othah American kids wouldn't go someplace wh-ah they don't speak English," Gratchev says. "I know all about that stuff. Doesn't bothah me."

Skokan has the best starter kit—in a t-shirt he's thicker through the chest, shoulders and arms than Fortier is in his pads and sweater. In the game that I saw he resembled the action hero from the movies who looks the part but calls in a stunt man for the tough stuff. Maybe he could be a killer on the cycle and I just caught on a night when he doesn't show it.

Still, if I have to bank on one player out of the four draft-eligible prospects here, on what I've seen, what I hear from them, what I hear about them, I'd bank on Fortier.

I'm not going to chance the drive out of Rimouski for another day. I check my voicemail messages at home. A call from Tai Aliu. He says his son has headed back to Sudbury. Mike Foligno has lifted Akim's suspension in time to get him into the line-up for the Wolves playoff opener against the Mississauga Ice Dogs. I phone up Tai and tell him that we'll catch up at a game in a few days.

March 23, 2007, Metro Centre, Halifax

HALIFAX 5 MONCTON 1

The sign-in sheet on press row tells the story: A large contingent of scouts has made it out to Game 2 of this first-round Q league playoff series. The Coyotes, the Flyers, the Blackhawks . . . practically every team that will miss the NHL playoffs has sent at least one set of eyeballs here. Before the game the Mooseheads present a trophy to the player those eyes will be trained on. The ceremony starts out conventionally enough. Arena workers roll out a red carpet onto the ice. Then they carry a table and place it at the end of the carpet and finally lug an oversize piece of silverware and place it on the table. Members of the team's board walk out on the rug and the announcement is made: The Mooseheads' rookie of the year is Jakub Voracek.

This surprises no one and nor should it. In 59 games during the regular season Voracek led the team in scoring with 23 goals and 63 assists.[30] But the ceremony does seem to catch Voracek off guard. He's supposed to pose for a photo and then place the trophy back on the table and skate back to the bench. Everything starts off well enough. He doffs his helmet and his messy shock of blond hair bounces as he skates over. But the event departs from the script when he's handed the trophy. At that point he raises it like the Stanley Cup and carries it over to the Mooseheads' bench where he hands it to a surprised trainer, asking him to put it in his stall in the dressing room.

It's a comic vignette, and a telling one. From the talks I've had with his teammates, the Mooseheads' brass and the scouts who've worked Voracek's games, a couple of themes recur: enthusiasm and energy. That may not sound like much—you'd expect a player to be enthusiastic and energetic. But often teenage players are at the rink or on the ice because they have to be—even if they love the game, they don't love it every minute.

"Jakub doesn't have any bad days," says Bobby Smith, the former NHLer and first-overall draft pick who owns the Mooseheads. "Off the ice he's positive about everything he does. Other kids, whether they come here from Europe or just out of town, look at some things as an inconvenience or a challenge. Jakub always has a smile on his face. He walks into a room and makes everyone happy. On the ice he takes a joy in playing the game. Whether he has the puck or is

---

30. Numbers that are virtually a wash with Angelo Esposito's this year: 27 goals, 52 assists in 60 games. Whenever I've asked a player in the Q about the two prospects, Esposito and Voracek, they've told me every time that the Czech kid was the much better player this season.

playing without it, he's working every second out there trying to make things happen."

That seems like a comprehensive scouting report. On his first shift he picks up the puck on the right wing, and in two or three strides he has Wildcat defenceman Nathan Weltan scrambling to catch up. It should be a basic one-on-one lock-up, a situation that has the defender at the advantage. Voracek's change of pace turns the dynamic around. This shift is the template for the rest of the night. Every time he gathers up the puck, a Moncton defenceman is taking a deep breath.

Voracek isn't a prepossessing physical package. He's rangy-looking—listed at six foot one and 187 pounds, he looks taller and slighter, like he's all arms and legs, like he would have a high centre of gravity and be easy to knock off the puck. It's a theory I have to abandon. The Moncton d-men are hard pressed to lay a glove on him in the open ice. On the cycle he gives more than he takes. Even the biggest Moncton defencemen can't push him around.

Voracek ends up with two goals and two assists and is named the game's first star. But the numbers only hint at his overall game. The Mooseheads feel like they're not getting their share of calls in the first period—they spend more than half the period killing off penalties, while the Wildcats get away with everything except rifling the gate receipts. Voracek takes shifts on the penalty kill. By the second period, when the whistles die down, he starts to impose his will on the game. I've seen other prospects this season have as big an impact, but only because they have runs on the power play—nobody has been as good as Voracek in five-on-five situations. It is, with Patrick Kane's performances at the world juniors, the most impressive stuff I've seen from a draft-eligible player in a winter's worth of games. How he's down all the way to No. 15 by the reckoning of Central Scouting is beyond me.

I see Jim Nill, the assistant general manager of the Detroit Red Wings, packing up his stuff in the press box at the end of the game. "Pretty special player," Nill says. When Nill says this, he sighs and shrugs. Voracek's far too special to be around when Detroit's pick comes up at the end of the first round.[31]

March 24, 2007, Metro Centre, Halifax

MOOSEHEADS PRACTICE

The next morning the Mooseheads skate through the drills with winners' exuberance—they realize that this series against last year's Memorial Cup finalist is there to be taken. For his part, Jakub Voracek goes about the line rushes at game pace, no coasting or floating. But it's game pace, not game face. Between rushes he's talking to his teammates and laughing, a high-pitched voice-still-changing rasp when he's winded.

Some Euros alienate their Canadian teammates within minutes of walking into their dressing rooms. Even before they arrive there's talk about the Euros' agents gouging teams for six figures and travel guarantees—more than enough to sour the honest workers like Myles Rumsey and kids playing out their contracts like Brady Leavold. And the demands don't end once the junior clubs live up to their end—a few years back, one junior coach told me about a Slovak kid who threatened to go home if the team didn't bring his girlfriend over. In that case the Slovak overplayed his hand and was soon packing for home. Still, stories of carpet-baggers and prima donnas have given incoming Euros an image problem.

It doesn't seem that Jakub Voracek has any baggage. Bobby Smith and others around the team have told me he hasn't tried to squeeze

---

31. The last time the Red Wings had a top-ten draft pick was 1991 (Martin Lapointe, tenth overall). In that time they've had only one other pick in the top twenty. Detroit landed the nineteenth pick in the 2005 draft when positions were determined by a draw after the lockout.

anything out of anybody and only told them how grateful he's been since he arrived in Halifax. That's backed up when I start canvassing his teammates after practice.

Logan MacMillan's take on Voracek is the consensus in the room.

"We heard a lot about him before he came here, that he was a real good player," he says. "We didn't know anything about him as person, though. He walked into the dressing room with a big smile and said, 'Hi everybody, my name is Jakub.' And we thought he seems okay and we started asking him questions — like when he got here, if he'd been in Canada before, who his billets were. He just stood there smiling. When he said, 'Hi everybody . . .' those were the only words he knew in English. Nothing else. Not one word. To him it wasn't a problem, and without any lessons or anything he just has been figuring it out ever since."

MacMillan's a good player, a smart kid with a veteran pro's understanding of everything that goes on at the arena. He fit right in on the summer under-18 team. He's as quick-witted off the ice as he is on it. At the Mooseheads' awards dinner last week, he was presented with the team's most gentlemanly player award, and upon being handed it he asked: "Do I have to accept this?"

Logan MacMillan's father, Bob, is a scout with the Calgary Flames but the son has seen more of Voracek than any scout — and from the vantage point that's most telling: ice level. Logan tells me Voracek is a different player than when he first arrived. "I think he was disappointed that he didn't get to play more at the world juniors, but when he came back to Halifax after that he was on fire," MacMillan says. "He just took his game to another level."

If you put the Mooseheads in a police lineup and you had to pick out the elite player, you'd pick MacMillan first and just about everyone else before you got around to Voracek. He looks dynamic on the ice but off the ice he looks average at best. He's not thickly muscled. Fact is, in his gym stuff he seems physically immature compared to a lot of other prospects. He doesn't seem to have much muscle definition at all.

MacMillan has lowered my expectations of coming away with anything useful in an interview with Voracek. I can't imagine he would have learned much English in seven months—especially when he was away for four weeks for the world under-20 tournament.

I start off by asking him about growing up.

"Jaromir Jagr is from Kladno, so he is the hero," he says.

"Do you play like him?"

"There is Jagr and there is everyone else," he says. The same way Nicklas Backstrom said of Peter Forsberg, "There is only one."

"Did you play other sports?"

Voracek says he played soccer and tennis as well as hockey until age twelve. "They are good for you," he says. "Only after I'm concentrating on hockey. My father was a player—not international but a player. I didn't know if I can be a professional [or] play for Czech [or] in Canada. I do it because it's fun. When I'm sixteen, an agent tells me that I can play here—Petr Svoboda [who] played in the NHL. Until then, I did not think about it so much."

"Is that when you knew you have a special talent?

When I ask this I can see his expression change as he parses and translates every word. I guess something is lost going from English to Czech back to English, but no matter—the answer to whatever question he thinks I'm asking sounds honest enough.

"I don't think I'm a special person because I play hockey," he says. "I am like my teammates and we're like other people. I'm good to them and I'm good to everyone—that's how you should be. I play hockey because it is what I like to do. I have fun doing it."

That seems consistent with everything else he says. He seems to prefer to talk about the team, using the first-person plural, rather than himself.

I ask him if he has talked to any NHL teams—it would be premature for clubs to talk to him directly, though it can never be too early to gather background. He tells me only one club has contacted him directly: the Los Angeles Kings. It wasn't just a chance conversation, either, not just paths crossing at the arena with the Kings' regional scout. Voracek says Kings general manager Dean Lombardi came down to the dressing room to speak to him after a game a few weeks back. It's just enough to get me thinking that maybe my trip out to Halifax might be a moot exercise with the Kings drafting ahead of Columbus (barring a trade). This might be background on a player destined to land elsewhere.

Voracek is utterly guileless. I don't think it has much to do with language, just his nature. Even when things come out wrong they sound right. One story making the rounds: Voracek's mother visited him in Halifax and someone with the club told him that he gets his looks from her. "Do you love her?" Jakub asked with a straight face.

Later I call Voracek's billets, the Murray family, Stephen and Dawnalda. They've been putting up Mooseheads players for about ten years now. It's clear that Voracek stands out among those who've stayed with them.

"He didn't speak a word when he came here, but he picked things up so quickly," says Stephen Murray, a sergeant with the Halifax police force. "You could have a conversation with him within a couple of weeks or a month. He likes steak. After a game, even in the middle of winter, I'd start up the barbecue and make a steak for him and he'd talk about the game. He's always positive about his teammates—if he scored a hat trick, he'd rather talk about a third-liner scoring. He just has such a great outlook on things. He's just a generous kid. When our daughter started running as part of her girls' hockey program, he asked us if she'd like him to run with her. That trophy he won the other night—he gave that to my wife—he said it was to thank her for helping him. When his sister stayed with us for a bit and his parents came over during the season—I told them what a great job they did raising their son."

For a half hour Murray regales me with stories of Voracek going out to play ball hockey with kids in the neighbourhood, or of looking after his responsibilities around the house. One description I circle in my notes: "Never acting like he was entitled."

The way Murray and the Mooseheads speak of Voracek, the way Voracek goes about things, inevitably breaking into a smile—it makes me think of Jaromir Jagr. Not the Jagr who went to Washington and later to the Rangers, not the veteran who seemed spoiled by hockey's biggest salary. No, the stories about Jakub Voracek remind me of the younger Jagr, maybe hockey's biggest talent in the mid-90s depending on Mario Lemieux's health and mood. During those days Jagr took unfiltered joy from the game. Every day at the rink he was like a child on the first day of his vacation.

The Jaromir Jagr story was one of hockey's best for a long time and maybe someday he'll recapture that former glory. If he can summon up his inner child, or maybe channel this kid from Kladno, that might do the trick.

March 25, 2007, Hershey Centre, Mississauga

MISSISSAUGA 4 SUDBURY 3

Mike Foligno has reinstated Akim Aliu, with conditions. The coach is dropping Aliu from the first line to the third and taking him off the power play. Aliu's expected to keep in line, be a soldier, not a star. He's expected to blend in, not disrupt. It's an exercise in control and humility. It's not an opportunity to showcase his game, just a chance to demonstrate that he can be a team player.

When I saw Sudbury a few weeks back I thought they had little chance to make it out of the first round. Now, though, the Wolves are poised to advance into the second round. It's not Aliu who's leading them but Marc Staal and Nick Foligno. Stefan Legein and the other Ice Dogs forwards hit a brick wall at the Sudbury blue line—Staal completely shuts them down. Nick Foligno heads up a troupe of Sudbury forwards who forecheck furiously and get bigger returns than you'd expect out of the few scoring chances that come their way.

The team's run in the playoffs would seem unlikely—then again, it doesn't seem any less likely than the scene in the stands, the section where Team Aliu is sitting. It's no surprise that his parents are there. Or that they're sitting with Akim's friends from Chaminade

College, where he went to school before heading off to play junior hockey. But one of his soccer coaches has made it out. So have his billets from Windsor. They've seen a couple of dozen of his games over the season and driven to arenas even farther from home. It has me thinking about what Doug MacLean said about Phil Kessel: "What if the stories about this kid aren't true?"

I file this report on Akim Aliu for Don Boyd:

Backstory: Father is Nigerian, mother is Ukrainian. They met in Kiev, married, had children (two boys, Akim the younger) in Nigeria and moved back to Kiev when AA was in an infant. AA's childhood and early adolescence was spent in Kiev. He spoke Russian at home, no English. He wasn't involved in sports at all, did not own a pair of skates until parents left Russia when he was age 12. He says the family left Russia "because my father would be stopped by police and soldiers all the time, even if he wasn't doing anything . . . harassment all the time, all of it racial." He says that he "was in a fight every day when his family first came to Toronto"—they lived in a one-bedroom apartment in a rough, mostly Portuguese neighbourhood. They lived on welfare when they first came to Canada. Father was trained as a geologist (went to university in Kiev), but had to find an office job (eventually working two jobs, real-estate agent on the side). Mother worked as a cleaner, jumped up to administrative position. First played with borrowed skates and equipment because family couldn't afford it. "I counted on friends to help me out getting to games and getting equipment second-hand," he says. He also played soccer at a provincial level—one of best players in province, according to two coaches I spoke to. He says that he didn't play soccer in Kiev.

His time with the Marlies, with Tavares, Sam Gagner and others: "John T is probably my best friend in the game. I liked playing with guys that good. If it meant getting less ice time, less attention, that was okay. And it was a challenge to try to match them and do better." Torn Achilles before going to junior, he says he had to stretch it out the first year after the injury but it's not a problem now.

About Downie: "No one heard my side of it. After Downie goes to the world junior tournament, it's like I was in the wrong. I wasn't. I wasn't going back there [for the hotbox treatment on the bus]. It's stupid. I wouldn't do that to someone else, nobody should tell me to do it. The assistant coaches and others knew what was going on and did nothing, like it was okay. It wasn't okay for me. At the practice Downie sticked me right in the mouth. I went to the dressing room and was spitting out my front teeth. That's when I lost it. I'm not going to take that."

Works out in the summer with Rick Nash. Says that he wants to be a combination of Rick Nash and Todd Bertuzzi. Asked who's the best defenceman in the league, he says "none . . . every time I have the puck I think I should beat whoever is there . . . I don't feel good about beating a 16-year-old sixth defenceman . . . I should beat him . . . I only feel good if I've beaten a guy who's been drafted." He says that before every game he looks for scouts in the stands—that being a high draft choice was his goal before the season.

Said that he hoped that he'd be in the mix for u-18s last summer—disappointed that maybe Windsor incident was held against him but not Downie. Said he hoped that he'd be considered for spring u-18s if Sudbury were knocked out ([Hockey Canada officials] told me there's no interest in Aliu whatsoever).

Before second-last weekend of the season, that he was "happy with the way things are in Sudbury . . . a good opportunity to play for a coach who knows what it takes to be in the NHL." Suspended after the third game in three days, a loss at St. Michael's, when he took a third-period unsportsmanlike for beefing about a penalty called on a teammate. (Sudbury was down 2–1 midway thru 3rd and St. Michael's scored on the 5-on-3 to put the game away. After the St. Michael's goal, Aliu came out of the box and skated over to the ref—who pointed him back to the box. Foligno went off on him in the dressing room after the game.)

Foligno: Was supposed to talk to me after the St. Michael's game but said: "I can't say anything about AA right now except that I'm disappointed in him as a player and a person."

[Ontario league coach]: "I had to look at him [before the OHL draft]. I called a couple of friends [who knew him pretty well] They told me to stay away from him."

[Wolves employee]: "Every day it's maintenance with Aliu."

[Wolves employee]: "He had trouble with his billets. They wanted him out. He ended up staying at the Folignos for a while. Trouble at his school too. Might have been suspended—I'm not sure."

[Ontario league executive]: "We looked at him after [the Windsor incident]. I spoke to his father and he had a chip on his shoulder. I was worried that if it didn't go right, he'd turn around and accuse us of being racist. I cooled off after that, but ours wasn't the right situation. When you have a problem like him, you have to play your problem to fix it—the way our roster was, we couldn't afford to play him the way you'd have to."

David Bova, high school best friend: "I wasn't surprised after I heard the story in Windsor. Akim would never sit and take something. He would always stand up for himself. He always speaks his mind. He'd be in fights at school when we were in Grade 9 and 10—but mostly because he would stand up for himself when older kids would be on him."

Sam Gagner: "He would physically dominate with the Marlies. He just skated right through and over guys. He was just an amazing talent. I think we lost four or six games all year . . . won over 70 games."

Dave Gagner (who was an assistant with the Marlies): "He had anger issues, but more on the ice than off. I don't think that he's a bad kid."

Paul Henry (a former NHL scout and a sports psychologist who is consulting on AA): "After the Windsor incident we talked about AA going to Russia to play in a program over there . . . just because [the Downie incident] was going to follow him everywhere. Foligno is going after him and it's not right. He's punishing him and he approves of the rest of the team dumping on him. He's gone to using him on the third line and put him in a situation that makes it impossible for him to succeed. AA has to get out of there but he's doing his best to get along since they brought him back."

From Boyd:

Some interesting stuff here. Hard to have too much info. A very interesting kid in a lot of ways.

Apri 16, 2007, Scandic Hotel, Tampere, Finland

"Have you heard anything?" Milan Tichy asks me.

It's a common question in scouting circles. Scouts crave the news a day before reading about it the papers or seeing play out on an evening sportscast. They fear being out of the loop and getting ambushed by events.

Rumours are swirling inside the loop. The loop is usually on the other side of the Atlantic, but rumours are floating around the Scandic Hotel, where scouts working the world under-18s have checked in. The Chicago Blackhawks won the lottery and own the top selection in the 2007 entry draft and are here in force, led by their general manager, Dale Tallon. So are the Philadelphia Flyers, who were the worst team all season long and whose bad luck held in the lottery when they fell to the No. 2 slot.

The Flyers' general manager, Paul Holmgren, is here, as are general managers of other hindmost NHL teams, including Los Angeles's Dean Lombardi and Edmonton's Kevin Lowe. (Given his team's late-season collapse and the heat that he has taken for trading the franchise icon Ryan Smyth, Lowe might be considering buying a place here.)

But Tichy isn't asking about any rumoured trades. He's asking about the one general manager who isn't here in body but is on the minds of many: Doug MacLean. Columbus's GM isn't staying at home to do his radio show and field calls from the media. No, this time it's Blue Jackets' owner, John H. McConnell, beckoning. A command performance. When I arrive, Tichy and Kjell Larsson, the Blue Jackets' scouts in the Czech Republic and Sweden, are loitering in the Scandic's lobby and are asking scouts from other outfits if they've heard anything about MacLean's status. Some rumours buoy them—that MacLean will be kicked upstairs to the presidency, where he'd hire a new general manager, that he'll survive against the odds as he had before. Some rumours terrify them—when they hear that Mike Keenan is in the mix, it sends shivers down their spines. And they try to piece the puzzle together on their own—if the owner hired coach Ken Hitchcock unilaterally, they assume that Hitchcock will have influence over MacLean's fate (that is, *toast*) and on the choice of his successor. A scenario like this would make it a matter of guessing which amigo of Hitch would be in play.

I tell Tichy I haven't heard anything. But I don't sugar-coat it. I tell him I exchanged emails with Don Boyd a few days ago, and the terse replies suggested to me that the news will likely be grim when he arrives in Tampere tomorrow. I tell Tichy I doubt MacLean will be able to hold onto his job or even last a week. It's not just a matter of optics. It's *sonics*.

"I just can't imagine that the owner is going to want Doug on the stage at the draft in the arena in Columbus in a few weeks and the crowd booing. The owner has poured in millions and he's booed for his trouble—I just can't see him standing for that."

I tell Milan and Kjell to hang in there. Easy to say in my position, since my job isn't on the line.

As I head to the door I hear Tichy ask a scout who's just arriving: "Have you heard anything?"

April 17, 2007, Scandic Hotel, Tampere

"How's it going?" I ask Don Boyd when I see him at the arena.

What else is there to say? I figure that he might not want to get into what he's heard. If Tichy seemed worried, Boyd is simply downcast. He's the defeated player who refuses to look up at the scoreboard.

Boyd's grimace is accompanied by a sound that might be either his knuckles cracking or the shattering of the enamel on his teeth. I'm not really sure. Not that it would be any less painful than the update he has to give.

"Well, I've been knocked down as director of scouting," he says. "Paul Castron's doing that now."

I don't let on that I already know. Boyd's sheepish and disappointed. The move is supposed to look like nothing more than a change in job title, but it's a demotion. Boyd's friends and peers know exactly what it is. He doesn't bother with the subtext, the fact that this move was MacLean's last-ditch attempt to head off criticism of his own record by pointing his finger at the scouting department.

It seems cold-blooded for MacLean to make a fall guy out of a hockey man who had been his mentor. Most scouts would know that when it comes to looking in the rear-view mirror, objects may appear closer than they are. MacLean had been Bryan Murray's assistant with the Washington Capitals and was a friend and protégé to the veteran coach for several seasons — just as Boyd gave MacLean his big break in junior, so did Murray open the door for him in the NHL. But when the Capitals went into a tailspin and Murray was fired, it took less than an hour for MacLean to walk into the general manager's office and announce that he should be the front-runner to take over behind the bench. The dumbfounded executive assured him that, yes, he was the front-runner for the coaching job . . . of the Baltimore Skipjacks, Washington's minor-league affiliate. Soon after, MacLean was pink-slipped.

MacLean was claiming that poor scouting and drafting were responsible for the team's failures, but it's hardly fair of him to slough off the blame on Boyd. Many scouts outside the Columbus war room have always presumed that MacLean had a lot of input and the ultimate sign-off on the Blue Jackets' first-rounder each season. (Most general managers give total authority to their chief amateur scouts or scouting directors.) After all, it was MacLean, not Boyd, who claimed that the team had ranked Zherdev the top player in the 2003 draft.

Maybe there was less intrigue to it. Maybe Castron had offers to go to other organizations. Friends from his time in Ottawa had been installed as general managers in Pittsburgh and Boston last summer. Maybe MacLean felt like he had to sweeten Castron's position to hold onto him. Then again, MacLean's priority at this point is not franchise-building but rather self-preservation.

April 17, 2007, Tampere Hakametsa

SWEDEN 3 CZECH REPUBLIC 0
FINLAND 1 SLOVAKIA 0

Jakub Voracek usually brings a fourth-liner's pent-up energy to a lead role on every shift, but in the Czechs' final game of the opening round he looks listless. So do the rest of the Czechs, whose loss to Sweden drops them into the relegation round. Winless so far in this tournament, the Czechs will need victories over Latvia and Germany to avoid demotion to next year's B pool, where they'd have to compete with the likes of France and Denmark. Scouts will be pulling for the Czechs in these remaining games, because they dread having to make a trip to the B pool tournament next spring—this year's edition was held in Poland. The 2008 site hasn't been announced, but the scouts aren't banking on it being in the south of France.

The scouts are down on the Czechs, but not on Voracek. Their top prospect is getting a pass because of jet lag. He arrived in time for the Czechs' loss to Finland the other day—when he made it to the rink the game was in progress—and he was best player on the ice. Today, though, he's surely paying the price today for flying economy class from Halifax to Montreal to Frankfurt to Helsinki, then sitting for a couple of hours on the drive out to Tampere. There's also a related fatigue factor—he's fresh off (but not fresh after) two rounds of playoffs in the Q, including a first-round victory over Moncton, which featured a Game 7 win on the road. This season he has played more hockey than ever before, and the most intense of it over the last three weeks. The scouts give him credit for showing up. Even if he was running out of gas, he was prepared to try to play on fumes.

Maybe Voracek would rise to the occasion if the Czech coaches had used him with better players. The Czech coaches, who wear matching, skin-tight red sweaters like a team of acrobats straight off of the Ed Sullivan show, display game judgment that's no better than their fashion sense. They had to drop a fourth-liner to make room for Voracek but neglected to shake up any of their other lines. One of the top three players in this tournament, Voracek is planted on the fourth line on a winless team.

Only late in the third period do the coaches move Voracek up to play with Stepan Novotny, a sixteen-year-old who led Shattuck–St. Mary's to a national high school title this season, a double-underager who's projected to be up there in John Tavares's draft class.

When I catch up to Voracek after the game it's as if he's bumped into an old friend. Given the circumstances, he seems impossibly sunny. "I have nothing," he says, mustering the strength to smile. "My sleep was very bad, very short. But I wanted to come and try. I want to be part of the [national program] in the next years and it's better if they think of me wanting to help. I was disappointed that I didn't play more in the under-20s, but I don't complain. Maybe I play more next year because I help here."

Voracek talks about getting a good night's sleep before the Czechs' next game. He talks about looking forward to going back to Halifax again and next year's Mooseheads. He talks about a host of other things but doesn't mention the draft. That's a healthy sign— not getting caught up in rankings and which teams are interested. He doesn't seem to have a clue.

I can't work up the enthusiasm to stick around for the third period of the second game. It's not jet lag like Voracek's, just the narcotic effect of two dull games near the end of a long season. I need to collapse on the rack before catching up with the scouts for a late-night bullshit session and getting the lowdown from Don Boyd and the rest of the Columbus crew.

The bar at the Scandic Hotel opposite the Tampere train station is standing room only. There's at least a hundred guys who pull down NHL paycheques, from high-powered general managers right down to part-timers who work in Scandinavia. It's an egalitarian set-up. A couple of general managers might go off to the side and away from the hoi polloi, but another exec will be mixing it up with his staffers or maybe a former teammate. The scouts who've spent their entire careers with one outfit could occupy one table in the room and leave the rest of the joint to those who know all about the knot in Don Boyd's stomach.

Boyd is at the bar standing beside Tim Murray, commiserating. Murray knows exactly what Boyd is going through. He was whacked in Anaheim a couple of summers ago when Brian Burke took over the Ducks. He's telling a story that he has told before — instant lore. The day his contract ended he went to a bar in his hometown of Shawville, Quebec, and knocked back a few beers to drown his sorrows. When he got home there was a message on his voicemail — the New York Rangers were asking about his availability. Reason for all to hope

Don Boyd is still putting on a brave face. If it's not quite three-beer courage, it's three-beer optimism. "There's a chance that Doug will hang on," he says. "He has two years to run. If he can get through this, he's on the clock, that's for sure."

Again Boyd trots out the talking points, the same ones MacLean will raise in his meeting with the owner. Last year it was the fact that Columbus had the fourth-best second-half record in the Western Conference. This year it was that the team was only five points out of the playoffs as late as February with emphasis on the 299 man-games lost because of injuries. It's all true, but it's not me or Tim Murray or anyone at the bar that Boyd has to sell. In fact, it's not Boyd's to sell at all. It's up to MacLean to convince the Columbus proprietor who has heard variations on these themes before.

The way Boyd tells it, MacLean might be drowned out by the chorus of critics in the Columbus media.

"They're killing us about our record," he says. "Well, Nashville didn't make the playoffs until year seven, and we'd be going into that next season. Is that going to help us?"

Probably not. I've been keeping up with the press MacLean and the Blue Jackets have been receiving, and "killing" is only barely hyperbolic. The bad press started early in the season when *The Hockey News* ranked MacLean twenty-ninth out of thirty NHL general managers. Then it turned nasty. *The Columbus Dispatch* all but dispatched MacLean at the end of the season. Just as the general manager could seize on a statistical talking point as evidence of the team's progress, so did the *Dispatch* make the case for his firing, pointing out that the closest the Blue Jackets ever came to making the playoffs was in their first season. Last week Bob Hunter, the *Columbus Dispatch*'s columnist, cited the talking points that MacLean trotted out on his local radio show and concluded: "The BS wears me out. Six years of non-stop BS has worn just about everybody out."

Another *Dispatch* writer, Todd Jones, kept up the hammering: "[MacLean] hired every coach and every scout until ownership stepped in and hired Ken Hitchcock. He signed every player, OK'd every draft pick and made every trade. And after six years, the team is still up to its nostrils in losses." Jones talked to five scouts outside the Blue Jackets organization and wrote that they all gave "bad marks" to the organization. When a member of the Blue Jackets' front office—Jones described him as "one of MacLean's trusted lieutenants"—expressed doubt about the story, Jones ratcheted up the mocking. He asked if the Blue Jackets were above industry criticism "because hockey people everywhere recognize the ingenious methods that went into building this hockey juggernaut?"

It would be tough press in any situation, even more so given that the Blue Jackets' owner owns a 10-percent stake in the *Dispatch*.

"They're killing us about our drafts," Boyd says. "It's easy to do. You cherry-pick things and it's easy to do."

Whether it's the Columbus media or other teams' scouts, the criticisms of the Blue Jackets' drafting record comes back to two unshining examples: Zherdev and Alexandre Picard.

Zherdev's is a plain case. Columbus chose Zherdev fourth overall in a draft deep in prospects who are already making an impact around the league. Dion Phaneuf, a defenceman who should be in the running for the Norris Trophy for a generation, went to Calgary with the ninth pick. A couple of forwards who are top-six forwards on contenders, Zach Parise and Ryan Getzlaf, went to New Jersey and Anaheim seventeenth and nineteenth overall.

Picard, the Blue Jackets' first-rounder in 2004, is a more complicated case, but still less than a score in the draft. Columbus selected the left winger from the Lewiston Maineiacs eighth overall and in 40 games with the Blue Jackets he has yet to score a goal and has racked up only one assist.

One scout I spoke with a few weeks back told me that he had Picard as a no-draft player. "I wouldn't have put him on my list," he told me. "There was no point putting him in the second round or third round—if you don't want him, you just don't want him."

Nearly three years later, with virtually no NHL stats—and not even decent American league numbers to support him—Boyd says he still believes in Picard. Maybe prospects start to look better closer to last call. Boyd still thinks it was a good choice in the circumstances, or at least a defensible one. He may be right. The class of 2004 was a collection of disappointments—not the top two slots, Russian stars Alexander Ovechkin and Evgeni Malkin, but rather the players from No. 5 through the end of the first round. Of those selected after Picard, only Nashville's Alexander Radulov looks like a certain first-liner.[32] Even a couple of players selected ahead of Picard look no better. At No. 5, Phoenix picked a Minnesota high schooler, Blake Wheeler, who hasn't impressed in NCAA play; at No. 6 the Rangers went for Al Montoya, a goaltender from the University of Michigan, who is only a marginal NHL prospect two years into his professional career.

"They were saying that we've had bad drafts," Boyd says. "We've had good ones. Is there any way that you can write that? Please, is there any way you can get that into print?"

---

32. Others who impress are Buffalo's Drew Stafford at No. 13, Colorado's Wojtek Wolski at No. 21 and Ottawa's Andrej Meszaros at No. 23.

The bartender drops the tab in front of us. I tell Don that I'll try to present a balanced picture when I tell my story.

April 18, 2007, Scandic Hotel, Tampere

Don Boyd is in the lobby of the Scandic Hotel. The breakfast buffet is set up in the dining room, but he doesn't have much of an appetite. He got the word: MacLean is done.

The Blue Jackets issued a press release. For once, MacLean is unavailable for comment. He will be leaving as he came. He was working as a general manager and president for two years before the team stepped on the ice, and he has two years to run on his contract as he cleans out his desk.

The Blue Jackets shuffle the deck. Jim Clark is bumped up to interim general manager, with the emphasis on *interim*. Mike Priest is installed as president. No matter whether he holds onto the title or steps aside for the incoming general manager, Priest is going to have clout in Columbus's executive offices.

I ask Boyd how he gets along with Priest, as if perhaps a personal connection might offer him an umbrella in the shitstorm. No such luck. "I've been with Columbus for six years and I've never met him," he says. It seems like MacLean was Priest's only contact with the hockey side, and if it comes down to pink-slipping longtime employees of the club, they'll only be so many faceless names on the payroll.

Boyd sits on a couch in the lobby and a few longtime regulars in the trade stop by to offer him well-meaning words of encouragement. He shakes their hands, but it has the feel of a receiving line at a memorial service. When they tell him to be strong and hang in and remember the good times, it seems to be as much for their own benefit as for Boyd's—everyone needs a reminder that his ticket can be pulled anytime. Not just MacLean, who appeared to have a bulletproof sinecure, but a loyal foot-soldier like Don Boyd.

Boyd doesn't talk about landing with another organization. That wouldn't be kosher—not yet. But he makes the under-18s sound like his farewell tour. "This could be it," he says. Could be that the Blue Jackets won't need him and his list. Not that he's asking for or accepting pity.

"They want me to come in for a meeting the day after I get back," he says. "This could be it. If it is, so be it."

Boyd and most on Columbus's scouting payroll signed two-year contracts last summer. They have a safety net through June 30, 2008, but like any high-wire act they don't want to use it. NHL coaches will often, even usually, collect the balance of a season or two remaining on a contract, the golden handshake they feel entitled to, no one begrudges them. For scouts though, it's insurance no one wants to collect. The longer a scout is out of the game, the harder it is for him to get back in. No matter the circumstances behind the dismissal, no matter how unfair, waiting out a paid vacation could earn a scout an adverse rep in a business that's supposed to be all about pride and work ethic.

The only good news is that Boyd and those who used to report to him know that change is in the air in Columbus before the combine, before the draft. So will other NHL teams. A last-second gassing—like the one in Buffalo last summer—would make it a lot more difficult to get word out in time for openings to be filled.

One of those who makes his way over to Boyd in the lobby is Grant Sonier. Sonier knows what Boyd is going through. He's one of the L.A. Kings scouts who were let go by general manger Dean Lombardi at the world juniors in Sweden in January. And Sonier has a real connection to Boyd. Boyd gave him his first break, a job as a poverty-waged assistant coach in Newmarket. Sonier assures Boyd that he'll land on his feet. Right now he seems more confidant of it than Boyd does.

"Bad things always happen when you're in Europe," says Sonier.

There's an awkward moment of silence. I try to fill it and lighten the mood by telling Sonier and Boyd about a weird coincidence.

"Over at the arena I picked up a guide for the Tampere team," I tell them. "Jason Bonsignore played a few games here and he hasn't played since."

Sonier grins, but Boyd's expression doesn't change. It's as if he has had a run of bad luck and now someone is pointing out a black cat crossing his path. At least Don Boyd's chances of being in the game are better than those of Bonsignore, the highest-drafted junior he ever coached.

Ten a.m., April 19, 2007, Tampere Hakamesta

The scouts won't show at the rink until the afternoon, for the quarter-final games, but I go out early for the Canadian practice. I figure it's a good chance to read players' work habits, study their skating mechanics and take the pulse of the team.

The optics are good. The practice opens lightly: the roster is divided into two teams, and with all players on the ice at the same time, the coaches throw a bunch of pucks onto the ice and a bit of shinny bedlam breaks out. A half-dozen games break out, players darting from one to another. After six or seven minutes, all the pucks are in the net save one. All the players descend on the lone puck in the closest thing that hockey would have to a rugby scrum, albeit one featuring a lot of the best of a coming generation of NHLers.

After that, the practice goes as practices have always gone. It's more of a skate than a heavy strategic session. Line rushes, break-outs. But banter and energy. Healthy signs.

Jim Hammett, Hockey Canada's scout and previously a scout with the Colorado Avalanche, talks up Trent Yawney, the coach brought in out of the cold for this under-18 team. Out of the cold, that is, in that he hasn't coached junior and isn't familiar with at least some of the players here. "How this guy doesn't have a NHL job, I don't know," Hammett says to me.

I don't volunteer to Hammett what I've heard over the past few days. Yawney didn't last long in Chicago because of a few moves that go beyond the unconventional into the downright bizarre. At one juncture, the story goes, Yawney decided to go with four lines all playing equal minutes. That type of troop rotation might work in war—or it might not. In a local house league it would quell the usual complaints from parents whose kids are shorted on ice time. In the NHL, though, this wasn't unorthodox innovation so much as outright socialism, especially when first-line forwards pull down salaries five, six and seven times those of a fourth-line grinder. It was a fast way to alienate the highest-priced talent on the roster. It apparently didn't sit well with the Chicago general manager, Dale Tallon, who made it plain that the best are paid more to play more.

Four p.m., April 19, 2007, Tampere Hakamesta

RUSSIA 4 SWITZERLAND 3 (OVERTIME)

At the end of a seemingly endless winter, this will probably turn out to be my favourite game, just because my expectations were so low beforehand and what took place was so unlikely.

This Swiss team is like most Swiss teams in this competition. That is to say, either skills-challenged or star-crossed. This team is like most that wear the white cross: big, disciplined, physical, mobile. The issue, as ever, is just a matter of giftedness. There isn't a Swiss player who inspires with either playmaking or sniping ability. There never has been before.[33] The one candidate here, Luca Cunti, shows some flash but not a lot of drive. As for the rest—it's like asking coal miners to cut diamonds.

Through the first five minutes, the game plays out as expected, the Russians running out to a 2–0 lead on goals by Egor Averin and

---

33. The one possible exception was the ill-starred Luca Cerada, who was the leading scorer in the under-18 tournament in 1999 and the Toronto Maple Leafs' first-round draft pick ahead of Martin Havlat among others. Cereda's career was stalled by an irregular heartbeat, and his prospects of playing NHL hockey ended in his early twenties.

Vyacheslav Voinov. To the scouts it looks like the rout is on—apparently to the Russians, too, because they begin to coast at this point. Denis Hollenstein scores for the Swiss a couple of minutes later and Switzerland starts to seize control of play. For the balance of the first period and throughout the second they take the game to the Russians but just can't finish off several glorious chances. Skyscrapers are raised in less time than it takes the Swiss to build up to the tying goal, Hollenstein's second of the game. It comes only at the end of seventeen minutes of unrelenting pressure. Not on a play so much as a shaggy-dog story. When Pascal Berger scores midway through the third period it looks like a mighty upset. The Russians haven't done a thing through forty minutes of play and their star player, Alexei Cherepanov, looks like he's out for a pleasure skate.

Alas, the story is too good to be true. Nikolai Klyukin scores with ten minutes left in regulation to tie the game. In the end an underage Russian, a dynamic winger named Nikita Filatov, scores seven minutes into overtime. Filatov powers in on the net from the left wing and dekes goaltender Robert Mayer. He skates to the far corner and makes a big theatrical turn, waiting for his linemates to mob him. None do. In fact, they skate away from him and form a little hugging / high-fiving trio. Filatov pays no mind to the snub and skates to the bench, where he receives a lukewarm reception—the treatment a banjo hitter will get sometimes from pranksome teammates when he gets back to the dugout after a rare homer.

U.S. 7 Slovakia 2

The other quarterfinal lacks all the drama but has its own humorous touch, when U.S. goaltender Josh Unice ducks a shot from outside the blue line and it goes into the net, just under the crossbar.

Four p.m., April 20, 2007, Tampere Hakamesta

RUSSIA 5 SWEDEN 4

Russia's struggles against the Swiss shouldn't have come as such a big surprise. The Russians are the youngest team in the tournament. Nine players are eligible for the 2008 draft (seven 1990 birthdays and two late '89s), and one won't be eligible until the John Tavares draft in 2009. Even those eligible for the upcoming draft skew young. Five of the twelve players who are up for the draft in Columbus were born in August or early September of 1989—they miss out on the 2008 draft by six weeks or less.

The scouts are forgiving of those players, but they're not cutting Alexei Cherepanov any slack. He was missing in action against the Swiss, and throughout the tournament the scouts have been unimpressed with his work ethic. Hard to imagine that he could be named the top forward at the under-20s and be a high-scoring firstliner against former NHLers in the Russian elite league yet fade into the background at the under-18s. In his first few shifts against the Swedes, the wonder is that the Russian coaches keep playing him—while his linemates are forechecking furiously, he cruises the Swedish end like he just wants to get a good look at the action. On one forecheck a line mate gets him the puck, wide open, at the face-off dot on the right wing, and Cherepanov whiffs completely, like a novice.

Given Russia's youth and Cherepanov's walkabouts, the Swedes have to like their chances in the first semifinal, especially when they run out to a 2–0 lead two minutes into the second period. At this point, though, Cherepanov takes over the game. On his next shift he stickhandles with impunity through three checkers and runs a lap around the Swedish end before dishing the puck to Evgeni Dadonov, who is unchecked on the far side of the crease. Two-one and, worse for the Swedes, Cherepanov is engaged.

Sergei Korostin and the underage Filatov add goals to give the Russians the lead at the end of the second period. The Swedes score twice in the third period, including a penalty shot by Mikael Backlund with five minutes to go in regulation to tie the game four-all. But over the last twenty minutes the others are playing in a game that Cherepanov owns. His first goal triggers a sense of déjà vu—it begins with the same set-up that he whiffs on in the first period, same forecheck, same spot, but this time there's a cold hard finish—and he fires the puck high on the short side, above goalkeeper Mark Owuya's glove.

It's an exquisite skill display but it has nothing on Cherepanov's game-winning goal. The Russians go on the power play with thirty seconds left in regulation. Cherepanov, Dadonov and Averin buzz around the Swedish end of the rink. Averin fires the puck from the half-boards, not to Dadonov so much as *at* him. It hits Dadonov in the leg and caroms to Cherepanov—who isn't looking for the puck but must be sensing that it's coming. When he puts it past Owuya, the scoreboard reads 19:59.[34] A play that's up there with Mario Lemieux letting the puck pass between his skates in the Olympic final in 2002—not an instance of hockey sense so much as an intuition. I'm sitting just a few rows up from ice level. If the play were choreographed and tried a thousand times without defencemen, without a goaltender, the best NHLers couldn't make it happen.

Seven p.m., Tampere Hakamesta

U.S. 4 CANADA 3 (SHOOTOUT)

The two teams met only a few days ago in the opening round with Canada registering a 3–3 victory in a shootout. You'd presume that would give the Canadians confidence, but they're as tight as frog skin to open the game. The hallmarks of Canadian hockey—big hits on a hard forecheck, establishing a high work rate and emotional

---

34. Scoreboards in IIHF tournaments count time up rather than down.

level and intimidating opponents—are nowhere to be seen. The Americans own a big advantage in shots on goal, 14–6, in the first period and Vincent Saponari's goal with fifteen seconds to go gives them a 1–0 lead.

The U.S. again dominates play in the second period, firing nineteen shots on goaltender Trevor Cann, but Canada scores three times on just ten shots. Zach Boychuk scores twice and then Kyle Turris, the BCHL player, scores his third goal of the tournament to give Canada a 3–2 lead going into the third period.

Turris didn't make much of an impression on me at the summer under-18s—all I can remember is how slight he seemed—but all season long I've heard scouts talk about his performance with the Burnaby Express. He burst onto the scene last season, leading his team to the national junior A championship, and this year has performed miracles regularly. His numbers are otherworldy: 66 goals and 55 assists in 53 regular-season games this year. Coaches in the Western league have ripped Turris, saying that he should have joined the Vancouver Giants, the club that drafted him, if he really wanted to develop as a player— that he was beating up on inferior competition in the BCHL. But the scouts' reviews aren't enthusiastic as much as rapturous. The most memorable game for many came in November in Yorkton, Saskatchewan, when Turrus led a Provincial A all-star squad past a Russian touring team—scoring four times and twice hitting posts.

A few days before coming over I called up Turris's coach in Burnaby, ex-NHLer Rick Lanz, and at the tournament I caught up with his father, Bruce, who was a lacrosse legend in his day. Both defended Kyle's decision to pay in the BCHL and to attend the University of Wisconsin next season. Lanz said Kyle weighed several factors in opting for U.S. college. "He's a highly intelligent kid who understands his game better than anyone else," Lanz told me. "He believes he needs the time to fill out and that college was a better fit for him. He also made a promise to his teammates that he'd come back this season. It was his decision and his decision alone."

Turris picks up his goal against the U.S. on his second scoring chance on a shift midway through the second period. Twice Angelo

Esposito sets Turris up. The first time Turris fans, the second time he roofs a shot from the slot.

Maybe the scouts are looking for Turris to step up. Instead, American forward James van Riemsdyk makes the rest of the game his personal showcase. Van Riemsdyk plays up to his billing as a candidate for the first-overall selection. He scores the tying goal in the third, and Canadian defencemen can't handle him on the cycle the rest of the way. At one point in overtime, with the teams playing four-on-four, he's Mark Katic's worst nightmare. He's a full head taller than the Canadian defenceman—not only can't Katic get the puck off him, but he probably can't see it.

Van Riemsdyk generates chances but can't win the game in overtime. But his goal in the shootout sends the U.S. into the final. He skates the length of the ice back to his teammates on the other side of the red line, passing the Canadian bench, taunting the crestfallen losing side. Most of the Canadian players have heads bowed, though I can see Brandon Sutter taking van Riemsdyk's number.

April 22, 2007, Tampere Hakamesta

The arena starts to fill up. A lot of scouts, maybe half of those who were here a couple of days ago, have gone home. Time management. They don't think it's worth the wait of two days to see two games. Don Boyd could have gone home. Maybe he thinks that he should have. It must feel like he's putting off the inevitable: what looks like his last day on the road with the Blue Jackets.

"I had things pencilled in," he tells me in the stands while the Canadians and Swedes skate in the warmups before the bronze-medal game. "I was gonna go over to the O and see a game in the Plymouth–London series this week. I thought I might even drive out to catch a game or two between Sudbury and Belleville. There was the USHL . . . figured I'd make some games in that depending on who was playing where. And I was going to go to the Mem Cup. The way it's looking, we could have four players in that."

A trigger word there: The first person plural. He says "we" but realizes soon enough that it could be "they" in short order.

"I'm not going to Memorial Cup and I don't think that I'm going to be doing much else," he says. "I don't know where I stand . . . what they want me to do . . . if anything. I'm just going to go back home. Gotta drive from Detroit. I'll know more during the week. But right now I don't know what my role is . . . if anything. I haven't been in a position like this for a long while."

Boyd fears he's through with the organization. And as unhappy and stressful as imminent unemployment might be, Don Boyd seems even unhappier coming off the road, even for the short stretch of the junior hockey season that remains. If he has to go down and go out, he wishes he could go down scouting. It's not just a habit he can't break. He's hurting because his reputation rides on this draft as much as all the others. He can't even rule out being told to sit out the draft entirely. Just last spring the Islanders' scouts had to sit at the team table, like movie extras with no speaking parts, while the team psychologist made the picks. The indignity attached to their final paycheque. It could be something that humbling for Boyd.

Milan Tichy is sitting behind Boyd and soon Kjell Larsson and Paul Castron will be flanking him.

"Are you gonna go to Belleville?" Boyd asks me.

"Belleville at least," I tell him. "I might end up going to Sudbury if it goes six. I might even try to get to London if that series stretches out."

"If you're going to Belleville, give me a report on McQuaid and Tangradi," he says.

If I had any doubts about going to Belleville, they're erased now. Not that I want or need to feel in the loop. No, I'd feel bad if I didn't do my part, my very small part, in letting Don Boyd feel connected.

SWEDEN 8 CANADA 3

Generalizations about the game are usually suspect. One, though, is unassailable: Canadian teams don't play for bronze. Just think of all the Hall of Famers—Gretzky, Yzerman, etc.—on the Canadian

Olympic team that lost to Finland in the bronze-medal game in Nagano in 1998. While other teams skate with their nations' hopes behind them, the Canadians skate with the weight of a nation's expectations on their shoulders. As soon as gold is out of reach, their failure is assured and they let down.

The suspense in the bronze-medal game is limited to the first ten minutes or so.

Just as they had in the semifinal against the U.S., the Canadians don't establish their forecheck. Those expected to fill that role, most notably Colton Gillies, just aren't finding the Swedes on the back wall and in the corners. Again, Esposito and Turris are trying to find their games. Those expected to carry the offence, to initiate and finish it, seem out of sync. Esposito makes one move too many and shies away from contact; Turris looks too slight to fight through checks and hold-ups that are going uncalled by a Slovak ref. Any chance to turn their fortunes around is killed by bad goaltending. The Swedes score an opening goal midway through the first period on a forty-five-foot floating, unscreened wrist shot that goaltender Trevor Cann fluffs. A batting-practice fastball that he gets only a piece of his glove on. The descent gathers speed.

The final two games are a second-guesser's delight, and no one is a more authoritative second-guesser than scouts here.

Fortier reprises his role as a penalty-killer and third- and fourth-liner, yet it's clear that Logan Couture is either physically not up to playing in this tournament or just in over his head. To move Fortier up into a more prominent role would seem a logical step. It's just one adjustment on the fly that the scouts would have liked to see Yawney make.

Even stranger, though, was one move that Yawney made but then abandoned. In the second period against Sweden, Yawney seemed to strike on a line that finally lit a fire under Turris, placing Colton Gillies and Brandon Sutter on his wings. For a couple of shifts in the second period, the hard-hitting Gillies and canny Sutter seemed to open the ice up for Turris. No goals, but chances and good shifts. Evidently, that wasn't enough for Yawney, who shuffled line assignments once more. The promising threesome was split up to struggle separately.

While the scouts take a dinner break before the final, I go down to the Canadian dressing room. Maybe the scouts will ask the Canadian players about the tournament at the combine—when the players will have had a chance to prep their answers. I'm looking for the unfiltered response. The players might still choose their words carefully. But their faces, their voices, are the real article. There's no disguising it with poker faces.

Turris, eyes red, voice cracking, is the most despondent. He had more to prove than any other Canadian player here, simply by reason of his playing against lesser competition in the BCHL.

"I didn't have the best of tournaments," Turris says. "It's tough. I started slow and I thought that maybe it was coming together at the end of the opening round, but I just didn't get it going. The coach kept playing me. He kept giving me a chance and putting me out there. Y'know, I thank him for that, but I don't think that I deserved to be out there. I didn't do my part for the team."

And of the players I speak to, the one most buoyant is Steven Stamkos, again predictable. While Yawney is giving a speech to the team after the game, IIHF officials peel Stamkos away from the Canadian room for a urine test. Just as the Canadian team struggled to perform on the ice, the underager struggles when handed a beaker and is occupied for nearly half an hour. Maybe the absurdity of it has him smiling by the time he comes out. Stamkos looks about as disappointed as a kid who goes on a school trip to Europe and ends up going to the Eiffel Tower on a rainy day.

"It was an honour just to get invited to the tournament," Stamkos says. "The under-17s was great, but there were a lot of us who had played together or against each other for years. We came up together. Here it was players I had never met, guys I had just heard about."

In the wake of the loss Esposito seems weary and resigned, not angered. "It's a learning experience for all us," he says. "You know, we learned that there are other good teams in the world and we learned about expectations."

Expectations. A loaded word. I was going to bring it up, but he mentions it without my solicitation.

"Personally, I've been dealing with expectations all year," he says. "I think Patrick [Roy] has been a big help to me in that way."

RUSSIA 6 U.S. 5

I sit with Dale Tallon, who was the Chicago general manager, for a stretch. Tallon knows firsthand the difference between a No. 1 pick and a No. 2. He was the No. 2 choice of Vancouver back when the Canucks joined the league. The history of the franchise would have looked entirely different if Buffalo had drafted Tallon at the top and Gilbert Perreault had fallen into the Canucks' lap.

I ask Tallon if his first pick overall is playing today.

"Oh yeah," he says. "Somewhere. Maybe here. Maybe in the Plymouth-London series."

That sets a few scouts around us talking about the London team. News from the Ontario league makes it all the way over here. The Knights, that most professional of junior teams, faced a far stiffer than expected challenge from their second-round opponents, the Soo Greyhounds.

In fact, when the series went to a seventh game, the Knights were looking for a competitive advantage and booked airfare from the Soo to London for five of their players, including Patrick Kane and Sam Gagner. That sets off snickering in the ranks—it might leave a few stars feeling a little fresher for the deciding game, but it would be bound to cause resentment in the ranks.

After van Riemsdyk's performance against Canada, it's hard to imagine that he isn't near the top of the Chicago list. And against the Russians, his play doesn't fall off: a goal, a couple of assists. The word around the arena has been that some scouts aren't impressed by his work ethic—not that he's lazy but that he picks his spots and waits for openings rather than seizing the initiative and imposing his will on a game. He seems fully engaged against the Russians as the U.S. runs out to 2–0 and 3–2 leads in the first period and goes into the third period tied at four.

The judgment on Cherepanov has been even more damning. It's a consensus scouting report: Does not play hard. If you focus on him for whole shifts, whole periods, he rarely strays in from the perimeter. Like he was against the Swiss and for long stretches against the Swedes, Cherepanov seems to be going through the motions.

Even those most critical of Cherepanov have to give him his due: more than any player in this tournament or in this draft, he is capable of taking over a shift and finishing a play with flair, stuff his peers can't even imagine. That's the case on the goal that decides this tournament.

With less than ten minutes to go, Cherepanov controls the puck on the cycle—defencemen Ryan McDonagh and Kevin Shattenkirk look like greyhounds chasing the mechanical rabbit, staying in his wake, knowing they'll never quite catch up. Cherepanov weaves in and out of traffic, dishes the puck to an open teammate on the point so he can set himself up behind the net. When centre Vitali Karamnov delivers Cherepanov the puck behind the net, Shattenkirk has the thankless, impossible task of giving chase. It wouldn't be an imminently threatening situation with anyone else in this tournament. Cherepanov skates out to the side of the net, ten feet out at a forty-five-degree angle, and, with indecent confidence, spins without looking and fires the puck between Shattenkirk's skates and above goaltender Josh Unice's glove into the top corner of the net. They look on at first dismayed, disbelieving, unable to figure out how Cherepanov has scored, how he put the puck blindly an inch under the crossbar from an acute angle.

At the end of the game the Russians celebrate. I ask Dale Tallon if he thinks Cherepanov is the best player in the draft.

"He'll be a player, all right," Tallon says. "Just not a Blackhawk."

On the way out of the rink I spot Don Boyd again, among a bunch of scouts heading for the parking lots and their rides back to Helsinki. I tell him that I'll get back to him with write-ups on the game in Belleville and my notes from the Canadian team.

Seven a.m., April 23, 2007, Helsinki Airport

I'm on the same flight from Helsinki to Frankfurt as the Canadian team. I'm in line with Angelo Esposito, who seems to be filling the role of team leader more naturally than he did last summer in Piestany and Breclav. The banter with players in two languages doesn't seem forced at all.

I talk to him and he seems relieved, that the worst is over. Though he has a day of travelling ahead of him—Helsinki–Frankfurt–Toronto–Montreal—he has some sort of closure. I mention to him to the story out of London with the five players on the charter. He looks at me in disbelief at first.

"Personally, I wouldn't take that flight if it was offered to me," he says. "I know what that would do with the others. It's just not worth it. You've got to be thinking how your choices affect the team."

It's a hell of an answer, and for the right reasons. Fact is, the beneficiaries of the elite Knights should have been mindful of how it would play with their teammates. Yeah, this was the first year that Esposito was the feature player on his team—he hadn't been that in Shattuck and he hadn't been that in his first season in Quebec either. The downside: maybe an uneasiness in the spotlight. The upside: maybe empathy for those in the wings.

It got me to wondering whether Nikita Filatov ever grabbed a charter instead of boarding the team bus.

April 25, 2007, Yardman Arena, Belleville

Sudbury 3 Belleville 1

I'm still reeling from the trip back from Finland, still paying the price for a seven-and-a-half-hour stopover in Frankfurt. The drive out from Toronto is 180 kilometres and about as many yawns. It would be an easy game to pass up. I could rationalize it away. I don't even know whether Don Boyd still has a job, never mind a voice, in the Blue Jackets organization. I sent off an email this morning, but I didn't hear back. I go out to Belleville for Game 5 of the Ontario league's eastern conference final anyway. That last night in Finland I told Boyd I'd send him back reports on Adam McQuaid and Eric Tangradi. One more view piled up on top of dozens of others, one from the least qualified and least trustworthy set of eyes. I'll keep my word on that, whether it matters or—almost certainly—not.

Belleville and Sudbury split the first four games and the Yardman Arena is sold out. The scouts who've made it out are lined up in standing room beside the press box forty minutes before the game. If they're late they'll be two or three deep, watching the game over a fan's shoulder. About twenty scouts are there when I arrive.

This morning, NHL Central Scouting issued its final lists of draft-eligible juniors, and they're the chief topic of conversation in standing room. The lists are a little like final marks for the honours students in their final semester of high school—the best of them have already been accepted by the universities of their choice, so their grades really don't matter that much. In this case Central Scouting's final rankings won't factor in the draft-day decisions of NHL clubs—no scouting staff will refer to them, the way some might have early in the season or in mid-winter, looking for marginal kids in leagues receiving little coverage. The final rankings are delivered with fanfare for the benefit of fans and to add to the mix of hope and dread experienced by the prospects themselves. It doesn't occur to the players that the NHL scouts pay scant attention at this point to anybody's opinion but their own.

At a glance the lists look much like those from any other year: a mosaic of assorted players in assorted positions drawn from assorted leagues in assorted countries. Even in memorable years the lists resemble those of others. They are, after all, just lists of numbers and names—each is like a straight line descending forty-five degrees on a graph, a perfect diagonal trajectory, from the highest point at the left to the bottom right of the page. The list doesn't give you any sense of separation—the idea that there was a hell of a fall-off in 2005 between Crosby and the No. 2-ranked skater in North America, Benoit Pouliot, or that the same might have been said of the Euros in 2004 between the first two skaters, Ovechkin and Malkin, and the next two, Rotislav Olesz and Ladislav Smid.[35]

Within this year's final lists there are clues that this season might be out of the ordinary—they're just not the clues that you might expect. When the media first reported on the release of the lists, the lead story was that Kyle Turris was the first player from Tier II to be ranked as the top player among North American skaters.

The festival standing arrangement—claim your place on the rail in back of the last row—leaves me next to Chris Edwards, a former linesman in the O and the American league who is now chief scout with Central. When I ask Edwards about Turris and mention that he never jumped out in any game at the summer or spring under-18s, he assures me the top-ranked player is deserving of the high marks. Edwards says that Turris is a hype-free No. 1, that he lit up a Russian team—"four goals and two posts, could have been six goals easy, against the Russians in the [World] Challenge game out in Yorkton in November."

Turris's emergence is interesting stuff, but more a measure of one player than evidence of a paradigm shift. There was a lot more to

---

35. Benoit Pouliot has yet to stick with Minnesota after being drafted No. 4 overall. Olesz, drafted No. 7 overall, has played two full seasons with Florida and scored 19 goals, compared with Malkin's 33 in his rookie campaign with Pittsburgh. Anaheim drafted Smid ninth overall but has traded the defenceman to Edmonton.   .

glean from the list if you cross-referenced it with the mid-terms. It wasn't just that Turris shot up from No. 5 to No. 1. An even bigger move was made by Angelo Esposito—from the top rank in the mid-term to No. 8. Esposito's fall was even more precipitous than that of Jason Bonsignore, who dropped from No. 1 in the mid-terms to No. 4 in the final. Then again, neither Turris's rise nor Esposito's fall are the most dramatic swings in fortunes in the draft. Brandon Sutter in Red Deer falls from ninth in the mid-terms to 28th in the final, while Stefan Legein from Mississauga shoots up from 32nd to 13th.

Scouts have been saying all season that there are few breakout talents, that the player drafted at No. 40 or No. 50 might be as good as the tenth pick in the draft. That mood seems to be reflected in the final rankings. Fact is, players who were in ranked in the top twenty dropped like anchors into the second twenty, while others moved weightlessly up into their places. Said one scout along press row out of Edwards's earshot: "Some of the movement could have, and probably should have, been even more dramatic. There might have been a little face-saving going on . . . not wanting some players to fall so far that they'd have you wondering how they ranked way up in the mid-terms."

Two minutes after I take my narrow place on the rail, there's a surprise, one that has me doing a double-take: Don Boyd and Jim Clark arrive. Handshakes and backslaps from the regulars, the kind you'd give someone who made it out of surgery, or who made it back from the front lines.

The teams are off the ice and the Zamboni is looping the rink before the opening face-off when I catch up with Boyd, who looks far happier than he did at any time in Finland.

"What did they tell you?" I ask.

"Just to carry on like normal," he says. "Keep on keeping on."

Normal. He'll have a voice at the draft.

Keep on keeping on. Right through to the Memorial Cup.

Who wouldn't take any consolation from those directions? From what I can tell, almost anybody else except Don Boyd and Jim Clark. They were so prepared for the worst that anything less feels like winning the lottery. Still, they don't have any illusions about their status. Boyd tells me that Clark will interview for the general manager's job and that he will, too, but he also tells me not to read the wrong thing into it.

"They're going to talk to a lot of people who have been in the organization and they're going to listen to a lot of people on the outside, too."

It's as much about the past six seasons as the seasons to come, post mortem as much as head-hunting. Especially for Boyd and Jim Clark. The Blue Jackets' owner placed a lot of trust in Doug MacLean, and only at this late date are he and the execs on the business side getting familiar with the hockey side of the franchise.

"You were gonna file that report on McQuaid and Tangradi, weren't you?" Boyd says.

"Still will," I tell him.

The template for the Wolves' success in the playoff is still in place. Marc Staal is the best nineteen-year-old defenceman in the world and he dominates play for the thirty minutes a game he plays. Nick Foligno plays like you'd expect a coach's son would, making smart decisions at every turn, winning almost every shift. Sudbury's little Danish goaltender, Sebastien Dahm, is playing out of his mind.

The game is tied at one in the second period and the Bulls trail by only a goal late in the second period, but at no time does it seem as if the home team will win the game.

It's 2–1 Sudbury in the dying minutes of the game when Akim Aliu gets his moment to shine. He gets loose of a Belleville defence-man, skates in on goal and bangs it home. He skates past the net and gathers speed along the boards as the crowd looks on silently. For that moment his troubles with the Wolves are, like the Belleville defenceman, behind him.

"I'll catch the Plymouth–London game and then we'll see what we're going to do from there," Boyd tells me as we head to the parking lot. "I don't know about the Memorial Cup still. John Williams and Sam McMaster are going to be there and we should have players out there, though it doesn't look like there will be any draft [prospects]. It would probably be good to meet out there, but right now I don't know."

Even though Boyd made it out to the game, I write up my reports as I promised—not that my evaluations of the two target players mean much; more to see if he thinks my readings of the players are even close.

McQuaid: Quiet, safe, effective game. Will hit. Complementary player who understands that less is more for him.
Tangradi: Didn't show any burst. Did not compete hard. No fire.

I wonder if I reward the kid on the winning team too much and if I'm unfairly punishing the player on the losing side. I might as well write, *Looks good playing beside Marc Staal* for McQuaid and *Can't beat a future NHL franchise defenceman* for Tangradi. Those evaluations would apply to almost any junior—then again, maybe that's all they are: average junior players with limited prospects of a playing at the next level.

May 21, 2007, Pacific Coliseum, Vancouver

MEDICINE HAT 4 PLYMOUTH 1

Day Four of the Memorial Cup tournament features a tilt between the champions of the Western and Ontario leagues. Both teams lost their opening games here. The Whalers were unlucky to lose to the host Vancouver Giants in overtime on Friday night. The next day the Tigers could only get one puck past Jonathan Bernier, the Lewiston Maineiacs' goaltender and the Los Angeles Kings' first-round pick in the 2006 draft. The way the Memorial Cup is set up, a team's bid for a national title, months and years in the making, can go up in smoke in 120 minutes or so. Two losses to open the four-team tournament leave a team needing help just to have a chance to get into the elimination round of games.

For all the drama, the atmosphere isn't electric. The Pacific Coliseum isn't full—it's the holiday Monday of the Victoria Day weekend. Neither team has marquee player like Sidney Crosby, who had been when he packed the stands at the Memorial Cup in London two years ago. Fans might come out to root for the Western champion Medicine Hat Tigers, but not the week after they knocked off Vancouver in a tense seven-game WHL final. And in other circumstances fans would come out to root for an Ontario league team to knock off the Tigers, but the OHL team is based in the U.S. A dilemma for fans.

No dilemma for the Columbus scouts, though. Not for Don Boyd and Jim Clark, who've made the trip after all the uncertainty. They're watching four of their own players in the game: defenceman Kris Russell and forward Derek Dorsett on the Tigers, Tom Sestito and Jared Boll on the Whalers. The Blue Jackets don't have pressing decisions to make on the prospects: all have signed contracts with the club.

No, the Columbus scouts can focus on the players they own rather than any they might acquire.

The two teams' styles couldn't be further apart. Plymouth will look for Sestito, Boll and James Neal to physically hammer the smaller Tigers. They intimidated Ontario league teams all season and will try to do the same here. Medicine Hat will look to skate right past the Whalers and to have Russell and Dorsett leading in very different ways—Russell with skill and cool, Dorsett with grit and fire. Russell was named the top player in the WHL last week, just days after Vancouver management accused Dorsett of biting Giants forward Kendall McArdle during a melée in Game 4 of the final. Though Dorsett denied sinking his teeth into McArdle, it seemed entirely in keeping with his hyper-competitive attitude.

Those elements—Plymouth's size, the Hat's skating—are in play, but almost as secondary themes. The Whalers' goaltending, a strength all season, betrays them. Michal Neuvirth, the Washington pick who had looked shaky in the Ontario league final against Sudbury, gives up two goals on the first two real shots he faces. The second of them squirts through the five-hole and produces gales of laughter. Behind the Plymouth bench on the scoreboard's video screen, coach Mike Vellucci looks stricken. Neuvirth out, backup Jeremy Smith in.

Through the rest of the first period the Whalers are the better team, but can't put the puck in the net. The idea that it isn't going to be their night starts sinking in during a Plymouth power play when Tom Sestito gets a rolling, fluttering puck beside the net with Medicine Hat goaltender Matt Keatley sprawled on the far side. Sestito swipes at the puck twice, and seems to get a piece of it both times, but can't push it over the goal line. From three feet out he finally pushes it wide. By the end of the period, Plymouth is still down 2–0, though with any goaltending and luck they could be up by the same score.

Russell is again a treat to watch. At the world juniors, I thought he was just an interesting player, a novelty, maybe a player who could make the NHL as a power-play specialist. At five foot nine and 160 pounds he just looked too small to take a regular shift in the pros. And even here he looks like a midget player skating out into a junior game; it seems as if he might get in harm's way. Once the puck is dropped, though, it's clear that harm won't find Russell—as quickly as any bigger player might close on him, he anticipates the play that has to be made and the best way to get up the ice.

It seems more a matter of quickness than speed—that is, Russell's hockey sense is so strong, so wired, that he can make his reads almost instantly. He makes play after play ahead of any pressure, but never seems to hurry. He's not hell bent to rush the puck on every possession, but when he does take off it can be breathtaking. The best example comes at one point in the second period: Sestito chases him on the forecheck in the Tigers' end of the rink, but Russell gets by him with a head fake and a spin. In three strides he leaves Sestito and another Plymouth player fading in his wake.

The Columbus scouts maintain that this isn't even Russell at his best. "He's really banged up," Don Boyd says. "From his shoulder to his wrist, his arm is one big bruise."

"Any team that's played Medicine Hat has gone after him hard," John Williams says. "The way Red Deer went after him in the opening round, seven games, was brutal. He's so game, though. He doesn't slow down. He leaves it all on the ice."

I watch the third period standing beside Boyd and his friend from his days with the Quebec Nordiques, Don Paarup. Paarup is a throwback the to scouts of Al Ritchie's era. He wears a houndstooth hat, just like the one Tony Lucadello used to wear. He doesn't use a Blackberry, just a ruled notebook full of unevenly scrawled notes. He has stayed with one outfit all these years—when the Nordiques moved to Colorado back in '95, they took Paarup with them. Beyond all this, Paarup reminds scouts of another time, better days, when teams had more fun on the job. Back in those days it seemed that scouts spent as much time plotting pranks as they did filing reports, and Paarup was the preferred dupe.

I first met him at the 2001 Memorial Cup. When I saw the houndstooth hat, I actually thought he was in costume for a piece of community theatre. Paarup was passing by the front desk of the Regina Inn when he saw Archie Henderson, then a Washington Capitals scout, checking in with his golf clubs beside him.

"Arch, when are you gonna get a chance to go golfing with all the games in the day?" Paarup asked.

"I'm going golfing tonight," Henderson deadpanned.

"Tonight?" Paarup said, not realizing the hook had already pierced his cheek.

"Yeah, night golf," Henderson said. "The provincial government and the Saskatchewan power authority got together and they set up lights on a nice little nine-hole course about ten minutes north of the city. Wanna come out?"

One thing led to another—Henderson assuring Paarup that they wouldn't have to line up, that prices were fair and that rental clubs would be available. And after the game that night, at 11 p.m., Paarup showed up at the front desk ready to golf, with a gaggle of scouts looking on across the lobby, convulsing in laughter.

Paarup has been the butt of a thousand snipe hunts. Boyd has told me that the Quebec scouts couldn't help themselves. They'd tell him that meetings were set up for one conference room at a hotel and then send him on a wild-goose chase by putting a sign on the door saying the meeting had been moved to a room where, inevitably, another similar sign had been placed on the door. Schoolyard stuff, but Paarup took it so goodnaturedly, responding with nothing stronger than a dopey "Aw shucks, guys" or "You got me again."

The last laugh has been Paarup's, though. As Western league scout for the Nordiques, he has been able to dine out on the drafting of Joe Sakic for a generation.

The Medicine Hat-Plymouth game has an ill-tempered end. The Whalers are frustrated. Boll starts acting out. Sestito goes after Russell twice. The first time, Sestito takes a run all the way from left wing to the far boards, but Russell ducks and it's Sestito who is sent sprawling. The second time is the more egregious. Behind the play, out of sight of the officials skating up the ice, Sestito slashes Russell across the leg, across the side of his left knee. Russell falls to the ice and then limps off before the trainer can come out.

In July, Sestito and Russell will skate at the Blue Jackets' development camp. In September they'll be at Columbus's training camp. They're probably destined to play together for the farm club in Syracuse down the line. Here, though, Sestito looks intent on having Russell carried off the ice on a stretcher.

Marriott restaurant, Vancouver

I catch up with Don Boyd, John Williams and Jim Clark at dinner after the game. Usually, the session would be a free-flowing comparing of notes, but it's hardly that this time because Ken Hitchcock has made the trip west. It's Hitchcock's first good look at some pieces that he'll have in seasons down the line: Russell, Dorsett, Sestito and Boll. Although he had about three-quarters of a season to study the bunch of

Columbus draftees who've made the big club, Hitchcock was still working in Philly when these junior draftees attended the Blue Jackets' training camp last fall. Hitchcock doesn't have that much to say about the two Medicine Hat Tigers while I'm around , but he does seem encouraged about the players on tonight's losing team.

"That Sestito does so many things like a pro," Hitchcock enthuses. "Boll always seems to be trying to stir things up."

Dinner's an awkward session. For the Blue Jackets it's not fine dining but rather humble hamburgers. No beers either. Boyd, Williams and Clark have to feel like it's not the draftees who are under review so much as the *drafters*, the scouting staff assembled by the general manager who was pushed out the door held open by Hitchcock. The scouts' job prospects ride on the whims of the Blue Jackets' next general manager, but Hitchcock still wields clout in the team's executive office, still has the owner's ear.

Hitchcock sees Clément Jodoin, the Lewiston coach, sitting by himself at table beside the bar.

"Lonely time, eh, Clément?" Hitchcock says and he waves. He turns to the scouts. "I know what he's going through. You're in this tournament and nobody wants to talk to you."

Hitchcock keeps describing the pressure-cooker of coaching in a championship. This strikes me, if nobody else at the table, as ironic. I remember covering the Dallas Stars when they were making their run to the Stanley Cup in 1999. During that stretch, nobody seemed to be having more fun that Hitchcock. In fact, he talked to me about trying to enjoy the experience because he didn't know if he'd ever get another chance to play for a championship. Right now, he has to believe that he's years away from the spotlight with the Blue Jackets.

As lonely as Hitchcock ever felt or as Jodoin might feel it must be as unpleasant for the longtime Blue Jackets scouts. It's hard not to notice someone looking over your shoulder, and that's what Hitchcock is doing. So Hitchcock's enthusiasm for Sestito is heartening, but no one at the table is reading too much into it.

May 22, 2007, Pacific Coliseum, Vancouver

MEMORIAL CUP OPENING ROUND
PLYMOUTH 2 LEWISTON 1 (OVERTIME)

Fortunes rise and fall with lightning speed at the Memorial Cup, the Whalers providing the best example in their last opening-round game.

Truth is, for more than two periods it's a brutal, uninteresting game — no goals, no passion, no beauty, the scouts grousing. After the Whalers' loss to Medicine Hat, Plymouth coach Mike Vellucci said he'd take the blame for his team "not being ready to play," but the next day his players still seem listless, looking nothing like the team that rolled through the Ontario league playoffs. Boll recklessly runs players from behind and looks astonished every time the ref whistles him. Sestito's game, Hitchcock's enthusiasm aside, isn't where it was earlier in the year — he looks more like a fifteen-goal plugger than a forty-goal first-liner. And James Neal, the stalwart, seems stuck in second gear.

The only reason that the game is at all competitive is that Lewiston can't generate any offence. The Maineiacs open with a flurry of shots in the first three shifts but then register only ten more over the next thirty-five minutes, none of them testing Michal Neuvirth (save percentage vs Medicine Hat: .600). Lewiston doesn't have a lot of options up front to start with — the foundation of its sixteen wins in seventeen Quebec league playoff games is goaltender Jonathan Bernier. So when a key forward, Marc-Andre Cliche, is sidelined with a shoulder injury in Lewiston's victory over Medicine Hat on Saturday, it's a safe bet that goals will be as scarce as Maine licence plates on the streets of Vancouver.

Play takes a strange turn in the third period, going from tight to ragged, probably out of a combination of weariness, frustration and desperation. Plymouth's season looks as though it will soon be over when the Maineiacs score with less than six minutes left in regulation. Boll angrily shouts at the defenceman beaten on the play. And the end of the Whalers' season looks to be a sure thing when

Plymouth takes a penalty with less than two minutes left in regulation. A team out of sorts, a man short, and up against perhaps the best goaltender in junior hockey: it's enough to drive the crowd and the scouts to the exits. Boyd high-tails it, having to drive to Seattle for a flight at dawn tomorrow. He misses a tying goal, against the tide of the game—by Evan Brophy, to this point an underachiever—and, even more improbably, a goal by Whaler forward Andre Fournier just three minutes into overtime. Plymouth has a life. Maybe Sestito and Boll will get another chance to show their stuff. Not that Hitchcock will be around to see it or that the Blue Jackets scouts will be able to point it out to him.

Cordero's Grill, a swank steakhouse on Vancouver's waterfront, is the NHL hangout of choice during the Memorial Cup. The big brass has blown in, and executive tastes and expense accounts run a little ritzier than the usual for the scouts. Lining up for a table, I catch up with Rick Dudley, the assistant general manager of the Chicago Blackhawks and an exec I first talked to when he was coach of the Detroit Vipers in the International league back in the mid-'90s. He invites me to join the Chicago crew for dinner. Just as the waiter drops the red snapper on the table, Dudley's boss, Dale Tallon, walks into the restaurant with Kyle Turris, the top-ranked kid on Central Scouting's list. There's no knowing whom else Tallon has broken bread with, though I suspect that he hasn't broken black bread with Cherepanov.

Dudley asks me if I've seen the teams in the tournament this season and I tell him that I saw a fair bit of Plymouth, including most of the games in the Ontario league final against Sudbury.

"Did you see Akim Aliu much this year?" he asks.

"Ten or twelve times during the season, right up to the final in the O," I say. "I went up to all three games they played up in Sudbury. Do you like him?"

"I really like him," Dudley says.

I could see that he would. Dudley spends more time in the gym than any NHL executive, and probably more than a lot of NHL players. His arms are as big as Lou Ferrigno's. Dudley was a hard-rock heart-and-soul forward in his day with the Buffalo Sabres, and an even better lacrosse player. He looks for athletes and athleticism — he'd be anti-*Moneyball*. Some scouts almost hold pure athleticism against a player — reasoning that what they do matters more than what they might become — in fact, to the complete exclusion of their athleticism. It's the divide between potential and performance. That's not to say that Dudley doesn't care how Aliu plays, but it's Aliu's athleticism that intrigues him.

I give Dudley the rundown on Aliu — the family history, training with Rick Nash, the meltdown at St. Michael's, right up to the Ontario final. I tell Dudley that Aliu wasn't in a position to show much when he rejoined the team. When I tell him how Aliu filled in Tom Sestito in one fight in the OHL final — flushing him with ten straight right hands, the last few with Sestito's back on the ice — Dudley's eyes light up. I'm not giving away privileged information — if I were a scout on Columbus's payroll, this sort of shop talk wouldn't be appropriate, I suppose. Still, it's stuff that the Blackhawks could drum up with an interview at the combine. I can rationalize giving a little to get a little. This bull session with Dudley is not just information giving but information *gathering*, too — I'm coming out of this with the knowledge that Chicago has an interest in him.

May 23, 2007, Pacific Coliseum, Vancouver

MEDICINE HAT 1 VANCOUVER 0

It's a small classic in junior hockey, in large part because the opponents are so skilled, so evenly matched and so clearly sick and tired of each other. These teams met on this same patch of ice in Game 7 of the WHL final, and the Hat prevailed 3–2 in overtime. In fact, three of the games in the final went to overtime. The teams don't just have memories of that series — they still have the bruises. All that would be the makings of a passion play but, fact is, it's much more than that. After a season spent in junior hockey rinks, more than seventy games at this point, I haven't seen a team as good as these two. It's like they're playing one game and everyone else another.

One Columbus draftee sets the stage for the game's lone goal, and the other delivers it. It starts with a seemingly innocent play, the home team icing the puck late in the second period. Kris Russell gives chase and pulls up after the whistle is blown. A Vancouver forward runs Russell into the boards. The Giants know that the Tigers' captain is banged up, and the Tigers know that they know, so a melée ensues. On the following power play, the puck comes back to Russell at the point and he finds Derek Dorsett in the slot with his back to the Giants' net. Fighting through the check of a defender, Dorsett spins and dekes goaltender Tyson Sexsmith. The game turns on those two plays. Prior to the penalty, the Giants had been coming on for several minutes and the visiting team was reeling. Maybe fate was tempted when, earlier in the period, the Giants fans roared when one of their legion beside the Medicine Hat bench held up a sign that said: DORSETT—YOUR MOTHER CALLED, SHE WANTS HER MOUSTACHE BACK.

The Tigers continue to take the play to the home team through the first ten minutes of the third period. Rather than just falling back and trapping and clogging up the middle, the Tigers dump and chase and pressure the Vancouver defencemen, especially Jonathan Blum, who's rated the ninth-best North American skater by NHL Central Scouting. The home team struggles with the furious pace. On a few shifts, Medicine Hat forwards like Darren Helm and Dorsett control the puck on the cycle, and you can practically hear the clock ticking down on the Giants' chances to step into the express line to the championship game. In the last ten minutes of regulation, the Tigers defend the lead more conventionally. They revert into a counter-punching mode, offering only token pressure on the forecheck, falling back into the neutral zone and stretching five-wide across the blue line. Led by the two Columbus draftees, Medicine Hat has made it into the Memorial Cup final.

May 24, 2007, Pacific Coliseum, Vancouver

PLYMOUTH 5 LEWISTON 1

The Maineiacs were the first team to qualify for the tournament and are the first here to get knocked out. It was tough enough when they lost Marc-Andre Cliche, a forward who played a prominent role on the Canadian under-20 team in Sweden. It's too much when Lewiston's goaltender, Jonathan Bernier, stays on the bench at the start of the second period with his team down 2–0. There's a hum in the corners of the stands—the scouts are second-guessing the move by coach Jodoin. Then they get word—Bernier says he's hurt. He did go down awkwardly on the Whalers' first goal, when Tom Sestito bore down on the Lewiston goal from the left wing and made a nice deke. When Bernier pushed hard to his left to stay with the big winger and then went to his knees, he tweaked a groin muscle. That's what he has told the coach. He didn't call for the trainer at the time, didn't make his way to the bench, didn't seem to favour any injury the rest of the period or when he skated off the ice. This has the scouts howling with derision.

"It better be falling off for him to come out," one scout says, watching a television replay of Sestito's goal. "That's just terrible."

Lewiston came to Vancouver with a goaltender's chance to beat any team, and that's how it has turned out in the opening round: the Maineiacs' victory over Medicine Hat on Saturday night was Bernier's solo effort. Now even that goaltender's chance at victory is gone.

The Dallas Stars might have James Neal in their lineup next season, but he's eclipsed tonight by Sestito. It's hard to imagine how much progress Sestito's made since Central Scouting had him No. 180 among North American skaters eighteen months ago. In a tilt between the champions of the Ontario and Quebec, Sestito is the best player on the ice. If Ken Hitchcock liked Sestito after an average performance in the loss to Medicine Hat, he'd be rushing him into the Blue Jackets lineup if he were here tonight.

One scout with an NHL team that finished out of the playoffs tells me that he'd trade his club's first-rounder in June, a lottery pick, straight up for Sestito—he might even sweeten the deal in order to close it. It would be music to Don Boyd's ears though he'd probably wish that the scout had been one of those who spoke to the *Columbus Dispatch* about the team's prospects.

May 25, 2007, Pacific Coliseum, Vancouver

VANCOUVER 8 PLYMOUTH 1

The Whalers have nothing left. Just shifts into the game, they know it—they're out of it early. Boll and James Neal and Sestito run the Giants—it worked for them in the O and against the under-manned Maineiacs—but the Giants are nearly as big, *and* better. Plymouth's bullies aren't intimidating the home team. The final is set, and it's what the fans want and what the scouts consider the best possible matchup: a rematch of the Western final.

May 26, 2007, Pacific Coliseum, Vancouver

Kris Russell told the local reporters last week that he wouldn't mind coming back to Medicine Hat to play as an overager, as Dorsett did this season. A few Tigers fans might have been thrilled by the prospect of the league's most valuable player returning. Most know that there's not a chance in the world, not with Russell having been signed by the Blue Jackets, not when he has accomplished every-thing he possibly can at the junior level.

After practice Russell is standing outside the Tigers' dressing room and in front of a video camera, soaked in sweat, in a stretchy black shirt and shorts. He's so short and sinewy, he could pass for a bicycle racer. As an action hero he's more Tobey Maguire than Vin Diesel. I ask him about the fight with his brother. "It was the first time in our lives we had ever played against each other," he says. "We were winning the game by a lot and I guess he wanted to get his team going. The guys on our bench wanted me to fight him, so I went for it. It wasn't something we talked about or planned. It just happened. Honestly. It was a pretty even fight."

Russell says he was "as surprised as anybody" when the Blue Jackets drafted him. "I expected to get drafted in the sixth or seventh round," he says. "I had talked to a couple of teams, but not the Blue Jackets. I didn't really believe it when I heard. I don't know that *I* would have drafted me this high."

May 26, 2007, River Rock Theatre, Richmond

Russell makes his way from the arena to the hotel/casino/dinner theatre complex for the CHL awards dinner. His hair is a well-organized mess—though it's a cultivated look, it is strand-for-strand the way it looked when he took his helmet off after practising. Russell's just one in a constellation of junior stars at the show.

Oshawa's John Tavares is the big winner. Reporters try to draw out of him any frustration at having to wait for the 2009 draft but Tavares doesn't take the bait. He blows off the suggestion that he'll seek another exception and apply to enter next year's NHL draft. Richest irony: the community service award goes to Kyle Moir, the goaltender who wanted out of Swift Current. It's not Tavares nor Moir but Patrick Kane I want to run down. Reporters ask him about possibly being the first-overall pick and stepping right into the NHL next season. I ask about the flight he and selected teammates took back to London after a game in the Soo while others rode the bus through the night and into the morning. If it's a gotcha moment he fails to notice or care. His expression doesn't change. He just keeps smiling, knowingly.

"It was too bad because the whole team could have gone," he says without skipping a beat. "There were enough seats. There weren't any [hard feelings]. The team was just doing what it thought would give us the best chance to win. The whole team would have thought that."

Maybe that's what his teammates would say if I asked them. Maybe it's one way they would try to rationalize the decision of the London coaching staff. But I can't imagine that it wouldn't cause resentment, and that's the prevailing wisdom among the scouts. I still like Angelo Esposito's take—that Kane and the others should have refused: Sidney Crosby could have used his clout to get preferred treatment, but instead went to every length to blend in and be one of the guys. When he signed his Reebok contract, he got his Rimouski teammates swagged out. If they come around with gifts, don't forget the team. Maybe Plymouth would have beaten London in the playoffs even if the Knights were the model of team spirit. Still that plane ride invites second-guessing.

May 27, 2007, Pacific Coliseum, Vancouver

Vancouver 3 Medicine Hat 1

"It's my last game as a scout," Lorne Davis says in the scouts' tent outside the arena. I figure that I'm in on a piece of history: the last game of the ranking member of the scouting fraternity. Seventy-seven years old, Davis first drew an NHL paycheque with the Montreal Canadiens. He was called up to step into the lineup one night when Rocket Richard was scratched. He ended up playing for four of the "Original Six" teams. When expansion came along he landed a scouting job with the St. Louis Blues. He moved on to Edmonton when the Oilers came over from the World Hockey Association and has stayed through five Stanley Cups and a near-miss last spring. He was one of the first scouts to work Europe—he had played there for Father David Bauer in international tournaments. His fellow Oiler scout Barry Fraser was a better known name, but Lorne Davis could stake a claim to scouting a bunch of Hall of Famers alongside him: Paul Coffey, Grant Fuhr and Jari Kurri, among others. By Davis's count he is closing in on 9,000 games scouted. He has kept on working through a management change and the loss of his wife a few years back. He spent whole weeks on the road these last few seasons even though he has physically slowed down a bit. A hitch in his giddy-up makes arena stairs a bitch to climb, and beers with the boys have become a lot less frequent. Maybe no one is surprised that he says this is it. "My last game," he announces again. The scouts don't look up from the free sandwiches they've piled up from the banquet trays. I figure that camaraderie is a casualty of the long season. It seems cold-blooded the way they're ignoring him.

I race around the arena looking for a photographer to capture this small piece of hockey history. I know Lorne's son Brad, also a scout for Edmonton. I'm sure he'd want a print framed. By the time I find a guy with a camera, Lorne Davis has disappeared into the capacity crowd.

I spot Craig Button, a scout with the Toronto Maple Leafs, and ask him if he's seen Lorne, telling him it's Lorne's last game.

"It's Lorne's last game *every year*," Button says. I feel like Don Paarup walking up to the tee for a round of night golf in Regina.

The refs let the Giants run the smaller Tigers all over the rink. They put their whistles in their pockets on blatant charges, strictly Texas Death Match stuff. The Giants lead all the way, but the Tigers keep it close right down to the empty-net goal in the waning seconds. In the end, Russell is just too banged up to play his game. That much is clear when he comes off the ice when the Tigers go on a power play in the third period. Bittersweet stuff.

It's Russell's last game as a junior. *My* last as a wannabe scout. Not Lorne Davis's last, though.

PART THREE

THROUGH THICK AND MOSTLY THIN

June 1, 2007, Park Plaza Toronto Airport

THE COLUMBUS WAR ROOM AT THE NHL COMBINE ISN'T open to me this time around. That much I knew when Don Boyd told me that he had been moved aside to let Paul Castron take charge of the draft. So, there's no perusing the lists, no asking the prospects questions. The situation is too unsettled, too delicate. The Blue Jackets still haven't hired a general manager. Jim Clark is still the interim GM. No one has a read on what the new team president, Mike Priest, might be thinking. No one is in a position to sign off on having a media interloper in the war room.

The club hasn't quite become a laughingstock because of the protracted head-hunting, but it's not far off. For the scouting staff, it's the stuff of gallows humour.

"On *Hockey Night in Canada,* they said it's down to four candidates: Bob Murray, Neil Smith, Jim Clark and me," Boyd says, grabbing a sandwich with Clark at the hotel restaurant between interviews, watching NHL scouts and the combine's prospects passing in and out. "And then they say it's those four, but there might be two others. What the hell does that mean?"

A rueful smile. Boyd won't read too much into his name and Clark's supposedly being in the mix. It might be a courtesy to them, a tacit endorsement of their work. It might be a ruse by the Blue Jackets' upper management, a bad tip intended to throw the media off the scent. Boyd won't presume that anything has changed that much in the five weeks since MacLean was fired. There's no knowing who'll be in charge when the draft rolls around. The latest hot rumour has Bob Murray, the assistant general manager in Anaheim, as Priest's first choice. If true, that would explain the delay—talking to Murray and negotiating a deal wouldn't be appropriate while the Ducks are in against the Senators in the Stanley Cup final. Whether it's Murray or anyone else outside the organization, no one on the Blue Jackets' scouting staff can be confident about his long-term job security. Maybe nerves aren't jangling the way Don Boyd's were at the under-18s in Finland, but that's the result of shock giving way to resignation. It's not that they're scared of the unknown, just weary of the not knowing.

I ask Boyd which of the top prospects are coming down to Columbus the way Brassard, Mueller and Staal did last June. Boyd dips his head.

"No one believes me, but since I switched positions I'm not in charge of our draft anymore," he says. "That's Paul Castron's job."

Until a new general manager is named, Boyd tells me, everything is scaled back. Fewer scouts have been brought in for the Blue Jackets' war room at the combine. Plans to invite prospects to Columbus for further testing and interviews won't be as ambitious. Doug MacLean liked to go first class. In his wake, the Jackets are in steerage.

This wouldn't usually matter to other clubs' scouting staffs, but because the belt-tightening Blue Jackets are the draft's host team, everybody's feeling the pinch. Traditionally, the host team's scouting staff is supposed to organize the fraternity's annual golf tournament, and many were looking forward to this year's draft because of the historic courses near Columbus. Some scouts even had hopes that the tournament would be held at owner John H. McConnell's private club, Double Eagle in Galena. McConnell isn't just a member; he's the owner.

Midway through the season, the word was put out that there'd be no golf tournament this year. The Blue Jackets cited scheduling. In the past, the tournament was reserved for the Sunday after the draft, which would run from lunchtime on Saturday until late into the evening. With the NHL going to a new draft format this year—with the first round being staged on Friday night and all later picks commencing Saturday morning—the Blue Jackets said that most scouts would start heading for home early Saturday evening. Still, McConnell probably would have found a way to hand the course over to his scouting staff for a day if the team had been heading for the playoffs.

Other scouting staffs used to laugh at the Blue Jackets for interviewing every kid who came to the combine. This year it's a more streamlined operation. Columbus will still interview more than most—there are just under eighty names on the schedule—but they're not talking to most of the Russian players. If a Russian player is already over here—for example, Ruslan Bashkirov with the Quebec Remparts—then the invitation is open. By being in North America, Bashkirov and others in similar situations are already freed of the shackles that could prevent them from signing with a NHL club. They've also displayed an eagerness to come over. Those still under contract to Russian league clubs are another story.

Like most NHL teams, the Blue Jackets are worried about drafting a Russian junior under contract to a club in his homeland and losing his rights if they're unable to sign him within two years. Under the previous collective agreements, NHL clubs retained the rights to drafted players in Europe until they felt moved to sign them. Now the meter starts running on draft day, just as it does with kids out of the Canadian major junior leagues.

Alexei Cherepanov is a unique talent who might be the first-overall pick if he had been born in Swift Current. Some of Cherepanov's draft-eligible teammates from the under-18s would be first- or second-rounders if they were from Toronto, Malmo or Kladno. But without an agreement between the NHL and the Russian federation that can guarantee the safe delivery of the prospects, the Russians are high-risk propositions. Last spring, Don Boyd and Doug MacLean and the rest of the Blue Jackets told me they didn't weigh the ability to sign a player in their evaluations. That notion is turned on its head here.

Boyd, Clark and Castron's uncertain status in the organization has to factor into the decision to steer clear of Russian players.

They're caretakers, and as such adverse to risk. They've been handed the wheel, but it's not their car. They don't won't to get into a street race when they'll have to hand over the keys and the ownership to the incoming general manager. There might be a temptation to gamble with other people's money, but if you lose recklessly you'll lose any chance of being handed other people's money again.

Alexei Cherepanov is coming through the physical testing in the basement of the hotel. His back against the wall, he's a quarter inch under six foot one. Body fat comes in under nine percent, a bit better than average. Not much on the upper-body strength—he manages only two reps with 150-pounds. Better than average flexibility. Dead-on average readings, right down to the fraction, as far as aerobic and anaerobic testing; nothing special as far as endurance or power. If you didn't know any better going in, you'd see nothing that would flag him as a special talent.

I tap one scout whose team has already interviewed Cherepanov. At the under-18s, I heard the same scout ripping Cherepanov as a coaster, another skilled Russian who'll sign for maximum money and give minimum effort. That's this scout's usual line—he has never been a fan of Russian players, likes to grind his team's Russian scout. I'd guarantee that the team put Cherepanov on its interview list over this guy's strenuous objections. So when I ask the scout how Cherepanov's interview went, I'm expecting sushi-quality cutting.

Instead, the scout admits he was impressed.

"It started off bad," the scout tells me. "The kid was slumped in his seat, low energy, distracted. I said to him, 'Are you sure you want to be here? We can end this now.' Talking through the interpreter, he said he was sorry—that he's normally not like this, that he has jet lag and hasn't been able to sleep. 'Go ahead, ask me anything,' he says. We asked him about his work [ethic]. He says that he hears about it all the time. Says he goes out on the first few shifts and sometimes it looks like he's not playing hard because he's looking for things, looking to see what players on the other team do in certain situations. He talked about looking for patterns [and] he said that he tries to think out on the ice and thinks a lot about the game. In just a couple of minutes he explained the way he plays."

I ask the scout about Cherepanov's contract status. I know he's represented by Jay Grossman, who has Ilya Kovalchuk and a bunch of other Russian players on his list of clients.[1]

"We didn't go there—it's Russia," the scout says.

To the scouts, it's an oblique, existential and incomprehensible war zone. "We didn't go there—it's Russia." It has the faint echo of Joe Mantell's words of cold comfort to Jack Nicholson in the classic movie: "Forget about it, Jake. It's Chinatown."

I tell the scout that I can't believe he didn't push the matter further—a deal in Russia that supposedly pays him $1.5 million might be up for discussion—but he has a ready explanation.

"If he has a contract [with a Russian league team], he just gives them two weeks' notice and he's out of it," the scout says. "You're going to have to pay off somebody, that's a given, but so long as you're willing to do it, fine. We didn't even go there because we don't think he'll fall as far as our pick. The team that drafts him will probably have something already in place. Some teams will be afraid that it would be hard to put together. Maybe someone's got it set up that everyone else is cut out."

Another Russian player, a lower-ranked, lower-profile forward, is generating a lot less interest than Cherepanov. He says he has five interviews lined up, though I think that might be inflated. I'm not sure he's doing any better than Bud Holloway, the Wal-Mart weightlifter from Wapella, Saskatchewan at last year's combine.

---

1. I have a frosty relationship with Grossman dating back to stories I wrote in 2002 about his agency luring players from other NHL agents. Kovalchuk, for instance, was originally a client of Scott Greenspun. Players hopscotching from agent to agent is the way business is done in Russia. You not only have to wonder whether you can get a player out of Russia, but whether the agent you're doing business with will end up representing the player you drafted.

I was first impressed by Vitali Karamnov when the Russians played the Czechs back at the summer under-18s. It was the second game I saw this long season, and all these months later the way he unselfishly threw the puck around and set up his linemate, Sergei Korostin, has stuck with me. When I saw him last, he was on the sideboards in the third period in the spring under-18 final, feeding the puck behind the net to Cherepanov moments before the winning goal was scored. Attention was always focused on Cherepanov, and to a lesser extent Korostin. I thought Karamnov didn't have the finishing skill of the other two, but I liked the way he worked. One scout called him "a greasy little fucker," which for him was a term of endearment, a suggestion that Karamnov would be unpleasant to play against. I sat beside Tim Bernhardt, the Dallas scout, at the semis of the under-18s and told him that I liked 12 and 21, Karamnov and Korostin, and he shrugged, like a pro handicapper who had been tipped by a little old lady who liked the sound of a horse's name. When Central Scouting's final lists came out a week later, I thought Korostin and Karamnov were undervalued at Nos. 8 and 19 among European skaters.

It turns out that Karamnov's father, Vitali Sr., was a draft pick of the St. Louis Blues in 1992 and played 92 games over three seasons for the club. The son has fond, if faint, memories of St. Louis, mostly of root beer. Vitali Sr. is now is a coach with Red Army, but he supports the idea of his son playing junior hockey in North America. Todd Diamond, a New Jersey agent, is representing Vitali. Diamond says he's closing a deal that will place Karamnov with a WHL club via the CHL import draft, which takes place the week after the NHL draft.

"Tell him he'll fit right in, the way he plays," I say to Diamond, who translates to his blankly smiling client.

Karamnov may play "greasy," but he looks more boy-next-door-ish than anything else. He's one of those Russian under-18s who only narrowly missed being a late '89 and being eligible for the 2008 NHL draft. Even without an agreement, I have to believe that an NHL club will draft him—he was on the top two lines of the team that won the under-18s. He's not going to sweat out the draft in Columbus, Diamond tells me.

"He's got a vacation booked with his parents to the seaside," the agent says.

Unlike Karamnov, the near-Russian player I've tracked closely is getting plenty of attention.

Akim Aliu first makes an impression at the combine not by anything he does in physical testing nor any question he answers in an interview. When a translator doesn't show up for a Russian player's interview with the Washington Capitals, Aliu is recruited by one of the Central Scouting staffers to help out. The Capitals' director of amateur scouting, Ross Mahoney, tells me later that it's "one of the more impressive things a kid has done here."

Aliu's testing is at least as impressive as his translating. The honest measure is six foot two, an inch less than what appears in the program, and his weight is 197, with body fat just over eight percent. I watch him go through the stations. His anaerobic measurements, his explosive burst, are near the top of all skaters. Same with his standing long jump. All other marks are just above average.

When I ask him about it later, his approach is telling.

"I watched what other people were doing and tried to do more," he says. He takes the same approach to testing as everything else in this draft year—he seems preoccupied by what others are doing and saying. He's aware of it and doesn't pretend otherwise.

Aliu says he has more than twenty interviews lined up, and at least one team has asked him back for a second interview. Aliu has been a subject of a lot of conversation, and not just because of his language skills. Word has it he'll be traded from Sudbury to the London Knights, that the Ontario league will make an official announcement any day now. "It's a perfect situation," he says.

True—at least for Aliu, it's a perfect situation to develop his game and erase the question marks beside his name. With two players, Patrick Kane and Sam Gagner, returning, the Knights should be a contender in the Ontario league. Kane and Gagner will get long looks at their respective NHL training camps, but they're almost certain to be back in London. For Aliu, the Knights will be the closest thing to the Toronto Marlies, where he worked with and was challenged by talented teammates.

It might not be perfect for London, though—or at least there's risk attached. If there is a rift in London between the stars and the soldiers, between those who flew home from the Soo and the rest who had to ride the bus, could London's dressing room end up divided about Aliu the way it was in Windsor and Sudbury? If he were one who had to ride the bus while others got star treatment, how might he take it?

Aliu tells me he's booked to talk to Chicago later today. I tell him about the conversation I had with Rick Dudley at the Memorial Cup and suggest that the Blackhawks might be a good fit for him.

Aliu seems more positive, more upbeat, than at any time since I met him three months ago.

After lunch, a Chicago scout tells me that Aliu was impressive in his interview with the Blackhawks, that he admitted making mistakes, that he accepted the blame, that he didn't make excuses. "A no-bullshit interview. A tough one, but a straight one," the scout says to me.

A little later, a scout for another team tells me that Aliu was a no-show for his scheduled interview.

June 2, 2007, Park Plaza Toronto Airport

The headliners of the 2007 draft were late showing up: Patrick Kane, Sam Gagner, Kyle Turris, James van Riemsdyk, Karl Alzner and Keaton Ellerby. The other night the six were feted on Coach's Corner on *Hockey Night in Canada*, basking in the glow of television lights and Don Cherry's blazer. They were out in Anaheim, taking in the Ducks' victory over the Ottawa Senators in Game 2 of the Stanley Cup final. Their connecting flight from Chicago to Toronto was delayed by stormy weather at O'Hare. This wouldn't be an issue at all, except that the meter is running for the two players heading to U.S. colleges, Turris and Van Riemsdyk—the NCAA allows them only forty-eight hours as guests of the NHL.

The Central Scouting staffers will have to scramble to fit in Turris's and van Riemsdyk's interviews, shuffling the schedules of the kids who watched *Hockey Night in Canada* in their rooms here at the Park Plaza last night. They'll have to make way for draft royalty.

I talk briefly to Angelo Esposito out in the lobby. He seems burned out, dispirited. If Don Cherry's draft showcase had been booked for *Hockey Night's* first game of the season, he'd have been there. He has to have heard the rumblings, that his stock is cratering, that he's out of the top ten, that he's in free fall. Scouts are telling me Esposito's interviews here have only been only okay. His physical testing hasn't even been that. His strength numbers, upper body and anaerobic explosiveness, are all below average. Then there are the red flags on his medical reports: two concussions. Being a front-runner has its advantages in a lot of situations. Not here. Not now.

Leading in the polls beats the alternative and any grandmaster wants to play white. But Esposito has to wish that he went into the season as No. 2 or No. 7 or even No. 12. He has to feel like he has played under the microscope—or maybe under a magnifying glass in the noonday sun. If he can take any consolation in it, he should remember that Sidney Crosby went through the same thing. It has to be tough for any teenager to be second-guessed so publicly by so many—and it must be hard for the prospective No. 1 to resist second-guessing himself. Some players who went No. 1—Joe Thornton would be an example—only emerged as top talents late in their draft season. Others like Lecavalier and Crosby have heard it for seasons in advance.

Cherepanov will find it easier to right things than Esposito, the captain of two Canadian under-18 teams and the leader of the Quebec team that won the under-17s the year before. Then again, Cherepanov made the world junior all-star team, racked up impressive numbers playing against veteran pros in the Russian elite league and had magical moments at the under-18s. Conclusion: Performance is the foundation for the rehabilitation of a prospect's profile.

—

At twenty after, twenty to and on the hour, the prospects pass through the lobby. They stand around, waiting for the scouts who'll shepherd them into the NHL teams' suites. Sometimes the scouts will be late, interviews running long. Sometimes the players have the equivalent of a spare on their class schedule. I've watched them in action all season; now, as they wait, in inaction. For many of the scouts this is a first opportunity to put a voice and personality to the name on the list. For me, I'm catching up.

Standing around the lobby in a recently purchased suit and with an expression more bemused than nervous, Patrick Kane looks like a kid dragged out of a pool hall for his first communion, making a half effort of feigning innocence. He remembers me asking him at the awards about the plane ride from the Soo, and wants to know when my story on him is going to run.

There's nothing feigned about Kyle Turris's innocence. It's all wide-eyed wonder. "My first season, we'd see a few scouts at our games, the same ones every time," he says. "Then, last year, we'd see fifty of them. One time there was something going on, and when we looked over it was Wayne Gretzky. He actually came out to one of our games."

I ask Logan Couture about the under-18s—I'm sure that it's come up in his interviews here. He acknowledges he had a bad tournament but makes it seem like a technical problem. "We had a whole bunch of centres," he says. "We needed someone to play wing. I haven't done that since I was an atom, but I thought I could."

I can't imagine that would go over with scouts on interviews.

One member of the Blue Jackets seems less fazed by the front-office uncertainty. Barry Brennan is still one of the guys. There just hasn't been any scaling back on his job as the strength and conditioning coach. He's off on his own more than the others. And if the others debate a player's virtues and weaknesses, Brennan is a stand-alone arbiter with a narrow focus. Others yield to his position on the single count.

In the testing room in the basement of the Park Plaza, Brennan is parked in front of the stationary bikes, where the prospects' explosive bursts are measured with the Wingate anaerobic test. He listens hard to hear the testers call out the readings to the staff who are booking the stats. More than that, though, he's eyeballing the scene. The other strength coaches come and go, but he's scribbling notes on everyone who passes through, each and every player who hits the two "gut" stations, aerobic and anaerobic. He'll give the other stuff a glance—the bench press, the jumps, push-ups, stretches. But when it comes to physicality, the players show it when they're pushing as hard as they can and when they're pushing as long as they can—two things that sound an awful lot alike but are as different as a 100-metre sprint and a marathon.

Brennan watches Vitali Karamnov mount the stationary bike for the aerobic test. The young Russian is smiling, but he's having trouble with the mouthpiece. He looks disbelievingly at the tube the runs from the mouthpiece to the imposing stainless-steel expanding drum. A Russian interpreter, a lanky, attractive blonde woman only a few years older than Karamnov, explains to him that he has to bite down on the mouthpiece, but every time he tries he gags. While this is going on, other combine staffers are taping Karamnov's feet to the pedals of the stationary bike—toe clips won't suffice. There can be no foot slippage at the risk of injury—and, Karamnov must be thinking, no escape either.

"It's not just what number the player registers, but how he gets there," Brennan says. "If there's a problem, if something damages the performance, you want to know."

That looks to be the case with Karamnov. Like a horse in a steeplechase, he has a couple of balks and then a refusal on the stationary bike—others here have been prepped for the combine. For Karamnov, this is all new. He's blindsided.

Brennan values the results but understands that they're only a starting point, the base that the players work from—and that he builds on.

"You want to see what the players can do here, and some of it is pretty impressive, but it's just a point very early on a curve,"

Brennan says. "It's all about maturing bodies and the willingness to work. You want to get an idea if a player will put out . . . if he's committed. You're just looking for some sort of sign that a kid has it in him to push himself. It's not like you're looking for [a prospect] who can keep up to the pros. It's amazing what the pros can do. The best kids here will get 1,200 to 1,300 on wattage/output, weakest kids probably in the 700s. Our best guys [in Columbus] test way over 2,000."

Karamnov gets 897 watts on the peak power (1,011 is the average among forwards) and 58.8 on the VO_2 (61.9 is the average at his position). Brennan marks an asterisk beside the second number. Gag factor.

Some of the results are what you'd expect.

For the past three years, since the sports pages around Albany first took notice of Nick Petrecki, he was inevitably described as a boy in a man's body. Stories mentioned him going to work with his father on a construction crew, working the business end of a wheelbarrow full of wet cement. It sounded like hype, stuff lifted from Gordie Howe's boyhood bio. As soon as Nick Petrecki walks into the testing area, it's clear the stories are based on facts as hard as the concrete he poured last week. As Petrecki makes the rounds of the testing stations, it looks as if a thirty-year-old longshoreman has slipped into the combine. Six foot three, 213 pounds, a condor-like wingspan of more than 77 inches.

The frail-looking Turris looks like a grade-schooler out for prospects' autographs, not the top-ranked skater in North America according to NHL Central Scouting. He manages only three reps with 150 pounds, less than half the average among forwards.[2] I remember watching Gretzky as a sixteen-year-old in the Ontario

---

2. The worst performer is the ridiculously soft-bodied Swiss forward Luca Cunti, who manages just one rep despite having nineteen pounds on the 170-pound Turris.

league, and Turris seems to have the same body type. A lot of observers doubted Gretzky would stand up to the physical grind then, in the days when players were more likely to hit a bar than grab a barbell. When Turris says he needs to put some meat on his bones, it's an astute reading of his situation.[3]

Some of the results, though, run counter to expectations.

I had heard those in junior hockey circles say that Logan Couture would be in for the shock of his life at the combine, but his numbers are average to above average.

Looking at Nick Petrecki, scouts expect him to set records on the bench and maybe bend the bar for fun. He manages ten reps, above average, and more impressive when you consider his sleeve length and the strict form the testers demand. But Mark Katic, spotting Petrecki thirty-seven pounds, racks up *twelve* reps.

Some of the results are contradictory.

I'm not surprised that Jakub Voracek's body-fat numbers are the worst among forwards: fourteen percent. And yet Voracek, pasty body and all, ends up registering the highest mark among skaters in the anaerobic tests, the measure of power his lower body can generate. He posted the best numbers for both peak and mean performance — what you might expect when you see his first step on the ice, the last thing you'd expect when you see his immature body in gym stuff.

And some of the results are incomplete.

Some players still have injuries sustained during the season and haven't been able to work out for weeks. They can't perform at some or all stations. These are small blows to their draft status, but they're mostly forgiven.

One U.S. college player is another story entirely.

Bill Sweatt, a swift, skilled forward from Colorado College, has garnered a lot of interest. Central Scouting ranked him 27th among North Americans, but he arrives at the combine with his

---

3. Strangely enough, Turris's grip strength numbers are far above average and well above Petrecki's.

arm in a sling. Sweatt tells the medical staff that he severed ten-
dons in his forearm, which would be distressing enough. When he
starts to tell the teams the history behind the injury, any concern
becomes ridicule. It wasn't a skate blade or a traffic accident or
anything in the household. No, Sweatt fell through a window at
his frat house, apparently pushed by a coed. The scouts can't
remember anyone showing up with a story like this. "Couldn't he
have just said that he did it working out?" one scout says. "Not too
bright for a college guy." Then again, if a kid can tell you that he
was pushed through a window by a coed, you don't have to worry
too much about honesty.

I find the most basic readings registered by Central Scouting the
most interesting. They fall under the category of Body
Development/Upper Body and Lower Body on the summaries written up by physicians brought in by the NHL. There are no percent-
ages or watts counts in the thousands or performances reduced to
two decimal points. It's a simple eyeballing by the doctors. There are
only four rankings: in descending order, Extensive (E), Above
Average (AA), Average (A) and Below Average (BA). It is the closest
thing to Honours, Pass and Fail.

The vast majority of kids get A for both upper- and lower-body
development. Mark Katic gets an A on both counts, even though he
gets the big number on the bench press. So does Jakub Voracek,
despite the high body fat. So does the rail-thin defenceman out of
Swift Current, Paul Postma. All four kids from Rimouski. Karamnov.
Cherepanov. Esposito. Kane. Gagner.

A grade of E, for Extensive, is the hardest to come by. That Nick
Petrecki doesn't rate it suggests that only a kid carved out of marble
need apply. In fact, among the hundred kids here, only three rankings of E are assigned—and German defenceman Denis Reul gets
two of them, one each for upper and lower body. At six feet four, 210
pounds, with his oversized musculature Reul would be an intimidating presence even if he had the countenance of a choirboy, but Reul
has alopecia, a condition that causes total hair loss. Without hair on

his head, eyebrows or eyelashes, Reul looks as if he has walked off the set of a science-fiction movie.[4]

Nick Petrecki is one of seven prospects who are ranked as AA in both upper- and lower-body development. The most surprising name on this list is that of Brandon Sutter, who looked like a creatine-free stringbean at the summer 18s.

A few prospects get AA in one category and A in the other. For instance, Halifax Mooseheads forward Logan MacMillan and Stefan Legein of Mississauga get AA in upper body and A in lower. Yannick Weber, a Swiss-born defenceman with Kitchener, is the lone prospect who gets A in upper body but Above Average in lower body.

Then there are those who are deemed lacking. Surprisingly, they include those at the top of Central's list. James van Riemsdyk may have been dominant on the cycle against Canada in the semifinal at the under-18s, but he wasn't using brute upper-body strength to do it—he's rated BA in upper-body, A in lower body. Finally, there are those unfortunate few who are BA/BA. They're doubly cursed. These include the top-ranked North American skater, Kyle Turris, and the continent's top ranked defenceman, Karl Alzner, who actually looks like a load.

The body-development rankings are interesting, but no more meaningful than anything else coming out of the combine's testing. That is, they're wide open for interpretation. BA/BA doesn't hurt Turris, and if you were a scout pushing to draft him, you could make a case that it actually helps him—if Turris is a dynamic player despite being physically undeveloped, he should be that much better with maturation and training. The irony: the only notation that might hurt a player is AA or E. If a kid isn't much of a player but grades out high in terms of body development and across the board in the specific

---

4. The other Extensive bestowed by physicians goes to Niklas Torp, a Swedish defenceman who receives E for his lower body and Below Average for his upper body, which suggests that he's built somewhat like a bowling pin.

combine testing, then he's got no place to go. He would be categorized as a good athlete who can't play—the kiss of death.

The doctors attach red flags to several players. A couple I've followed with interest have heart murmurs that will require echo cardiograms.[5] Another has a bad hip with troublesome clicking that will require an orthopedic exam. Angelo Esposito is flagged for his two concussions, though they're also marked as resolved.

It's not a definitive look at the medical histories. For instance, there were discrepancies between teams' counts on Toews's concussions last year—some had him down for two, others three. In the same way that Central's rankings serve as a list of leads for scouts, the medical reports are a matter for follow-up. If the interviews are like looking for a home and going to an open house, then having the doctors check out the medical histories is like bringing an inspector through to look at the wiring and plumbing prior to closing the sale.

Watching the players go through the stations, I'm convinced that Brennan is right: How (attitude, willingness) is deserving of at least equal weight with What (performance). How they take on the aerobic and anaerobic testing, their effort, is like a tell in poker. It seems a lot of hard science and expensive hardware for the sake of intuitive conclusions, but so be it. After all, the biggest decisions here don't fall to kinesiologists but most often to hockey executives whose high school marks were dragged down by weeklong road trips with their junior teams, men who've never set foot on a college campus, never mind a lab.

I suspect that Tony Lucadello wouldn't care much about the numbers as much as the How. The same can be said for many of the older scouts in the Park Plaza basement. Lucadello and scouts of a

---

5. I recently spoke to a cardiologist who told me that he's treating a player—he wouldn't say who—who's trying to keep a condition under wraps from teams, which sounds like an ill-advised risk.

certain vintage would be more interested in what the prospects do around the combine than at the stations.

Akim Aliu is the instructive case. His test results are meaningful enough. The scouts will take note of his nine reps on the bench and an anaerobic test that's near the top of the class, but nothing in the results posted by Central Scouting will answer their questions about him. *How* he goes about the tests, yes. If he's getting along with the other players in his test group, if he's co-operative, polite, social—this is the stuff that counts. How he talks about the tests— watching others, trying to do more than them, rather than simply pushing himself—is worth noting, too. It would recommend an approach to working with him—that he'd work better when part- nered with a hard-driving peer rather than if he were expected to push himself. The scouts would read more into Aliu hanging out with Sam Gagner, meeting him later in his room or grabbing lunch with him, than all the statistics logged in his session. Maybe more than his interviews, too, because it is what you do and not what you say that counts.

For years it struck me as odd that the scouts would gather in the basement of the Park Plaza to ogle the players during the testing— why they would need to see up close performances detailed in the readouts. It's for the same reason that they go to games rather than scout from statistics. Statistics are enough for Billy Beane and his *Moneyball* crew in Oakland, but not very meaningful here—not scoring statistics, and not testing numbers either. For the scouts, the basement at the combine is where they can catch a glimpse of char- acter. In the basement or in suites or out in the lobby, character is revealed in vignettes. Character, like courage, is a devalued word, worse off than the Mexican peso. More like Enron stock. Still, given Grant Sonier's six-chip, three-stack measure, character ranks up there with game sense and skill—and skill might be the stack you'd choose to go short on in some cases.

Over the season, I never noticed scouts trying to get down to ice level to see the expressions or to hear the voices of the players. Practices—well, scouts couldn't see any value in that. They'd dismiss it outright. They'd figure they saw all they needed to see about Logan Couture at that game in Mississauga back in February—I'm inclined to believe that seeing him crawl off the training table would have filled in the picture. Maybe Daniel Doré thought he saw all he needed to about Aliu when he started bitching at the ref late in the game at St. Michael's in March—but maybe seeing him walk red-eyed and remorseful out of the dressing room would factor into a scouting report. In lieu of those moments and hundreds of others, they have this close-up inspection in the basement, the players in an unfamiliar, high-pressure situation, none with advantages. If you could only have one shot at looking for tells on character, you could do worse.

Last June it was Brassard with his head buried inches from the handlebar on the stationary bike as he pushed in the VO$_2$ test while Kessel bailed out early. Now it's Turris, knowing that he has struggled on other stations, pushing the same way Brassard did, and it's Esposito looking disappointed again when a tester reads back his numbers.

Maybe the scouts are confident that they glean almost everything they need to know about the players in their day-to-day routine—that they can tell the character of a player by how he plays. They may be right. Still, it does seem funny to me that so many operate at such a distance during the season. And it seems funny that they'd soak up the conventional wisdom about prospects and the innuendo about a player like Aliu, but otherwise work in a vacuum.

I sit down for lunch with Jakub Voracek and David Skokan. Voracek hoovers back a Caesar salad and Skokan is laying waste to a steak. Seeing them sitting there, you'd swear that Central Scouting had it right at the mid-terms, when it ranked Skokan at No. 15, Voracek at 16.

Skokan looks like the athlete. With no interviews booked for the next couple of hours, he's walking around the hotel in a tight white t-shirt, like Marlon Brando in *A Streetcar Named Desire*. He tells

Voracek that he's going for a workout this afternoon, even though he has his combine testing tomorrow morning.

"He's crazy," Voracek says. "All he cares about is the gym."

That shows up in Skokan's testing, though not as much as he probably hoped—a little better than average in the straight upper-body testing, right on the average for lower-body stations.

"I started work in the gym hard this year," Voracek says. "I need to do more."

Some of Voracek's test numbers are as soft as his love handles. But it's his anaerobic test that's the revelation, the one aspect of testing that places Voracek out in front of Skokan and everyone else.

The players' plans after the combine hint at the fact that Voracek has passed Skokan as a prospect, CSS's mid-term rankings notwithstanding. Voracek will head off to California to work out with a personal trainer on agent Petr Svoboda's ticket. Meanwhile, Skokan will head back to Slovakia and will make his way to Columbus the day before the draft.

From their table, Skokan and Voracek watch Kane, Gagner, Turris and the other top prospects walk by. General managers of clubs—Doug Wilson of San Jose, Doug Risebrough of Minnesota, Doug Armstrong of Dallas—and others walk by, but these two don't seem to have any idea who they are.

Voracek and Skokan are a complete contrast to Akim Aliu. They're not preoccupied with the buzz; they neither know nor care about insider baseball. They're doing what they're asked to, and they're not worried about things they can't control.

I ask Voracek about his trip to Toronto and he tells me that it was "easier than going to Helsinki" for the under-18s.

"After that tournament, all the flying and games, I did not do anything for a week but sleep," he says. "This time easy—Prague to Montreal to Toronto."

I mention to him a story that's in the news—about a U.S. tourist who flew from Prague to Montreal even though he had been diagnosed with a virulently infectious form of tuberculosis. The word "tuberculosis" is a bit of a stumbling block, and I'm not sure that the word in Czech sounds remotely like it. It doesn't stop Voracek from getting the meaning, though.

"I was on that flight, I think," he says. "I have to go to my room to look at the Internet before my next interview."

Skokan doesn't look up from his steak when Voracek leaves the table. He tells him that he'll sign for the meal. Only when Voracek is at the elevator does Skokan look up.

"I saw the story," Skokan tells me. "Not the same flight as Jakub. But I don't tell him."

The conventional wisdom is that hockey is a young man's game. It's not quite true. Here at the combine, young men are trying to get into the game and old men are try to hang on to their places in it. Outsiders would presume that the old are more desperate than the young, but then again, no one seems more anxious than Akim Aliu.

You don't really see this contrast in the arenas. Neither do the players and the scouts. From the stands, the scouts can't see how young the young really are. The players are within a bubble, inside the plexiglass, behind visors and masks. From the ice, the players can't get a good look at the scouts who are up in the far reaches of the arena. If the players do look up before a face-off, there's a good chance that the scouts have their heads down during the stoppage and are taking notes.

Only at the combine and at the draft do their paths cross. The scouts coming down to the lobby and tapping the players on the shoulder, shaking hands, showing them the way to their next interviews. It's a routine that's just part of the game renewing itself.

For the players, the process is one of the rites of initiation, knowing that Crosby and Ovechkin and all the famous names have done this very same thing. The players are almost in a dream state, eyes on the horizon, nervously optimistic. For some there's a whiff of entitlement, like the faint scent of mostly unneeded aftershave. They want to seem old beyond their years, trying to trick themselves with tattoos, trying to bluff the scouts with their cool poses.

For the scouts it's vicarious living, making their teams

younger—and themselves, too, if only for a day. In the suites, the scouts will either make the prospects feel like part of the team or press them with hard questions, as if challenging them to drop the gloves and defend themselves. They want to be transported back to their playing days, and hair colouring, weaves, pieces and clothing styles years too young are their vain attempts.

There's excitement on both sides, but sadness, too. Some players, not those at the top of the lists, not those invited to stand beside Don Cherry, know enough about hockey to realize that they're longshots to make the NHL. Some scouts know, and almost all of them fear that they could be on their way out.

Daniel Doré is loitering in the lobby. He's not looking for a prospect; he just doesn't want to spend any more time in the Boston suite than is absolutely necessary. It's uncomfortable there, with everyone knowing he's on his way out. He talks in a low voice even though the lobby is almost empty—nobody around but a couple of Russian teenagers on the couch.

Doré says he's not going through the motions, says he's going to do his job as well as he can. He doesn't seem sour as much as wistful.

"If that's it, then I'm looking to do other things, new challenges," he says. "Maybe it's meant to be. Maybe it's just time. New players come in, a new class, and so do new scouts."

The scouts like to think of their trade as a fraternity. It might seem that way from the outside. But in the case of Doré, the new class coming into the executive offices in Boston is casting the alumni out.

The scouts like to think of their business as collegial, everyone getting along with few exceptions. But Doré is proof that an organization is only collegial when your friends are in charge.

The Blue Jackets' staff are interviewing another player on their list when one of the scouts steps out of the suite to make a phone call. The scout—not Boyd, not Clark, not Castron—was really just looking for an excuse for a break. He sits at the other end of the couch that I'm parked on, watching the comings and goings of prospects and scouts.

"It's been tough," he says to me. "It's not the same team feeling anymore. Is it winding down? Maybe it feels that way . . . that there's going to be big changes. Not today, not tomorrow, but before we're here next year. I guess change is inevitable in this business, and we had it good for a long time. It's hard to do your best work [when] there's a guy looking at our whole operation [whom] we've never met, not even when we've been in Columbus. Nobody knows who this guy is."

The scout is talking about Mike Priest, who is John H. McConnell's hired gun. It's galling to the scout that the hockey department is being evaluated by a non-hockey man, a pure business-school type, a guy who's more impressed by an MBA than decades of experience in the game. I've done a little background research on Priest and his every pronouncement is couched in business-school double-speak—if you only looked at his quotes, you wouldn't have a clue whether he was talking about a widget factory or the Blue Jackets.

The scout has me thinking about the grand arc of the game.

The ennui of the Columbus scout reminds me of those kids in Swift Current who went into junior hockey with big hopes and have been passed over the NHL draft. All his work, like all theirs, has brought them up to a void.

I've seen it happen to other scouts. He has, too, only now is it hitting home. John Stanton was let go by Los Angeles and Archie Henderson by Washington—two veteran scouts, two old pros. Neither thought it was a crisis, just a tough break. They went home and waited for their phones to ring. And they never did. They had been around the game long enough to know that nothing is forever, that there are no lifetime contracts. Still, they thought years of work, friendship, good citizenship, would get them second chances. That's hockey. That's scouting.

It has me thinking about Lorne Davis's "last game" in Vancouver. There's probably a rationale for the gag, for the charade, that maybe even Lorne Davis can't explain. Hockey is such an unreliable business that you tempt fate when you ask too much of it—if you bank on the worst happening, maybe you guarantee a good turn. For Lorne Davis, his mock retirement is like telling an actor to break a leg.

The scouts who are interchangeable and disposable will be interchanged and disposed of, unless, like Lorne Davis, they speak out loud about it. They announce their fatalism in search of permanence.

June 22, 2007, Columbus

A week before the draft, the Blue Jackets introduced their new general manager. It wasn't Bob Murray. The job was his for the taking, but Murray declined, saying that family issues made the timing all wrong. Few accept the explanation at face value. There are just too many side issues: Sergei Fedorov's burdensome contract, Nikolai Zherdev's bad attitude, the long shadow cast by league powerhouse and divisional rival Detroit . . . the laundry list goes on and on. Another factor may be a condition that Mike Priest has supposedly imposed: that the new general manager work with the existing Columbus staffers, specifically Jim Clark and Don Boyd.

Scott Howson, Edmonton's assistant general manager, ends up taking the Columbus job. He wasn't one of "the final four" as reported on *Hockey Night*, nor even one of the unnamed two others. Howson bears an uncanny resemblance to David Hyde Pierce, and in his manner he's not too far removed from Niles Crane. To the shock of no one in the NHL or at his introduction to the Columbus media, Howson describes himself as "a conservative person by nature"—that's exactly how he looks and exactly what Mike Priest is looking for. A caretaker.

The Blue Jackets staffers have seen him at games and events over the years, but they have no sense of him. Their reports on their new boss all read the same: Very quiet, keeps to himself, the Anti-MacLean. Again, Howson is exactly what Priest is looking for. Instead of good cop–bad cop, the Jackets were looking to go loud cop–quiet cop. A little less charisma wouldn't hurt, and would be a lot closer in spirit to John H. McConnell's preferred corporate culture.

Howson was a canny, high-scoring centre with Kingston in the Ontario league but wasn't drafted coming out of junior. The knock against him was his skating—it was almost painfully bad.[6] He beat the odds by signing a free-agent contract and eventually making the NHL with the New York Islanders in the mid-'80s. After eighteen NHL games he realized that he was up against it to stick with the big club. Hockey sense got him that far—common sense then prevailed. He made a pragmatic decision, giving up the game and opting to go to Osgoode Hall, York University's law school. After practising law for a few years, Howson joined the Oilers staff, running their farm teams and negotiating contracts. He expanded his portfolio, rising to the rank of assistant general manager to the Oilers' Kevin Lowe.

Howson sounds like the voice of reason coming in. When he talks up the prospects in the Blue Jackets' system, he might as well be reading from a script written by Boyd and Clark. Maybe it's a case of Ken Hitchcock having gone to bat for Clark, Boyd and the staff—that the coach was shooting straight about liking Sestito, Boll, Russell and Dorsett, the Blue Jackets' draftees at the Memorial Cup.

Still, on the eve of the draft, the storm clouds haven't quite blown over. Howson's hiring has bought Clark and Boyd time, but not security. It would have been a lot to expect any vote of confidence from Howson, and it would have been unrealistic to expect a wholly unqualified one. His public message is that he'll trust the draft to his staff—he'll offer up his own opinions. The story as he tells it—he hit the road as soon as the Oilers fell out of the playoff race this spring and started eyeballing the draft class more than an NHL assistant general manager normally would. Howson was doing field work tied to the Oilers' acquired in trade, including the first-rounder that

---

6. In fact, Howson went undrafted twice—he also passed through the Ontario league draft without a sniff.

came over from the Islanders in the deal that sent franchise icon Ryan Smyth to Long Island. He is claiming "an almost dangerous amount of knowledge" on the top picks. He also vowed to "have some input because I do know some of the players I am interested in [and] some of the players I am not interested in . . . I'll be interested to hear [the staff's] take on those players."

The irony isn't lost on the scouting fraternity. Not many teams could claim to have a worse draft record than the Blue Jackets, but the Oilers during Howson's time there surely did. Others in the Oilers organization, old-timers like Lorne Davis, could associate themselves with the drafts that were the foundation of Edmonton's Stanley Cup winners, but Howson arrived well after the fact. With its first-round selections between 1997 and 2000, Edmonton picked four players who played a total of 80 NHL games. Then there's Jesse Niinimaki, the fifteenth-overall pick in the 2002 draft. He met up with Lowe for dinner at the Scandic Hotel a few weeks back during the under-18s, and that had scouts in other organizations shaking their heads. One cracked: "If I'd spent a first-rounder on him, I'd poison his beer." It's not that Niinimaki made it over to North America for twenty-four minor-league games (and one goal) a couple of years ago—he was let go by his hometown team in Tampere afterward. A team that gave Jason Bonsignore a last chance bailed out on Jesse Niinimaki, the hometown hero. Later in that draft the Oilers selected a Slovakian player who wasn't even eligible. Everyone else on the floor of the arena seemed to know that the Slovak and several of his teammates hadn't filed the necessary paperwork with the NHL in time.

On the morning of the draft there's all kinds of cross-talk and scuttlebutt about Columbus's plans for the seventh pick overall. One thing is certain: The Blue Jackets would feel much better about their pick if it were sixth, and all the more so at No. 4 or even No. 3. The way the Blue Jackets and a lot of other teams see it, there's an elite group of six draft-eligibles: Kane, van Riemsdyk, Turris, Gagner, Voracek and Alzner. If it came down to talent alone, Cherepanov would be in that mix—but Columbus wouldn't pick a player in the first round, in front of their own fans, who wasn't a safe bet to sign with the team. It would hardly be a first move typical of an executive who describes himself as "conservative by nature." Maybe one of the other teams who pick before Columbus will go for him, but it's hard to imagine that teams out of the playoffs will be much inclined to gamble with, and maybe burn, a lottery pick. After this group, there's a significant fall-off. Last year, the Blue Jackets ranked seven players as "Top Tens." This year, just six made the grade, a seventh with an asterisk.

If the top six slots are filled as expected, a number of names will be in play for the Blue Jackets at No. 7. Maybe it's Minnesota high school defenceman Ryan McDonagh. Or Kevin Shattenkirk from the U.S. under-18 team. Because of all this uncertainty, there's speculation that the Blue Jackets might even try to convert their seventh-overall pick into a couple of later picks. One theory: Montreal, which has two first-round picks, might be in the market to move them to secure Angelo Esposito. (The first time I saw this in print, I thought back to Esposito telling me that going to Shattuck took pressure off him. If he landed in Montreal and was stir-fried by the press there, he'd probably be looking to see if he had any credits to catch up on at Shattuck.) But everything the scouts are saying suggests that Esposito will be there when Montreal picks at No. 12—or even later.

I meet up with one scout at breakfast at the Hyatt. He tells me a story that I'm a little skeptical about. He tells me that one of the top prospects in this draft—not one who was on my list of prospects to profile for Don Boyd—has OCD, obsessive-compulsive disorder. "Like Jack Nicholson in As Good As It Gets," he says. "The kid takes off and puts on his skates three or four times before skating. Walks around a car four times when he gets out of it, every time."

I hear out the scout. I suggest that OCD could be a little disruptive in a dressing room. The scout says it's more than that. "It affects his play . . . or at least it has," he says. "When he was in an all-star game he had trouble because it was an unfamiliar arena, an unfamiliar room, different linemates than he's used to. He's a kid who needs stuff that's familiar . . . it's trouble if he's out of that comfort zone. He gets really agitated, hyper. So how's he going to be going to a new league, new arenas all the time? How's it going to be if he's sent to the minors, like a lot of kids are?"

I tell the scout it's enough to scare teams off, but he maintains that his team has an interest in the player. It occurs to me that the scout might be running a negative campaign, trying to float a rumour that might scare a team off a player at the last minute if they got wind of it and weren't able to follow it up. Like a bad word about a company just before a speculator aims to buy up stock.

The scouts says he's giving me the straight goods. "We've done our homework," he says. "We like him."

At lunchtime on draft day, I take a walk around downtown Columbus and take a lap of the state legislature building. It's the last place you'd expect to find several million dollars' worth of hockey talent, and the good people of C-bus lined up at bus stops and the Subway sub shop wouldn't suspect that the three teenagers on the bench outside the legislature are just that. Steven Stamkos, Alex Pietrangelo and Michael Del Zotto are just hanging out a few blocks from the hotel. Unrecognized, they've walked past autograph collectors standing on the sidewalk. This isn't their draft year—that will come next June in Ottawa. If the draft for the class of 1990 were held today, these three would be in the top five picks. If they forged birth certificates and made themselves eligible for this year's draft, they'd be lottery picks.

It's a curious thing. Stamkos plays for Sarnia, Pietrangelo for Mississauga and Del Zotto for Oshawa, but the players have known each other for years, their families have travelled together and they all are signed with the same agent.

"Our agent brought us down and let us sit in on interviews just to see what it's like," Stamkos says. "And we get to see what it's like inside the arena at the draft."

I tell him I can only suppose it'll be one thing to watch others waiting to hear their names called, another when he's waiting for his own to echo around the arena.

The background work-ups that I was aiming to do for Boyd are incomplete — about as incomplete as Boyd's own season heading up to Columbus's draft. When we first talked about the assignment, the idea was to circulate the information I rounded up among Boyd's scouts. But they are no longer Boyd's scouts, they're Castron's — and for that matter, for the last week or so, Howson's. Rather than being a background checker, I've become more of a bird dog, Boyd's personal one. Just one source in a network of dozens of people a scout might sound out. An old-time scout like Al Ritchie would have had hundreds of them across the Prairies. I feel like each of them must have felt, that I have been playing a minor role but at least I'm in the game. The only payment Al Ritchie needed was to hear Foster Hewitt call out the names of the New York Rangers on *Hockey Night in Canada* radio broadcasts. I'm sure the same went for his bird dogs. For me, my sense of satisfaction would ride on hearing the name of the Blue Jackets' first-round pick. If I relayed any information that might factor into a later pick, so much the better. 'Tis to dream.

Originally, the idea was that I'd get a read of the players in the mix for Columbus's first pick. Originally, the target was the top fifteen or twenty players eligible for the 2007 draft, along with a few others who might have been of interest. Those numbers, of course, reflected the optimism of the Blue Jackets back in the summer of 2006, when they thought the franchise was well positioned to turn the corner and make the playoffs for the first time. Maybe that was tempting fate about Don Boyd's job security and the team's prospects. By the world juniors, it was clear that the playoffs were once again beyond the team's reach, and by March it was clear that Columbus would be picking in the top ten. I whittled the list down once more after the lottery was staged and Chicago came away with the first pick and Columbus the seventh.

There's only so much that an amateur, even a devoted one, can do when he's not on the team's payroll and not getting his expenses covered. In the end, I didn't do a work-up on James van Riemsdyk because I assumed that he'll be gone by the time the Blue Jackets' pick rolled around. Boyd said as much to me at the under-18s. I also assumed that, because he was playing in the U.S. development program in Ann Arbor, Paul Castron's base, the Blue Jackets would have a pretty good read on him if somehow he fell to No. 7. The same applies for any of the kids who rolled through the U.S. under-18s, including Shattenkirk and McDonagh, who joined the team that went to the spring under-18s.

Karl Alzner, the big defenceman with the Calgary Hitmen, remains the most significant hole on my list. I only spoke to him briefly at the under-20s and I didn't chase background on him that hard. I feel I'm up to speed on others Columbus has rated as Top Tens, though. Not that there were significant red flags on the projected Top Tens. Hours before the draft, then, I'm in scouting limbo, not knowing whether anything I've done over the course of the season will have any impact. Of course, many scouts are in exactly that same position. They have that sinking feeling that maybe it will be all for naught. At least for me and for most of them there'd be some suspense in it—it wouldn't quite be like Earl Ingarfield's last draft, when he sat for hours on Day One while every other team but his Islanders had their picks.

The upper bowl of the Nationwide Arena is filled when the Blue Jackets' owner, John H. McConnell, makes his way to the podium to deliver a brief speech before the draft. Back in the spring, the worry was that the restive crowd would boo the Blue Jackets—and Doug MacLean in particular—after missing the playoffs once again. When McConnell tries to speak, the cheering of the Blue Jackets' fans drowns him out, twice forcing him to stop and regroup. He thanks "the fans, who have stuck with us through thick and thin, mostly thin," and the crowd roars. When the owner bought out MacLean's contract, he bought himself this moment.

At the Columbus table, beside the stage, Howson is deadpan, while Boyd and his crew wince and laugh.

As tough as the seasons have been on the Blue Jackets fans, not even the worst defeats were as tough as this night will be on most of the draftees here. Drafts have always been hard on the teenagers. Even as he parades the top few draft-eligible players on Coach's Corner, Don Cherry in another segment warns players against going to the draft armed with hope rather than knowledge—that is, hoping to be selected rather than knowing it will happen. The warning falls on deaf ears, of course, and every year disheartened players and their families and friends sit in the stands while whole rounds pass. Often the players who come out for the biggest night of their lives go unselected. Day One—Night One, actually—has another level of cruelty built in. This year the NHL is adopting a new, made-for-television format. The draft was previously either a one-day (all-day Saturday) or weekend-long (rounds stretching over Saturday and Sunday) event. This year, though, the draft will start on Friday night—the first round only, just the top thirty picks. The night will be short for the lucky first few, who also have a pretty good idea of where they'll fall. But for others, even elite players, well-known names, the not knowing is torturous. For those on the bubble, it will be even tougher.

Ten minutes before the first pick is going to be made, I'm on the arena concourse talking to a couple of junior coaches about European players they're hoping to line up for the CHL's import draft. At that point I see Akim Aliu and his father and mother making their way to the section reserved for players, families and agents. Aliu is so anxious and agitated, he looks ready to jump out of his skin. A nervous reaction, he races when he talks, almost impossible to understand.

"Have you heard anything about where I'm going to go?" he asks.

I see his agents, Mark Guy and Pat Morris of Newport Sports, standing by. I tell him that a lot of teams I know have an interest in him, that Chicago does maybe more than the others.

"I just want to go tonight," he says. "I want go in the first round."

—

The puzzle of the draft starts to be pieced together on Friday night. The first two picks of the draft are predictable stuff.

1 Across: Chicago. The one who seems all along to know he is The One. The Blackhawks select, from the London Knights, Patrick Kane.

Dale Tallon waits for Kane on the stage. He'll say Kane's play at the under-20 was ultimately the deciding factor in the pick—that Kane was better against the older players than any of the others were against players in their own age group.

The general manager knows the difference between No. 1 and No. 2, between being The One and The Other. He was the latter, a good player chosen second overall in the wake of a Hall of Famer, Buffalo's Gilbert Perreault. For his part, Kane seems to know the difference, too. He looks old beyond his years, just a little too self-assured to be even remotely boyish. He looks like the child star who asks for and gets meetings with producers. I half expect Kane to go backstage with Tallon and seal the deal with a couple of Montecristos. Kane knows exactly who he is, what got him here and what's out there for him. He comes from upstate New York, but Jason Bonsignore he's not.

Some at tables other than Chicago's again voice their reservations— there always seems to be an issue with Kane. First it was the foot-dragging and negotiation to get him to the Knights. Now it's going without an agent. They'd all take him, though.

2 Across: Philadelphia. The Flyers wanted a power forward from New Jersey two years ago, but couldn't trade their way up in the draft to take Bobby Ryan, who went No. 2 to Anaheim. They have no obstacle this time. The Flyers select, from the USA Hockey Development program, James van Riemsdyk.

Van Riemsdyk walks across the arena floor in front of the section reserved for the draft-eligible players. The wonder is that he doesn't taunt the Canadians who have to wait. Then again, there's no need to pop his sweater, to wave the flag. Not when the NHL is ready to do it for him. By the time van Riemsdyk dons his Flyers sweater on stage, the NHL media-relations staffers are passing out press releases heralding the fact that American players have been selected with the top two picks for the first time in the history of the NHL draft.

3 Across: Phoenix. Wayne Gretzky walks up on stage. The fans give him a standing ovation. He was a third pick once (in the Ontario league draft). Twice he readies himself to speak; twice he's drowned out. His Coyotes didn't hear many ovations this year, and Gretzky as a coach is nowhere near the instant success he was as a player. He works with shopworn veterans, mediocrities in what passes for their primes, younger players of limited potential. No wonder the Coyotes and Gretzky would be looking for a player in his own mould. The Coyotes select, from the Burnaby Express of the BCHL, Kyle Turris.

It's a fit, and everyone should have seen it coming. That No. 99 turned up at Burnaby games. That Turris played lacrosse, like Gretzky did. That Turris's father has a sports pedigree, like Walter Gretzky. There are differences between them. Gretzky went the junior route and went the hard way, going to the Soo, one of the less attractive destinations in the Ontario league, and playing for a middling team and a young coach, Paul Theriault, who inspired more head-scratching than confidence. Turris passed up playing close to home for the powerhouse Vancouver Giants in the Dub and a coach, Don Hay, who took teams to Memorial Cup titles and sent a score of players to the NHL. Turris has been committed to Wisconsin from the start. Maybe it's a paradigm shift, though. Maybe Gretzky is the old school and Turris the new. Word is that Gretzky and Kevin Lowe are looking to send their sons to Shattuck–St. Mary's and that U.S. college would be the next step from there.

So far, no surprises.

4 Across: Los Angeles. General manager Dean Lombardi shocked the scouts throughout the league (but most of all his own) in January when he pink-slipped the crew he had signed up to two-year contracts just six months before. The way the Kings' drafts have fallen recently, it looks as though they'll draft a piece for their blue line. If the scouts at the other tables had to bet, they'd make Karl

Alzner the favourite and Keaton Ellerby, the other defenceman who stood next to Don Cherry on Coach's Corner, the second choice. Few would feel enthusiastic, though, if they had to pick between them. Neither would Lombardi. The Kings select, from the Seattle Thunderbirds, defenceman Thomas Hickey.

The Kings, with their overhauled scouting staff, go outside the box. Hickey, a kid from Calgary, is ranked No. 26 among North American skaters on Central Scouting's final list. A scout I talked to told me he had Hickey higher than Central, higher than the other forecasts, just not *this* high. I remember him vaguely from the spring under-18s and the Top Prospects Game—if he is really deserving of a slot this high, he has virtues I missed completely.[7] Lombardi has his explanation. "In today's game, being able to skate and get up and down the rink is becoming more and more important," Lombardi tells reporters. "The way this guy skates, the way he goes east to west, he's not just a straight-ahead skater, he can make plays."

The selection of Hickey represents a ray of daylight for the Columbus Blue Jackets. They have Jakub Voracek in the fourth slot on their list. The draft in their home rink is playing out like the one in 2005, when Boyd and his staff didn't expect to have a chance to select Gilbert Brule, but the Canadiens' unexpected tapping of Carey Price was a Columbus prayer answered.

The names fall into place.

5 Across: Washington. Some have an inkling that Cherepanov might be a complement to Ovechkin and Alexander Semin and Semen Vrlamov. *Nyet.* The hole at the top of my list is patched. The Capitals select, from the Calgary Hitmen, Karl Alzner. Ross Mahoney, the Capitals' amateur scouting director, is based in Regina and would have seen a lot of Alzner.

For Columbus, it comes down to Edmonton's pick. A coin flip, really: Voracek and Sam Gagner are still there, both of them higher

---

7. I make a point of looking for him in the video of the Top Prospects Game. Hickey looked solid, but didn't really stand out.

than No. 7 on the Blue Jackets' list. If Edmonton goes out of the box or thinks Cherepanov can be signed, Columbus would then have a choice between Voracek and Gagner.

6 Across: Edmonton. Brad Davis is based in Kitchener and sees a lot of the Ontario league. The Oilers select, from the London Knights, Sam Gagner.

I've heard a couple of scouts wonder whether Gagner will be anything more than a great junior, whether his professional career will be much closer to his father's than what you'd expect of a lottery pick. The thinking is that his statistics shine brightly because he and Kane do their best work on the power play, that he might find it tougher slogging when he gets to the pros and is playing five-on-five against bigger players. The scouts speculating about Gagner weren't in a position to draft him, so gentle ripping is par for the course.

At the Columbus table, weeks of dread about job security have given way to something approaching religious ecstasy. Milan Tichy wouldn't fight hard for many Czech players, but for Voracek he'd go to the mat. Not necessary, though. It's a pure and easy consensus. No last-second deliberation. No last-second calls from clubs looking to move up. No last-second calls to clubs, with Columbus looking to move down and acquire extra picks.

7 Across: Columbus. Another ovation, any boos pre-empted by Doug MacLean's firing. The former general manager is sitting under hot television lights on the set of TSN's broadcast of the draft. He watches his successor, Howson, lead the Columbus contingent up to the stage. Howson makes the announcement. The Blue Jackets select, from the Halifax Mooseheads, Jakub Voracek.

Up in the stands, Voracek rises to his feet. He hugs his parents, who remain seated, crying motionlessly, as he heads for the stage.

Voracek frames my season. He played in the second game I saw this season, 320 days ago. In just under a hundred games I took in this year—not quite half a scout's standard workload—his performance against Moncton was the best thing I saw, though Kane at the under-20s and Cherepanov's medal-round games at the under-18s would be right up there. Funny thing: not counting the Top Prospects game, I saw Voracek play six times this season, and his team won only once.

The prospects have to walk under the stands and past the Blue Jackets dressing room and training facility to get to the media room. When Voracek is led there, he walks past Barry Brennan, who has a few Columbus players—Rick Nash and Derick Brassard, among others—in the weight room. The strength coach introduces himself to Voracek and shakes his hand—the newest Columbus player doesn't quite understand Brennan's role with the team, and almost certainly won't remember his name. It occurs to me that scouts might profess to be the most objective observers of the game, but that distinction would have to be Brennan's. He's like a mechanic, looking at players when they're on the hoist or with the hood open. Personal tastes don't matter to him. Old-school allegiances aren't a factor—don't tell me that Don Boyd's heart doesn't race when he sees a player in a Bowling Green sweater. But for Brennan, it's only performance that counts.

Of the players at the top of this draft (and throwing Cherepanov in for good measure), Voracek jumps out as the only one who brought a special physical quality to the table: his explosive burst, peak performance in the Wingate anaerobic test, was the best of the skaters tested. His numbers were far, far ahead of Kane, Turris and Esposito, who would have been in the bottom twenty percent of all skaters tested. What makes Voracek's performance even more impressive is that he doesn't turn eighteen for another six weeks—he is one of the younger players here and, to the naked eye, one of the least physically mature. That's what Brennan sees and values.

"It's a great base for him," Brennan says. "We'll get him on a program. It's amazing what these kids can do once they get here."

With the pick of Voracek, with the Columbus fans slowly vacating the upper bowl, the focus of the night turns from the rollout of the first post-MacLean Blue Jacket to the watch for the elusive Cherepanov and the fast-fading Esposito.

The picks go by in a flash.

8 Across: Boston drafts Zach Hamill, centre with the Everett Silvertips.

9 Across: San Jose drafts Logan Couture. History repeats. Sharks general manager Doug Wilson taps the Ottawa 67's pipeline for the second straight draft. Couture billets with San Jose's second-rounder last year, Dan McGinn.

10 Across. Florida drafts Keaton Ellerby, the Kamloops defenceman. Still no Cherepanov, still no Esposito.

11 Across: Carolina drafts Brandon Sutter. Calgary Flames general manager Darryl Sutter had only faint hopes of drafting his nephew. Brandon's father and coach, Brent, was the No. 16 pick in his draft year.

Now Montreal is on the clock. During a disappointing season, the cry went up for the Canadiens to tap a star from Quebec. On sports talk radio and in the bars on Crescent Street, they reminisced about the glory days and the Québécois stars who carried the franchise to greatness. Easy to see why, with Sergei Samsonov a $3.5-million healthy scratch, with Alexei Kovalev an enigma, with Sheldon Souray looking to the horizon as a free-agent-to-be. One of the names the commentators and fans floated was Columbus's first-rounder last June, Derick Brassard, who lit up the Quebec league when he came back from a shoulder injury that kept him out more than half a season. Esposito is there when the Canadiens' first-round pick comes up. They don't have to trade up to have a shot at him.

12 Across: Montreal drafts Ryan McDonagh, the defenceman from Cretin–Derham Hall high school in Minnesota. He might have been Columbus's pick if Los Angeles had tapped Voracek instead of Thomas Hickey.

A rumble. Cameras are trained on Angelo Esposito, who tries to look phlegmatic and fails. When did it start to go wrong? Was it back in Piestany and Breclav, where he pressed so hard, where he tried to force things that had happened in the flow of the game before?

The picks fall like leaves from a tree on a windy autumn day. No. 13: St. Louis, Lars Eller, a centre with Frolunda's junior team and the first Danish-born first-rounder. No. 14: Colorado, Kevin Shattenkirk, a defenceman with U.S. under-18 program. No. 15, the pick that came to Edmonton from the Islanders for Ryan Smyth: Alex Plante, a defenceman with the Calgary Hitmen. No. 16: Minnesota, Colton Gillies, the rangy, hard-hitting forward with the Saskatoon Blades.

The watch for one of the marquee players ends.

No. 17: New York Rangers, Alexei Cherepanov, the wonder of the under-18 tournament and almost certainly the prospect who has the biggest bank balance here. The Rangers didn't balk last season when Artem Anisimov was telling teams he had a five-year contract. They took him with the No. 54 pick. Nor do the Rangers blink when their turn comes up this year. Almost immediately the word goes out that the Rangers have a deal, that Cherepanov will be at their summer rookie camp, that he'll be at their training camp in the fall.

No. 18: St. Louis, Ian Cole, another defenceman with the U.S. under-18s. No. 19: Anaheim (from Minnesota), Logan MacMillan, Jakub Voracek's teammate with Halifax. Back in the summer, Esposito was projected as the top pick. Now he's going to be the third player from the Quebec league selected.

No. 20: Pittsburgh, finally, Angelo Esposito. "I am not disappointed at all . . . I have never been happier," Esposito tells reporters in the media room, though appearances throughout the night—and even now—suggest it's not exactly the case. "I could not say this before the draft, but the Penguins were always a team I could see myself playing for when I was growing up." He couldn't say that before the draft, but I think back to the start of the season when he told me that his time at Shattuck took "a lot of pressure off" when he was just coming out of eighth grade. He won't have to worry about being out in front with any team that already has Sidney Crosby, Evgeni Malkin and Jordan Staal. Ray Shero, the Pittsburgh general manager, trots out a variation on the old line: "We didn't think he would be available." But there's a piece of evidence that makes it believable: the Penguins haven't prepared a sweater with Esposito's name on the back.

Ten more picks remain in the first round, the first night, but the major questions have been resolved. Just more names to check off. San Jose goes for Nick Petrecki at No. 28. And with the last pick of the first round, Phoenix taps Nick Ross, the Regina Pats defenceman. Sleepless nights are guaranteed for thirty or forty draft-eligible players who are hanging onto that last slim thread. I watch Akim Aliu stand up and head to the exit, unresponsive to the pats on his back from his parents, expressionless, almost catatonic.

June 23, 2007, Nationwide Arena, Columbus

At 9:30 a.m., a half hour before the scheduled resumption of the proceedings, I see Akim Aliu on the concourse again. He has changed suits, but he can't put on a brave face.

"I wanted to go last night so bad," he says. "Have you heard anything?"

I tell him that I still think it will be Chicago, and that with Patrick Kane it would be a nice fit—the Blackhawks' scouts would get added value heading up to work London games.

"Chicago's next pick is 38, right?" he asks.

Off the top of my head I don't know, but he's the one who was up all night going over the lists.

The draft picks up where it left off, and gathers speed. Picks are made faster. There's no clutter, none of the hype that goes with the broadcast first round. The names are less recognizable—at least to those who aren't sitting at the teams' tables on the arena floor. I figure I've talked to more than half the players in the first round and seen all but a few play. With the second round, though, it's fits and starts. That's how it will be through to the very last pick.

31 Down: Buffalo selects T.J. Brennan, a defenceman with St. John's in the Quebec league. I had lunch one day with the player and his father. They're from Philly. T.J. went to St. John's on a cold tryout

last fall—so lightly considered was Brennan that the Fog Devils' management told him not to get his hopes up. When he told me his story I thought his experience—from Philly, landing in St. John's as a teenager—must have been surreal.

35 Down: Boston goes with Tommy Cross, the defenceman who jumped from high-school hockey in Connecticut to the under-18 teams in the fall and spring. I thought he'd go higher than this until I heard that he injured a knee—a torn meniscus—playing baseball. The Bruins wanted him badly enough to trade their second-rounder, the thirty-eighth pick, and their third-rounder, just to move up three slots. He's planning on enrolling at Boston College after a season in the USHL.

37 Down: Columbus's second pick, their first of two second-rounders. The Blue Jackets go with a player I saw ten times this season, Stefan Legein, the right winger with Mississauga. Beyond cocky. The Blue Jackets tell the local reporters that he's in the Darcy Tucker/Sean Avery mould, and he doesn't balk at it.

38 Down. Chicago's first of two second-rounders. I watch Akim Aliu in the stands. Dale Tallon announces the selection of the kid who came to the combine with a lame arm and a lame story, Bill Sweatt from Colorado College. Aliu's head dips.

42 Down. Anaheim takes Eric Tangradi from Belleville, a scouting assignment Don Boyd gave me. Obviously, someone saw something that I missed entirely in that game.

51 Down. Pittsburgh takes the big forward from Victoriaville, Keven Veilleux, who almost took Voracek's head off at the Top Prospects Game.

52 Down. Los Angeles takes Oscar Moller, the Swede who played in Chilliwack, tore up the Top Prospects Game and looked solid at the summer and spring under-18s.

Columbus is up again. I'm thinking that maybe, maybe, Aliu is in play. The Blue Jackets go in an entirely different direction.

53 Down: Columbus, with the pick that came over from San Jose last year when the Blue Jackets traded down to take Tom Sestito, takes a defenceman from Gaylord High in Michigan, Will Weber.

The draft staff have to assemble his name to post it on the draft board—it's not one of the two hundred they have ready. This pick, like Sestito last year, has Boyd's and Castron's fingerprints all over it. Another pick from Michigan, from Castron's backyard. Another pick bound for U.S. college.

56 Down: Chicago again. Finally, Akim Aliu. When he's brought beneath the stands, he holds court for reporters, telling them about his family history, about his game, about having to wait until late in the second round. "Ninety-five percent of the players drafted here have played twice as much hockey as me," Aliu tells them. It's a conservative estimate. A few minutes later, while Akim is taking questions from Russian reporters in his first language, the Chicago media ask Dale Tallon about Aliu's history, his troubles and his talent. He says the fact that London traded for him was a character reference—those who knew him there thought they could work with him. He says Aliu could be "the home run" of the draft. "We did our homework," Tallon says. He points at me in the crowd. "He knows. We talked to him."

A mixed feeling. I'm supposed to be helping the Blue Jackets, yet another team in their division is saying they sounded me out about Aliv. That's not how it's supposed to work.

From the third round on I'm just tracking names from games a few weeks ago and games ten months ago.

Third Round. 62 Down: the Islanders go for Mark Katic from Sarnia. Within five picks of the slot where Columbus took Kris Russell two years ago. 64 Down. Dallas makes a daring play, selecting Sergei Korostin from Moscow Dynamo. I talked to Tim Bernhardt a half dozen times about Korostin and Vitali Karamnov, and he never let on that he had an interest in Korostin *or* that his club was doing the work-up to bring him over. 65 Down: Montreal takes Olivier Fortier, the first player from Rimouski to go. 69 Down: Chicago goes for Fortier's teammate and roommate Maxime Tanguay, who doesn't look happy about having to wait. 71 Down: Florida goes for another Russian player, Evgeni Dadonov. Maybe there'll be a run on players from the

Russian under-18s. 75 Down: Tampa Bay goes for the player with the least beach-ready body, Luca Cunti, the one-rep bench-press wonder from Switzerland. 85 Down: St. Louis, with a pick landed in the loan of Keith Tkachuk to the Atlanta Thrashers, tags Brett Sonne, last seen scoring five goals at the summer under-18s. Sonne scored 21 in 71 games with the Calgary Hitmen during the regular season. 86 Down: Chicago takes Josh Unice, the U.S. goaltender last seen trying to figure out exactly how it was that Cherepanov scored on him in the under-18 final. 91 Down: San Jose picks Tyson Sexsmith, the Vancouver Giants' goalie.

Fourth Round. 94 Down: Even though the Blue Jackets stayed away from Russians at the combine interviews, Columbus selects forward Maxim Mayorov from Leninogorsk. Evidently Howson isn't quite as conservative as he appears. To the triple digits. 106 Down: the Islanders go for a Russian who won't need a translator, Maxim Gratchev from Rimouski. 118 Down: Pittsburgh takes a Nova Scotian who, like Sidney Crosby, was the first pick in a Quebec league draft, defenceman Alex Grant from the St. John's Fog Devils. Grant goes more than eighty picks after T.J. Brennan, who was supposed to have no shot at making St. John's.

Fifth Round. 123 Down: Phoenix goes Russian, with defenceman Maxim Goncharov of Red Army. 130 Down: Boston takes the foreboding Denis Reul, the German defenceman with the Extensive development. "He's a driven kid," says Bruins general manager Peter Chiarelli. "He impressed all of us at the combine. He's a project. He's going to come over to North America. He's a warrior and he's only going to get bigger."[8] 149 Down: Dallas selects left winger Michael Neal of Belleville, the little brother of Stars draftee James Neal of Plymouth.

Sixth Round. 158 Down: Columbus takes goaltender Allen York, a big college-bound kid who plays Tier II for Camrose in the

---

8. The Lewiston Maineiacs will select Reul in the CHL's import draft a few days later.

Alberta Junior Hockey League. 163 Down: Montreal takes Nichlas Torp, the defenceman with the rocky lower body and sponge upstairs. 166 Down: the Islanders select a defenceman from Waterloo of the USHL, Blake Kessel, Phil's brother. 169 Down: Boston selects Czech defenceman Radim Ostrcil, No. 18 on Central Scouting's list of European skaters. 170 Down: Minnesota picks a Finnish defenceman, Harri Ilvonen, No. 21 on NHL Central Scouting's list. 177 Down: New Jersey picks Vili Sopanen, a forward with the Pelicans of the Finnish league, No. 72 on Central's list. The floor is opening under Vitali Karamnov's skates. 178 Down: Detroit drafts Zack Torquato, a centre with the Erie Otters, a selection to the Canadian teams at the summer and spring under-18 tournaments and one of the more impressive physical specimens at the combine.

Seventh (and final) Round. 190 Down: St. Louis drafts centre Trevor Nill of Detroit Compuware. Nill is the son of Detroit assistant general manager Jim Nill, who asks the Red Wings not to put him on their list. 193 Down: the Rangers select Rimouski's David Skokan, whom Central Scouting had at No. 15 in the mid-terms, one slot ahead of Jakub Voracek. 194 down: Toronto selects defenceman Carl Gunnarsson of Linkoping in the Swedish league. Gunnarsson didn't even show up on Central Scouting's list of European prospects. 205 Down: Atlanta selects Swift Current's skinny defenceman Paul Postma, the first Bronco to be drafted this year. If Postma needs any perspective about his selection, he can look to Myles Rumsey, the Swift Current captain. The Flames selected Rumsey in the seventh round two years ago and just a couple of weeks ago told him they weren't planning to sign him. His hopes of making it are about done, and Postma's are looking as slim as his marathoner's physique. 211 Down. Before making the last pick of the draft, Don Boyd thanks the fans who have stuck it out. He might also offer condolences to those who are hanging on to a last desperate hope. Boyd then announces that, with a pick acquired from Anaheim, Columbus selects Trent Vogelhuber, a right winger from Dublin, Ohio.

By the time Boyd's voice and Vogelhuber's name echo around the arena, all but a few teams have vacated their tables on the draft floor. The fans have gone home with their hopes topped up. Families and agents have made themselves scarce — some triumphant, some trying to seem so, some unable to conceal their disappointment. There's never a shortage of that, but there might be more of it this time out than in recent memory. In the days leading up to the draft, both the commentators in the media and NHL executives described the draft as unpredictable. Drafts are, by nature, predictable — you can count on surprises.

It was a surprise that Thomas Hickey soared into the upper reaches on draft day from the much lower slots assigned him by Central Scouting, the other scouting outfits and media outlets. It was a surprise that Angelo Esposito fell to No. 20. But those are the surprises of a regular sort, a movement up or down of within the margin of error.

Rankings and predictions aren't like political polling — none can claim to be accurate within 3.5 percent nineteen times out of twenty. It wasn't that they were off the mark, but the degree to which they missed.

Some of the misses had mitigating circumstances — that Cherepanov fell from the top five to the second ten and other Russians fell by whole rounds was, on some level, understandable. Some amount of drag on their draft placement because of questions about the ability to sign them seems reasonable. Likewise, I can understand teams shying away from a player like Alexander Vasiliev, the winger who scored a hat trick in the second game I saw this year, the Russians' win over Jakub Voracek and the Czechs — Vasiliev wasn't on the roster by the spring under-18s.

With few exceptions, where you finish the season is a lot more meaningful than where you start. Still, it's hard to imagine how the Vogelhubers were selected, but not several Russians who were major contributors to the world-champion under-18 squad — including Vitali Karamnov, the team captain. Even harder to figure are other prospects who were on the draft map and dropped off. Eric Doyle, a defenceman traded from Seattle to Swift Current in midseason, was ranked No. 19 in North America by the NHL Central Scouting's midterm rankings, was selected for the Top Prospects Game and the Canadian team at the spring under-18s, and invited to the NHL combine. He wasn't drafted. In the final rankings, Doyle had dropped to No. 69, two behind Swift Current teammate Paul Postma, and one behind Brendan Smith, a defenceman with St. Michael's Tier II team and the Detroit Red Wings' first-rounder, twenty-eighth overall. Just that pocket of the ranking shows the volatility of the draft. Some scouts stayed on the floor in the seventh round after their teams' last picks just to see who would go unselected and might be worth a phone call to invite to a pro camp as a free agent.[9]

In the fall, NHL Central Scouting placed Branislav Rehus and Travis Ehrhardt on its "Players to Watch" list. Rehus, the Lativian kid playing in Peterborough, ended up 191st on Central's final list of North American skaters, while Ehrhardt, the Moose Jaw defenceman who had five assists one night against Swift Current, is No. 202 out of 210 ranked. Neither was drafted. Trent Vogelhuber's name wasn't on any of Central's lists.

Oh yeah, the player who is supposed to have OCD—the team that employs the scout who tipped me about the prospect ended up drafting him—good tip or smoke and mirrors, I don't know.

The tables on the arena floor have been vacated. A lot of scouts have offered up their last opinions, heeded or mostly ignored, with clubs that owe them one last cheque and no other loyalty. A lot of the scouts know that it's over with their clubs—Daniel Doré in Boston, for one. There's no knowing what the future holds in Columbus, save what you can glean from optics.

Scott Howson and Don Boyd are the last NHL executives making the rounds with the media—at this point, only the local reporters are

---

9. The week after the draft, Doyle accepted an invitation to attend Dallas's summer development camp.

on hand. Despite his protestations that this wasn't going to be his draft, Don Boyd is the one who has walked downstairs with Howson, not Paul Castron. The new general manager and the holdover from the previous regime are asked about Vogelhuber. They're asked about Mayorov—Howson says the Blue Jackets felt he was a gamble worth taking, even if his agent is Rollie Hedges, the agent for Nikolai Zherdev. A red flag, but the draft weekend in Columbus is all about futures, new beginnings. The reporters lob questions about each and every pick on the second day of the draft, but eventually they wend back to the first pick, to Voracek.

"How often did you see him?" a reporter. "How did he play?"

"The last time I saw him, frankly, he struggled," Boyd says. "At the world under-18s in Finland. He was good for a game, the first game he got there, but then it caught up to him . . ."

At this point, Boyd turns to me.

"What did Voracek have to fly to get to the under-18s?"

I rhyme off Voracek's itinerary: "Halifax to Montreal. Montreal to Frankfurt. Frankfurt to Helsinki. Two and a half hours in a car from Helsinki to Tampere, straight into the lineup when the game started."

"And he was the best player on the ice that game. It caught up to him later in the tournament—couldn't sleep, then couldn't stay awake—but it says a lot about him that he was willing to give it a try. A tough trip."

Boyd allows himself a smile—the reporters can take down their notes, and Scott Howson can read the quotes in the newspaper tomorrow, but they'll never know how tough that trip was and how many sleepless nights there were—for Voracek *and* for those who put his name on Columbus's list.

ENDNOTE

A SEASON IN HOCKEY IS A STORY IN AND OF ITSELF. With *Future Greats and Heartbreaks*, I have tried to capture one season in the lives of a few characters, some of whom will be among the game's biggest names in a few seasons, while others who will be out of the game entirely. More than that, I tried to capture one season in the lives of the men who occupy the corner seats at arenas hundreds of nights every season.

I have no illusions about the work you hold in your hands. It's a story of a season, but it couldn't possibly be the whole story of those you find in the pages. There were many more stories than available space to tell them. For the players, their careers are either just starting or near the end. For the scouts, their work goes on . . . they hope. I can't think of one character whose story is resolved by the last page—your author included. So, for readers and hockey fans who are remotely interested in what happens next—or for anyone who has an interest in the game and scouting—I'll regularly update a blog I have set up.

http://scoutshonourbygarejoyce.blogspot.com/

It's a place where I can revisit the characters and backstories and answer questions you might have about *Future Greats and Heartbreaks*.

ACKNOWLEDGEMENTS

THIS BOOK WOULD NOT HAVE BEEN POSSIBLE WITHOUT the time, consideration and friendship extended to me over the years by too many NHL scouts to list here. I owe a huge debt to Doug MacLean for opening the door to the Columbus war room. I also owe many thanks to the Blue Jackets' crew who let me get a good look at their business: Don Boyd, Jim Clark, John Williams, Sam McMaster, Paul Castron, Milan Tichy, Kjell Larsson and Artem Telepin, among others. Scouts and executives from other organizations who generously helped me out include Wayne Smith, Jim Benning and Grant Sonier with Boston; Mike Sands, Tomas Jelinek and Tod Button with Calgary; Dale Tallon, Rick Dudley, Bruce Franklin and Mark Kelley in Chicago; Ted Hampson in Colorado; Tim Bernhardt and Les Jackson with Dallas; Jim Devellano, Jim Nill, Joe MacDonnell, Mark Leach and Hakan Andersson with Detroit; the Davises with Edmonton; Scott Luce in Florida; Dave Taylor with Los Angeles; Doug Risebrough and Guy Lapointe with Minnesota; Paul Fenton with Nashville; David Conte with New Jersey; Tim Murray now with Ottawa; Don Luce and Inge Hammarstrom in Philadelphia; Shawn Simpson and George Armstrong with Toronto; and Chris Edwards with Central Scouting, among others. Among those who are free agents, I'd like to thank Daniel Doré, Archie Henderson, John Stanton and Bob Tindall. I learned something from all of you.

I couldn't have written this book without the help of many teams in the Canadian Hockey League who opened their doors for me. The same goes for dozens of players—some of whom made it into the pages here, some of whom did not. I hope that my book sheds some light on the junior game circa 2007 and that maybe a few more fans will be drawn to the game. Likewise, I could not have written this book without the help of officials and friends with Hockey Canada—Brad Pascal and Andre Brin first and foremost—who managed to find a seat for me at their events and keep me in the loop.

Friends in the media end of the business have helped me out in sundry and various ways: Mark Giles, Jay Lovinger, Jeremy Schaap and everyone else at ESPN and espn.com; Terry Koshan at the *Toronto Sun*; Tim Wharnsby at *The Globe and Mail*; Bill Beacon with Canadian Press; Montreal sports-talk-radio legend Mitch Melnyk; Jim Kelley of Rogers Sportsnet; Ken Campbell of *The Hockey News*; and Damian Cox of the *Toronto Star*, among others.

Even with the help of all of these people, I would not have been able to get words to page without the unflagging spirit of my editor, Tim Rostron. And I wouldn't have been able to get anyone interested in the idea if not for the editor of my last book, Nick Massey-Garrison, and my agent, Rick Broadhead.

Finally, once again, I'd like to thank my Significant Other, Susan Bourette, for waiting up when I'd be driving back from Sudbury in the dead of night in mid-winter. And, once again, I'd like to thank my daughters, Ellen and Laura, for their patience and tolerance when searching for me under a mound of papers, programs, credentials, media guides and deadlines.